C000277241

LONG VOYAGE HOME

LONG VOYAGE HOME

True Stories from Britain's Twilight
Maritime Years

TIM MADGE

SIMON & SCHUSTER

LONDON·SYDNEY·NEW YORK·TOKYO·SINGAPORE·TORONTO

First published in Great Britain by
Simon & Schuster Ltd in 1993
A Paramount Communications Company

Copyright © Tim Madge, 1993

This book is copyright under the Berne Convention.
No reproduction without permission.
All rights reserved.

Simon & Schuster Ltd
West Garden Place
Kendal Street
London W2 2AQ

Simon & Schuster of Australia Pty Ltd
Sydney

A CIP catalogue record for this book is
available from the British Library
ISBN 0–671–71054–0
ISBN 0–671–71589–5 (paperback)

Filmset in Sabon by
Selwood Systems, Midsomer Norton
Printed and bound in Great Britain by
Butler & Tanner Ltd, Frome and London

To NJHM –
The fixéd star I steer by

CONTENTS

ACKNOWLEDGEMENTS

I am immensely grateful for all the assistance I have had from many, many people involved in every area of maritime life.

Some names stand out. Especially, I owe a lasting debt of gratitude to: Richard Woodman, Dave Ramwell, Clive Madge and John Moore.

Among the books I have raided shamelessly for ideas as well as facts those of Ronald Hope, Paul Kennedy and E.H.H. Archibald stand out, the latter for his works on English sea painters as well as on fighting ships. Janes, as usual, provided masses of hard facts about warships.

I am very grateful for all those who gave me time, in both formal and informal interview, and to the many people who have helped but who wish to remain anonymous. The list I give here is, therefore, incomplete. Thanks to Sir James Eberle, Jeremy Larken, Jeremy Black, Jeremy Stuart, Stuart Wallace, Andrew McNeil, Stuart Bradley, Commander Ranken, Captain Orr, Ian Middleton, Simon Sherrard, Ian Thompson, Bob and Sue Bushnell, John and Helga Thorpe, Gordon Scott-Morris, Les Walker, Julian Parker, Donald Davies, David Tomlinson, Sir Jeffrey Sterling, Daphne Lawry, Chris Freer, John Manley, Linda Dennison, Captain John Pilling, Mr Martin, Mr Griffiths, Peter Luff, Mr Cornish, Captain Denman, Brian Miles, Michael Everard, Mr Hornby, Mr Waage, Mr Bond, David Harris, Richard Hill, Robert Beattie, Eric Shawyer, Charles Walker, John Cooper, Bill Anderson, Captain Banner, Arthur Dawson, Ricky Calderley, Doug Foy, Dick Logan, Tim McCoy, Len Townend, Ken Long, Mike Reynolds, Pat Milner.

At a critical moment in the production of the book, Stephanie Boxall stepped in and transcribed a number of vital interviews; she saved my sanity and I cannot thank her enough.

I have had much encouragement from my publishers – in the early stages from Nick Brealey and Leslie Toll; latterly Carol O'Brien and Nick Webb. Many thanks to them and to Bill Hamilton, at A.M. Heath, who first saw the possibilities of the whole project.

My family, as always, have had to suffer another swerve in the old man's course: I hope the result, as well as the new library of books we have acquired, makes it all worth while. My wife, Nicola, made the right comment (she knows when) at a turning point in the book's life; to her more than gratitude.

Finally, this book is not quite yet the funeral oration I believed I was writing when I started. But it remains a damned close-run thing. Long may Britons continue to ply the world's oceans; long may we be, if not ruling the waves, then continuing to sail on them, enjoying and appreciating the environment of one of the planet's most precious assets: the sea.

INTRODUCTION:
THE SILENT SEAS

'I see the procession of steamships.'
Walt Whitman, *A Passage to India*

If you stand on the cliffs overlooking Dover on a clear day and gaze across the narrow sea that separates us from France for anything more than a few moments one thing will be abundantly apparent: ships. They come in all sizes, many different shapes; with binoculars you can see they are the messengers of many nations.

But very few, today, carry on their stern the 'red duster', the British flag. Even the ferries, plying back and forth, may show a Bermudan rather than a British flag at the stern; in 1990, the chairman of the Council of British Shipping, Sir Jeffrey Sterling, had to admit the P&O fleet's largest container ships were no longer British registered. It simply was not 'economic'.

The decline in the British shipping register has been dramatic. Yet this is the land which produced Ralegh and Hawkins, Anson and Drake, the land that created the *Pax Britannica*, that hundred years between 1815 and 1914 when the world was mostly at peace, largely out of the strength of the Royal Navy. Surely not. Sadly, any amount of rhetoric – and there has been a lot – cannot disguise the awful truth. After 500 years of a deep-sea maritime culture, we have turned back to being a nation of largely coastal sailors.

This retreat is general, applying to all branches of maritime life: the Navy, fishing, pilotage. For the Navy, it has been the worst of times, and the process is by no means yet over. Royal Naval officers – some recently retired and a few still serving – lament the slow and painful bleeding of the fleet; the old fixed-wing aircraft carriers have all gone, as have the cruisers, those archetypes of world naval power. The number of escorts, destroyers, frigates and mine sweepers has continued to fall. There are between forty and forty-five right now and likely to be far fewer.

Around the coasts of Britain, fewer and fewer fishing boats work

the harbours. Off-shore the growing fishing fleets of other nations –
Spain, France, Holland and, of course, Poland and the former Soviet
Union – vacuum the sea. Pilotage, which used to operate with British
ex-mariners in the great harbours of the world, now is generally
confined to British waters. There is talk now of finding soon a Malay
or Filipino harbour Master in a British port. Only the yachts multiply,
especially along the south coast, now apparently determined to evolve
into a giant marina from Dungeness to The Lizard. Is this it? Is this
the final episode of Britain's maritime history: a huge leisure park by
the sea?

The long-term decline of Britain's registered merchant fleet, from
the end of the First World War, continues. And it is generally true
that if the trend line is moved a decade or so ahead, Britain will cease
to have *any* deep-sea merchant fleet by 2000 for the first time in 400
years.

The *Independent* published an article in 1990 headlined, 'Proud
Men Sailing Close to Oblivion'. It went on to point out that what
made the *Remuera Bay* so unusual was that she was one of only a
dozen British registered deep-sea ships sailing with an all-British crew.

It has happened without most of us knowing it, this great sea-
change. The Press, radio and television, with few exceptions, have
hardly touched upon the passing of what most of us probably still
sincerely believe to be an enduring and central characteristic of the
British: that, in some indefinable way we still 'rule the waves'. The
sea is part-myth, part-folk memory, part of our way of life, people
will tell you. Seafarers say 'if it was ever true, it is true no longer'.

And if this is the case, what are the implications for our future?
More than 95 per cent of all our imports and exports still come in
by sea. My parent's generation was aware of the stark reality of that
in 1942 and 1943 when a few score U-boats nearly destroyed that
link with the outside world. A few weeks only stood between this
country and absolute defeat because we could not control the seas
that surround us. Now, fifty years later, it is as if we have handed
over control once more.

Apart from charting the many and often puzzling changes that
have occurred in British shipping in the last thirty or so years, this
book is also a personal journey for me. What I have found out has
surprised me, more than I was at first willing to admit.

Brought up in the 1950s when it was still possible to see the River
Thames full of steamers flying the red duster, I, like so many of my
contemporaries, had an early love affair with the sea and ships. Much

of that love has remained with me. I took succour frequently from books about the sea; I particularly remember reading of the epic struggle of Captain Carlsson to save his ship, the *Flying Enterprise*, after she began to list on a voyage across the Atlantic. The attempt to tow her into Falmouth by the ocean salvage tug, *Turmoil*, in January 1952, which ended when the *Flying Enterprise* sank sixty miles short of safety, lives with me to this day. Carlsson and the crew of the tug were national heroes in Britain and the plot was followed day by day in the Press, including all the tabloids.

At primary school my class adopted a Royal Navy ship; in those far off days there were plenty to choose from and ours was a light cruiser – HMS *Superb*. Some of us were privileged to make a visit when she was docked in Chatham, then one of the biggest of Britain's naval bases. There was an intimacy of shared purpose in all this. *Superb* had returned from a visit to West Africa; her trip tied in with our school projects (though that was not what they were called then) on the Empire. And the Empire, of course, was the key to it all.

In 1990 I returned, more than thirty years later, with my six-year-old son, to the 'Chatham Historic Dockyard' theme park, where the memories lay thick among the leaves on the ground and in the patterns of rippling water filling the now empty quays and the mast ponds. Chatham Naval Dockyard was – and remains – a beautiful setting. But now the grey ships that lined its quays have all gone. A terrible silence reigns.

In the 1950s British shipping was in the middle of a post-war boom. The Atlantic was crossed primarily by sea; not until 1958 did the number of people crossing the Atlantic by air exceed those crossing by sea.

The acceptance then by most British people that we had a long and enduring 'public' maritime tradition was unquestioned. The evidence was clear for anyone who cared to journey to the centre of London and the River Thames. London Pool, between Tower Bridge and London Bridge, was packed with mostly British ships; down river the density of commercial traffic grew, spilling over from the docks. On the northern bank: St Katherine's, Tobacco, Regent's, India, Millwall, Royal Victoria, Royal Albert, King George V; on the southern: Surrey, Canada, Russia, Greenland, Quebec. Each one told its own story.

I remember crossing the Thames at Gravesend when it was possible to see rank upon rank of tall-funnelled steam-powered tug-boats, moored to mid-river buoys, waiting patiently to work ships up and down London's river – then one of the world's greatest trading rivers. Ships – big British ships – were everywhere. Some of those buoys are still there because a sailing crony, Jack Crofton, hit one with his yacht a few years ago. But they are now the greater hazard; the tugs once moored to them have gone.

More memories crowd in: of Navy Days at Chatham, row upon row of frigates, destroyers, submarines, upon which my cousin and I would clamber, raising and lowering the Bofors guns in imaginary pursuit of low-flying enemy aircraft. Thousands of people would crowd into the dockyard on these days to see some of Britain's naval might, perhaps back from exotic tours in the Indian Ocean, or from Singapore or China. Join the Navy and see the world, the recruitment posters said; they did not lie.

Travelling through the Mediterranean then you might have caught a glimpse of a British task force, carrier steaming alongside cruiser, flanked by a destroyer flotilla and fussed over by auxiliaries. By and by a British cargo liner would steam past, later followed by a British tanker, then another, and another. They had almost as certainly been built in Britain, too. They ran on steam – by the 1950s the bigger cargo liners on turbines, some of the older on the fantastic triple or even quadruple expansion steam reciprocating engine. Some – too few as it turned out – were using oil as fuel and diesel engines as machinery. The old story of Britain's industrial ruin runs here too, like a thick strand. First in most innovations to do with the sea, we allowed our inventive genius to peter out, whilst the much despised foreigners, like the tortoise of the fable, slowly overtook us.

It was the world's first Industrial Revolution in Britain that had created the steamship, whether its power was, as 150 years later, directed through those incredibly beautiful triple expansion reciprocating engines, or through the more mysterious turbine. All had been British in invention; few questioned that, for until the turn of the century what was British was usually best.

That merchant fleet, with its serried ranks of warships, was potent in its time because it was the physical manifestation of what, as youngsters, we were taught to believe. Britain still could pretend in the fifties that she ruled the world, by trading and influence, if no longer by direct force.

But it was an illusion that we, as a nation, have taken a further thirty years to uncover; even now, many cannot believe we have not been conned in some way, cheated of what we had. Of those, many are merchant seamen, the last of those back from the world out there, where an Empire once was. They are home because most of their ships have passed into history. They are often bitter men, deprived as they see it of their life's work, spilled onto the pavements of public indifference.

Their cries for a merchant fleet flagged under British rules, for the necessity of a strong carrying capacity for defence, have seemed of late more desperate than reasoned, hollow, insubstantial. They beat against a public whose interests have long turned elsewhere. It is unimaginable today that our lack of warships, in comparison with the old Soviet Navy, could spark a violent national public outcry as it did eighty years ago when an outraged British public demanded more battleships to match Germany.

The British have retreated from the Empire, the soldiers have returned from all bar a few odd corners. Now our sailors are coming home, forced to work the short-sea trades, or in the howling wastes of the North Sea, angry, embittered, confused. Often in their voices I have heard an echo of my own: less a what happened, more of a why? And, always, how could the situation change so fast? In my own memory the changes from thirty years ago to now have become compressed. Reality tells a different story: change in the shipping industry is relatively sedate, like the movement of its principal players. In my mind it all happened overnight. From visibility came invisibility; from a mighty presence, a timid and faltering absence.

By the late 1980s – as now – it was possible to sail on the River Thames and see no British ship of any size at all; in the English Channel, to cover the distance between the Dover Straits and the Wolf Rock and to sight only foreign-flagged ships. A British captain, master of a foreign-flagged cargo ship in the Far East, noted at the end of 1989 that in three months of 'busy shipping' he only saw two British-flagged ships – both P&O as it happened. The same story is told from all over the world, whether it be in places the British merchant fleet was always strongly represented or not.

To witness the once mighty P&O apparently reduced to short-sea trades and a few deep-sea container ships is also a shock. But it is in the slow realisation that the ships have gone that the hardest blow comes. Where did they go?

What this book is about is an interweaving of the story of Britain in the last few decades with the reality of seafaring, what is was, how it still lives among many of our seafarers, how it has changed, with a very personal painful uncovering of the mythological baggage I have carried with me for most of my life. Many of the people I have

spoken to in the course of writing this book carry much of that
baggage still.

It runs far deeper in their lives than mine, for they have been to
sea, they understand the poet who says 'my heart is now restless in
my breast, my mind is with the sea-flood over the whale's domain'.[1]
That was written over a thousand years ago by an Anglo-Saxon
seafarer but it could have been written by any of the men quoted in
what follows.

It is the romance of the sea, its restless eternal call, that confuses
the base economic and strategic elements surrounding any debate on
shipping. Even the hardest heart can be swept away by the poetic,
especially if it has been out there, in a storm at sea, arriving at a
foreign port in the early dawn, returning home through the English
Channel after a long sea voyage.

The passenger is as affected by this, in the short term, as the
professional sailor, the inshore fisherman as the weekend yachtsman
or woman. And all of us can recall the heroes of the sea: Drake,
Ralegh, Hawkins, Frobisher, Nelson.

The qualities that the sea brings forth excite not just our imagination; we want to be like that. 'Hardy he was, prudent in his under-
taking; his beard in many a tempest had its shaking,' explained
Chaucer more than 600 years ago, of his shipman. More recently,
this: 'The Captain carried them all ... He was a tower of strength,
holding everything together by sheer unrelenting guts.'[2]

Then, in 1990 Britain ceased to be an island, after 30,000 years of
separation from the European mainland. Eighty years ago, Britain
could believe she was at the centre, not the periphery of Europe –
and the world. Her ships carried the product of British manufacture
to every part. Her coal fuelled tens of thousands of ships, ran railways
in South America, Africa and Asia. Her merchant navy was the bench-
mark for the world's fleets.

The sea, for an island race, is never that far away. For the British, the
sea has until very recently been our lifeblood, carrying in its salty
heart the food we needed to eat; taking away the goods we sold to
pay for that food.

The coming of the Channel Tunnel is a symbolic moment, and it
puts what follows into a larger perspective. For Britain has ceased to
be physically isolated. After one tunnel there will come others. The
physical importance should not be overlooked, either. With the
Tunnel we can for the first time envisage not needing the sea as

means of transport. When you set that alongside the knowledge that Rotterdam considers herself Britain's third port, and that 25 per cent of Japanese exports to Europe arrive by rail across the Soviet Union, the focus sharpens acutely. Oil could be piped in; more tunnels *could* undercut that 95 per cent-by-sea imports figure drastically.

Some of this is unlikely: transport by sea is cheap compared with other methods and the size of ships ensures that bulk goods can be moved in quite incredible amounts, far more than could be delivered by road or rail. But this may not help seafarers, as we shall see.

What is quite clear is that there will never again be a British-flagged merchant navy that could dominate the world's shipping register as it once did. Sixty per cent of the world's total tonnage was once owned and operated by Britain, at a time when we were building most of it as well.

Many of the traditions of the older seafarers will now only live in memories and, increasingly, in books, tapes, museums and theme parks. The great twentieth century revolutions in shipping: the development of the highly efficient marine diesel engine, the cheap, welded, prefabricated ship; total transformation of cargo handling by containerisation; the growth of national shipping lines; cost of training and of manning – all lend to inevitable inexorable change.

Gone too, though more slowly, is much of the maritime 'culture' we once had. Much of that culture was mixed with imperialism, with the dusting of the red on the global map, far more than with the carrying of that red duster by tramp steamers.

Like many great historic myths, our landside attitude to the men who went to sea was often less than enthusiastic. We liked them best when they were away voyaging, or dying in Hardy's arms. Two examples here will suffice.

After English sailors had saved their countrymen from the delights of the Spanish inquisition, towards the end of the sixteenth century, one author wrote of them, 'their usage hath been so ill that it is no marvel they show unwillingness to serve the Queen. For if they arrive sick from any voyage, such is the charity of the people ashore that they shall sooner die than find pity.'[3]

Three hundred and fifty years later the public still exercised its indifference. A ship's carpenter (a category the Elizabethan sailor would have saluted), having suffered enormous hardship after surviving the torpedoing of the cargo ship *Wayfarer*, came home from

Port Said on the troop ship *Queen of Bermuda*: 'We were treated like criminals and our official reception in Liverpool was in no way welcoming.'

It is possible that in both cases it was guilt that prevented a greater display of public gratitude. Seafaring has always been one of the hardest of trades. Dr Johnson, writing in the eighteenth century, expressed it best: 'No man will be a sailor who has contrivance enough to get himself into a jail; for being in a ship is being in a jail, with the chance of being drowned ... A man in a jail has more room, better food and commonly better company.'[4]

But we were proud of our ships. Perhaps most of all in the twilight of the golden age of British passenger shipping. The one sea voyage that never failed to capture the imagination was the transatlantic run, from the Old World to the New. Not least because so many emmigrants to the USA made that stormy passage, undoubtedly also because it led to the creation of the largest and most beautiful artifacts industrial society has ever created: the great passenger liners. From the early part of this century, from the time the turbine was invented, they grew and grew in size. Notwithstanding the appalling loss of the *Titanic*, came the ships which did not sink: the *Olympic*, the *Berengaria*, the *Mauretania*, the *Majestic*, the *Aquitania* – and the *Queens*. They epitomised a particular kind of success: the sheer bravado of millions of rivets. Somehow they exclaimed they had been truly 'built' in a way welded ships simply cannot. Every one of those rivets was banged into place by a man. There is a startling modern parallel: it is with space travel and space craft. People watching a great liner pass may well have had a similar sense of awe as when the Space Shuttle takes off. But there is one vital difference; we could all have travelled on the *Queen Elizabeth*. The ships were technological marvels but they were accessible – built for the people.

In their huge interiors designers could go completely for the grand effect. Huge ballrooms, restaurants, staterooms, opulence outdoing opulence. And yet, despite the extravagance of their fittings, inside and out, many of these great ships made money, year in and year out. Others achieved a fame all of their own: the *Queens*, shipping over a million and quarter men across the Atlantic in the Second World War, unescorted because they were so fast. The echo of that came back to many when the *QEII* and the *Canberra* sailed to the Falklands with their quota of troops.

It is in the human connection with the sea that we all most feel the loss: seafarers, from the ancient mariner on, have in one way or another transfixed us with their tales. Today, with mass air travel, that too has gone for ever.

Some memories of the sea and its part in our history remain fixed; many become encoded into something half-forgotten. What child of our times, for instance, really knows what he or she is celebrating each year at the Last Night of the Proms? Each September (and how appropriate for our story is an autumn date), in one of the most regal public spaces among the imperial emblems still to adorn London, thousands of people gather at the end of a great music festival. They wait expectantly for one quintessentially British moment, beset as it always is with pride, nostalgia, hope.

The soprano never disappoints and the Albert Hall once more rings to the shouted exultation that 'Britons, never, never, never, shall be slaves ...'

The song is, of course, *Rule Britannia*. The words were written, and set to music, in the eighteenth century, just 200 years ago, at the dawn of the first great Industrial Revolution which pitched the United Kingdom, relentlessly, into a largely unsought role as the world's first superpower.

The eighteenth century was the moment when Britain became Great; at the time, as so often happens, few realised it. But the seeds had been sown, and the harvest was about to be garnered. Whatever native genius for invention there was, the principal financial factor which led the country so rapidly towards being, for a few heady decades, the manufacturer for the entire world, was contingent on the nation's ability to trade.

That foundation was laid, deeper still, in the keels of the ships, and in the hearts of the men who went down to the seas to sail them. The strength of the British position lay in the British merchant trading fleet, protected by a burgeoning Royal Navy, itself heir to a swelling list of battle honours against the Spanish, the Portugese, the Dutch and the French, with the odd skirmishes against the Swedes and the Russians thrown in.

Behind the Navy and the traders lay a long history, common enough for an island race, of coastal trade, fishing and ship-building, coupled to the certain knowledge that if an island did not trade it could not grow, and might even die. For nearly 200 years though, those coastal waters lapped the shores of a giant among nations. To those same seas, through the narrow and rock-strewn channels off the British coast, came the trade of the world, largely carried in British ships. Great Britain was able, by the end of the last century, to claim that she alone among the powers had the power to keep the world's peace: *Pax Britannica*.

At the great Spithead Review in 1897 to celebrate Queen Victoria's jubilee, the Royal Navy, arbiter of this might and keeper of the world's peace, lay at anchor, secure in the knowledge that it was at least as large as the next two biggest navies combined. And at that same review, as a reminder of Britain's national technological strengths, a new invention was paraded. The *Turbinia*, the fastest ship afloat, heralded the onset of turbine-driven ships; a decade later, and the British Navy launched the *Dreadnought*, the first all-big-gun battleship afloat.

In the early part of the twentieth century Britain, although she was inexorably losing the world trade war, maintained the world's biggest navy and the biggest merchant fleet. But, as we shall see, like British industry much was founded on a bed of sand. The failure to keep going, the self-deluding effect of being on top, the arrogance of the winner, the burden of colonies, would wear us down, as would two world wars in forty years. It would take those wars and appalling loss of life, both at sea and on land, to begin to affect some of the changes we needed; other change would not come until it was too late.

When the *Herald of Free Enterprise* sank off Zeebrugge in 1987 we leapt to condemn the master and crew: not the owners, at least not at first, and not ourselves for demanding an ever faster and more frequent service to get us and our cars to and from Europe. The sea, like the air, is an unforgiving environment on which we impose our time-obsessed society at our own peril.

Those short-sea trades are now of increasing importance to the future of the merchant service. Times have changed indeed. It was in the short-sea trades that the English and finally the British shipping industry was founded. In the treacherous waters off the British coast, seafarers learned the skills and techniques of seamanship which would give them the confidence to venture right round the globe.

We know that it was in trade, not in war, that shipping began. Its origins are largely obscure but we know that between England and Ireland, the coast of Northern France and Benelux, and to Scandinavia, Iceland and the coast of Greenland, those early voyagers went. Eventually they reached North America (before William conquered England some Scots at least may have landed somewhere on that coast).

The tenacity of these early sailors was extraordinary. But their boats were strongly built and their knowledge of navigation built up over many years of coastal trading. Iceland is six days north of Ireland; Greenland almost that from the coast of Iceland. In a time when dragons and sea monsters were real, to make a journey into the unknown was a very brave act.

These are characteristics which traders have to have if they are to thrive. Our more modern tenacity of purpose, which took British sailors across the known world and into the further reaches of unexplored oceans, worked with those native virtues to ensure that we garnered a rich harvest in goods and land.

So much has been lost – particularly territory – it is hard to imagine at times what Great Britain was, until at least the end of World War Two. So much of that national self-identity was tied to the sea, through our ships and their trade. And yet, because the nation's traumas have in the past forty years been perceived as national, the loss of that great trading fleet – in tonnage terms as recently as just ten years ago – has passed almost unnoticed.

The truth, as we enter the last decade of the twentieth century, is that Britain is close to seeing herself as just the largest island off the coast of Europe. For the first time in 500 years our Royal Navy cannot defend us against invasion by sea, or prevent the cutting off of supply routes across the Atlantic. For the first time in hundreds of years it seems as if we no longer care about the sea, no longer believe in the necessity to sail, other than for pleasure.

It may not matter. At least, if we count trading futures; if we count our new strengthening alliance with Europe and the end of the Cold War; if we perceive our destiny as land-based and local. But the British, it could be argued, have hung together by looking outward, by having to face those journeys through treacherous shallow seas, by pulling together. The impetus to escape these shores, to seek out the rest of the world, stood us well as a national obsession. It brought wealth, it brought diversity, it bought us the riches which made us the most prosperous nation on earth, and keeps us still, though ever more precariously, among the top developed countries of the world. There is an argument that our retreat into these islands has made us narrower, nastier and, in general, crueller to others and ourselves. The generosity of spirit which had us policing, not at all always to our advantage, half the world, has subsided into a sometimes whey-faced desperation as to how we could have ended up in such a mess. That we are in a mess could be disputed, but that we remain uncertain of our national identity, and our future direction – despite the siren calls from Europe – is not at issue.

It is my contention, and one I hope to demonstrate, that at least part of this loss of identity is caused through our loss of our historic intimacy with the sea. That, rather than being a result of our general decline, maritime decline has precipitated much of our economic woe, and that a turning away from the sea has occasioned a deeper, possibly more fatal, perception – an ennui spreading through our pysche like a plague. The sickness of men and women who hanker, indeed 'after the sea-ship, after the whistling wind'.

If so, the decline of maritime power in all spheres is leading to the destruction in meaning of a massive portion of our own history; to a failure to locate a considerable portion of our culture – in literature, in drama, in art and in music.

A lack of interest in adventure, in the achievements of our current explorers, as well as our past, dismissed by media pundits as boring or foolhardy, suggests this ennui. The great Antarctic walk by Mear and Swan in 1985 was attacked for being wrong-headed; its principals were vilified, not lauded. We had come to a sad end, here. Exploration of the Antarctic is inextricably linked to exploration of the sea.

In turning from the sea, I believe we turn from an essential part of our true nature. Perhaps it is not too fanciful to read something into our role as the polluter of Europe; as we no longer live in harmony with the sea, as we no longer need it, we scorn it and fill it with garbage.

It is easy to get carried away on a tide of lost opportunities, missed courses, failures. The intriguing part of the story is we still have an opportunity – albeit a rapidly narrowing one – to strike out again and seek the sea.

I have tried to make what follows not just a chronicle but also a celebration of indomitable will, of the power of the sea to inspire, not just those who use it as a medium of transport, for influence and power, or as source of food and raw materials, but as inspiration for art, music, poetry and literature. That brings us back to the seafarers, the men – and lately, women – who go to sea still to 'the vagrant gypsy life'.[5]

PART ONE

The Threads that Bound us:
Britain's Victorian Armada

I

'THE DREAD AND ENVY OF THEM ALL!'

James Thompson, *Rule Britannia*

It did begin with Drake and Ralegh; in a very real sense the schoolbook histories of thirty years ago were quite right. The buccaneers of the sixteenth century – Europeans from Italy, Spain, Portugal, the Netherlands, France and England – all opened up the world for plunder through shipping. The discovery of gold and silver in South America, the beginnings of the slave trade, the spices brought by sea from the East, created a transport system, and the colonial system. In the very early days the English took the easy route, stealing from the efforts of others, their most successful mistress, the pirate queen, Elizabeth I.

Out of this ferment came colonies of our own, trade, and trade wars. By dint of savage courage, tenacity and often just savagery, by accident as well as design, the English found their first great talent in seamanship. As befits an island, perhaps, but this one was blessed with another enormous asset: the geography of Europe determines that the British Isles dominates the approaches to all the west coast sea-ports of the continent. The easy route to those lies through the English Channel, whose narrowest point is a mere twenty-one miles wide.

It took time for the British to rise to unmatched power if not glory – nigh on 200 years – but eventually it happened. The accretion of North America in the eighteenth century was the greatest single boost to British trade. Its loss 200 years ago hardly interrupted the by then unstoppable trend to more and more trading wealth.

For British shipping too the birth of greatness lies in the eighteenth century, in the addition of more and more colonies. The greatest prize after the Americans broke free was India but Canada remained as a resource. In any case, as we shall see, colonies were not the source of wealth – trade was and that continued unabated with both North and South America. Both of these continents were to play a pivotal role throughout the nineteenth century as Britain continued to exploit historic and imperial connections.

The engine of it all was industrial power in Britain, based on coal, iron – and through them, steam. The workshop of the world was also a kitchen of inventions out of which poured a succession of raw and manufactured goods, to provide a world hungry for novelty. It was always going to be challenged sooner or later. But a century of peace, from 1815 to 1914, ensured that the real challenge would not come until our century. It was part of the illusion, though, that peace was in some way *enforced* by the Royal Navy.

> *'Stout seamen, come away,' never be daunted*
> The Boatswain's Call

What follows is a drama, there is no better way to describe it. The first act – the defeat of Napoleon's France – is followed by a steady growth of wealth and power, colonies and influence until, towards the end, *Great* Britain becomes the world's first superpower, the organiser of more of this earth's people than ever before. This is not the place to discuss the merits, or otherwise, of this. Plainly, it happened; the costs were high, domestically and abroad. In becoming as rich as she did, Britain did not solve her own fundamental problems of poverty and social division. But it has become fashionable to use this to berate the Victorian era as if those living within it had the benefit of twentieth-century social consciousness.

Judged by the standards of the time, and those of the developing nations of Europe and the USA, Great Britain was the measure to which all others aspired. And this was as true of her governance as of her industrial production and economics. For decades, the British were able to present themselves as the most civilised, most up-to-date, most *liberal* society the world had ever seen.

British shipping played a central role in all this; without those ships, backed by the reputation of the Royal Navy, rather than its actions, not much would have happened. Above all else Britain had to trade to survive; that much at least has not altered in 200 years. All the elements were in place by the year 1800, though for the British, fighting against the might of France, the new century must have looked a grim prospect. Britain was powerful, even at that moment, for her trade was still growing and her Navy had come close to reaching a pinnacle it would never reach again.

The defeat of France: 'Now up my lads!'
Henry Newbolt, *The Old Superb*

The last of the wars against France was the longest and hardest of all, stretching from 1793 to 1802 and then, with hardly a pause, from 1803 to 1815, a twenty-year hard slog which might well have debilitated a lesser nation. As we shall see, Britain's trade *increased* during these years, although the National Debt soared. In 1815, triumphant, Britain was the most powerful nation on earth and set to conquer further and faster for another half century.

This astonishing feature of the wars should not be forgotten for, in the aftermath of the loss of the American colonies, and the conditions imposed at the subsequent peace treaty, Britain herself had paused for what some thought to be her last gasp, not just a deep breath. The mercantilists believed Old England to be finished: 'the fountain of our wealth ... the nursery of our naval power' the eighteenth century statesman, Lord Chatham had declared of North America. Now, with the French Navy helping the rebels, it had been thrown away.

The reasons why the loss of America was not a death-blow to British ambition are complex and were little understood at the time. One academic has suggested that it was because by the end of the eighteenth century, Britain was her own best strength. A large and expanding population, good communications (internally as well as externally), a well-founded (and reformable) government, strong armed services, and the most advanced economy of all, with financial reserves and City know-how, combined to reduce the impact of this setback.

More critically, in view of the two major wars fought by Britain in this century, wars 200 years ago were not fought with the total national commitment they have been in the last 100 years. A war could be fought and trade expanded quite easily. The key factor, though, in comparing Britain and, say, Holland, was that Britain could retreat to her island fortress to recover, unthreatened by any land army and therefore not needing one herself. Today, when aircraft span the world, when ballistic missiles make nonsense of any distance, and when the Channel Tunnel has been dug, this simple barrier has less significance than ever in its history; then it meant security, seclusion, a chance to take that vital breath.

Apart from her natural frontier, Britain was enjoying the first fruits of the Industrial Revolution. Demand for her manufactured products – the first of their kind the world had seen – were to

outweigh any other factor. Trade with America, for instance, was
growing faster than with anywhere else after 1785; rejection of
colonial rule did not prevent demand for the old oppressors' products.
It was this immense and growing economic power that France con-
fronted. Too often historians have tended to paint Britain as the
defensive nation, fighting for her life. Yet although the wars were to
threaten invasion, and although by 1808 Britain was isolated, she
was in considerably stronger a position than she was to be in 1940.

What this inexorably led to was Britain's naval mastery, a position
unchallenged in any decisive way until the end of the nineteenth
century. Of the main engagements by the British fleet of the French,
either alone or in combination with Dutch and Spanish warships, all
were victories for the Royal Navy. In these, numbers were often
equal – or to the enemy's advantage. What told was superior British
seamanship, better guns and gunnery, and audacity. Never before or
since has the Royal Navy depended on such a superb group of
great sailors and military tacticians: Troubridge, St Vincent, Howe,
Douglas, Jervis, Duncan – and Nelson.

The Royal Navy gained, too, from being at sea much more than
its enemies. The long, hard patrolling along the Atlantic coasts and
into the North Sea and Baltic meant that the British were hardened
to a continuous life of sailing and fighting. They were supplied at sea,
they repaired their ships at sea, they knew its currents and its moods.
They worked over greater distances, too, crossing and re-crossing the
Atlantic to the British colonies in the West Indies, seeking out the
French along the Mediterranean coasts, convoying merchant ships to
India and beyond. Thus, they were better navigators, their charts
more thorough and more up to date.

Tactically, their experience told when, for instance, at the Battle of
the Nile, Nelson's ships ran *inside* the anchored French, closer to the
shore, taking their old adversaries completely by surprise, and leaving
them gasping. It was Nelson, of course, who first broke the line at
Cape St Vincent against a larger and more heavily armed Spanish
fleet, thereby inventing a new naval tactic that was to pay handsomely
at Trafalgar. The British spoiled for a fight; like the Allies in the Gulf,
in 1991, they wanted the enemy to come out; he tried hard, on the
whole, to steer clear.

The other side of all the glory was impressment of seamen. The
twenty years of war created a terrible shortage and the Press Gangs
had to reach further and further. As many as 50 per cent of sailors
on a man-of-war might have been 'pressed'. What the Navy needed

was qualified seamen; many on their way home after a long voyage were seized from merchant ships in the Channel. Part of the cause of the 1812 war with the United States was that the Royal Navy seized men it suspected of being British from American ships. The situation worsened considerably in 1807 when HMS *Leopard* fired on the American warship *Chesapeake* killing three sailors; she was then boarded and the four men considered to be British were taken off. One of them was hanged.

Conditions on board Royal Naval ships were generally atrocious, alleviated here and there by good-hearted captains. Men lived, fought, were wounded, and died by the guns they manned, torn to bloody shreds by appalling weapons fired at point-blank range as ships closed. The sheer destructiveness of it all was aimed at men (and the rigging) – not the ships hulls. The massive three-deckers were almost impossible to sink unless a lucky shot hit a magazine. More ships were lost to weather at Trafalgar than to weapons. It was the crew you tried to maim and kill, or induce to surrender.

There was a good measure of incompetence among officers, as commissions, as in the Army, could be bought. Men, impressed or not, never knew when they might see a home port again; if they did they were liable to be seized once more. Prize money for captured men-of-war might have been some kind of incentive; as for the rest we can only speculate that it was the devil seamen knew – the cat for minor crime and the noose for cowardice, and a hundred other, lesser, offences were common punishments – that kept many fighting on. Life on land could be even harsher: the war years included many where the British rural labourer and his family were starving.

Of all the great battles that were fought at sea, we remember Trafalgar best – fought on the 21 October 1805 – because after it the command of the seas by the British was not to be seriously challenged again around these shores for over 100 years. There were other battles, notably off Copenhagen, and in the skirmishes against the Americans in the war of 1812; they were footnotes. Trafalgar was, in twentieth-century terms, Britain's Midway, or, perhaps more accurately, her Tsushima. Never before or since have we had such a naval victory.

In the Napoleonic Wars (1803–15), the French tried to hit at the heart of Britain's naval strength, which was being used to blockade the whole of Europe, an incredible task for one nation to undertake. The French failed, although their privateers took many ships (as many as 11,000 over the course of all the wars, 1793–1815). The French attacked in this way across the globe and the British replied in kind, including the first known use of 'Q' ships, warships disguised to tempt raiders.

The convoy system – used by medieval sailors as protection – was re-introduced, by law, along with expeditionary forces sent specifically to root out nests of French piracy operating from bases in Martinique, Mauritius and Guadeloupe. Most privateer attacks took place closer to home – in the Channel, the North Sea, Baltic and Mediterranean. The vulnerability of British ships to this hit-and-run tactic, coming as they did from all over the Western world, and from much of the Far East, was shown up starkly. The size of the Royal Navy and its operations expanded enormously as a result. By 1815, and the Congress of Vienna, the Navy had 214 ships of the line and nearly 800 'cruisers', the frigates and one-deckers of all kinds which could be used for detached operations, like anti-privateer work, worldwide. The frigate, as a design of warship, was shown to be the best for long-range scouting work, and for general duties. Her modern equivalent came to be the armoured cruiser, one of the two warships most associated with colonies, the other being the river gunboat. There was a transformation, and not just in size. The Navy, henceforth, would have a global role, and one not ended, formally, for 150 years until in 1967 the Royal Navy withdrew from east of Suez (only to return there in the 1970s). The numbers of ships on foreign station increased throughout the nineteenth century, rising from sixty-three in 1817, to 129 in 1848. Gunboat diplomacy had arrived.

'And England's far, and Honour a name'
Henry Newbolt, *Vitaï Lampada*

The defeat of France meant more than a re-drawing of the map of Europe. Although Britain's role in Vienna was to try to ensure the practical application of the theory of the balance of power, the wider result was that the 'second' British empire was now a fact. More even than that, Britain had become the embryonic first superpower, a nation to which others would increasingly turn for any number of reasons: raw materials, manufactures, support, military help. Britain was now to impose, willy nilly, her language and customs on the world.

The full extent of territory Britain directly ruled in 1815 was not great. After the loss of the American colonies, her greatest potential colonial land area was in Canada. In 1815 most of this had hardly been explored. Similarly in Australia: the First Fleet, which had landed in 1788, had been sent to investigate the use of Australia as a colony for convicts, now that America was lost for this use. Its members only just survived and Australia was still a pretty desperate place to be, even thirty years on. Of the great colonies, India was most obviously an asset, although in 1815 it was for the British still a series of trading posts, with her influence waxing but yet to make its full mark. Any sense of India as the jewel in the crown of the Empire was only to emerge much later. For the rest, Britain had a string of islands, many in the West Indies, others scattered across the globe. It was the latter, however, which provided the web which the British came to recognise as their greatest asset.

Latterly, it has become a received wisdom in some quarters that the British Empire happened as if by accident, that in many cases we were 'asked' to take over. It is certainly true that in some remote corners, tribes beset by overweening local enemies did ask for protection. Some received it; others not. It is specious in the extreme to suggest Britain did not recognise the possible gain from colonies: there were too many tracts, too many parliamentarians, too many religious zealots proclaiming as loudly as they could the benefits of colonisation, in one form or another, for it not to have been perceived in Britain that there were immense benefits. Equally, there remained sceptics all through, who saw the colonies as an increasing burden, and one Britain would one day have cause to regret.

It was not accepted that colonies meant great expenditure from the centre. Their abiding quality was their subservience, their openness to British goods, their raw materials which could be used either at home or for re-export. Strategically, in one form or another, far way colonies *were* a burden, with long open frontiers and recalcitrant natives, always on the verge of revolt,

The island bases, however, were a different matter. At and after the Congress of Vienna Britain gained a priceless set of minor jewels to add to her collection. Put another way – by Admiral John Arbuthnot (Jacky) Fisher – the bases constituted the keys which 'locked up' the entire world. They straddled the sea-lanes, they provided fuel and shelter for the British fleet. Britain had Heligoland, Malta and the Ionian Islands (including Corfu, where they still play cricket as a result of our brief encounter). These were added to that invaluable choke point – Gibraltar. With the Channel Islands, and the Orkneys and Shetlands, Britain in a very physical sense now surrounded Europe.

She had a string of Caribbean possessions, 'locking up' Central America; Bermuda (1609) did the same for the southern United States. Now were added the Atlantic islands of St Helena, Ascension and, in 1833, the Falklands, today the key to immense oil, mineral and fishing wealth in the Antarctic region. In 1819 Britain took Singapore, in 1839 Aden and, in 1841, perhaps the greatest still of these Far Eastern prizes, Hong Kong. Only in the Pacific did she lack, by this last date, a particular island base; then along came Fiji.

Of course, to this list have to be added any number of land ports: Lagos, Alexandria, Mombasa and, further away, the great sea-ports in Canada and the superb natural harbours of Sydney and Auckland. The acquisition of treaty ports on the Chinese mainland, the huge base in Ceylon (now Sri Lanka) of Trincomalee, arguably the finest harbour on earth, all embossed the basic design. And all for trade, to enable, above all, this island's traders to move at will across the globe buying and selling.

The Great Exhibition: 'nations not so blest as thee.'
Rule Britannia

In 1851 the specially erected 'Crystal' Palace in Hyde Park became the focus of the entire developed world; the wonder of the age. Queen Victoria had been on the throne for fourteen years. In that time she had already given her name to history: the world knows the greater part of the nineteenth century as the Victorian Age. The reason is easy to find. By the year of the Great Exhibition (itself the first 'world' fair) Britain was producing nearly 70 per cent of the world's coal, half its iron, five-sevenths of its steel, half its cotton cloth and 40 per cent of manufactured goods. Never again would one country so dominate the world (although Japan, today, bids fair to try). The watchwords, the new thinking behind this extraordinary achievement, were free trade; the Navigation Acts had been repealed, the Corn Laws had gone. Britain could well afford this entry into open markets. Along with the vogue for *laissez-faire* economic policy at home, their worth was plain for anyone to see. To take just our theme, shipping; by 1880, thirty years after the Great Exhibition, Britain had more registered tonnage than the rest of the world put together, and the fleet was entirely insured in London, earning enormous sums for the invisible exports which so long were to keep Britain rich.

The great Industrial Revolution of the latter part of the eighteenth century had created the framework for all this. First and foremost the mechanisation of the woollen and cotton industries; the inventions for refining and working iron; then the invention of steam power. Many other elements went to make up the sum of these parts and their collective impact on society. Transport had been continuously improved with the growth of canals for the transport of heavy goods, the turnpike roads for light. The real breakthrough came with the steam engine, first as a fixed pumping and winding engine; then, in its greatest manifestation, as mobile steam power.

Marine steam came at the very beginning of the nineteenth century, but then took a long time to develop. Steam engines for railways came later (they had less room to fit in) but developed much faster. By 1851, when Daniel Gooch's Great Western steam engine, *Lord of the Isles*, was exhibited at the Crystal Palace, the railways already provided a substantial national network. They provided, too, an export. British railways eventually spanned the world, as did British bridges, British roads, British canals, sewers, drains, mains water pipes and the purifying plants that made the local water safe.

Everything invented and used here was exported in one form or another, either as raw material, like pig-iron or steel bars, or as prefabricated parts, for assembly in some corner of the world. Complete bridges were sent out that way for in the prefabrication of iron the British demonstrated a special genius, transcending commerce and turning it into art. Although the Empire provided one extremely valuable market it was by no means the only one. Indeed, it was a minor partner in this century of economic expansion. This is so easily forgotten and yet it remains the most crucial link in the chain, the core of Britain's economic strength: over 60 per cent of British exports and over 80 per cent of her capital employed abroad went to destinations *outside* the Empire in this golden age.

It was virtually all carried in British ships. Even when they carried away raw bulk material, like coal, these ships were earning money. Capital, re-invested here or abroad, poured into and through the system. Never again would the British enjoy such a run for their money. There was a price. The rapid industrialisation of any country creates terrible disruption. Any developing area today demonstrates that – close at home the cities of East Europe, further afield, Mexico City, Jakarta, São Paulo. There was enormous misery in the cities of Victorian Britain, as Engels and Marx were to discover. No wonder that they identified a new Apocalypse whose 'scientific' development through the 'inevitable' revolution, would cleanse the pollution of industrial life from mens' souls.

Death from disease in those early crowded streets killed millions; death and injury from industrial accident killed many more. Women dragged carts of coal, naked, through the gloom of Victorian coal-mines until 1842; their ragged and exhausted children, saved by the same Shaftesbury Act, had fanned the same pits, often in the pitch-dark, for up to eighteen hours a day. The wealth that flowed out of these noxious pits, that spun off the looms of Lancashire and from the spinning machines of Bradford and Leeds, the iron that cascaded from the smelters, the myriad tin and fancy goods, the crockery, the finery and the frippery, which kept a burgeoning middle class in luxuries, cost the nation dear.

Victorian Britain, in 1851, was a society in a tremendous state of flux, where everything was for sale, where the conscience of a few had only slowly begun to penetrate into the central consciousness of the nation. Slavery had been made illegal in Britain and her colonies, finally, in 1807; in the next few decades the Royal Navy were to spend much effort on chasing, stopping and searching foreign ships. At home more than half her people were daily enslaved by an economic system which seemed unstoppable, God-given and ordained. And abroad, although her subject people might enjoy some of the most advanced manufactured goods ever seen, and in greater and greater quantities, the bloody end of the Indian Mutiny would shortly see British soldiers tying native mutineers across the barrels of their artillery, before blowing them to pieces. It was, as never before, 'the best of times, the worst of times'.

'Then come so many ships ...'
John Masefield, *Ships*

The long wars against France had far from checked British trade, but the organisation of that trade through 'venturers' was coming to an end. The main form of ship ownership was through partnerships. Ships were divided into sixty-four shares; any number of these could be owned, and captains might well have some. The long voyages were still hazardous; many effectively took a year to complete; on the Far East runs to China this was stretched to eighteenth months per trip, assuming nothing went wrong. Voyages had to be timed to avoid the hurricane season in the West Indies and the Monsoons in the Far East and although the Admiralty's charts were improving all the time, navigation across the large oceans was still a mixture of science, experience, art and conjecture for most merchant skippers. Throughout the French wars changes were taking place, codifying and classifying – ordering – British shipping. In 1797, the Manifest Act instructed all British ships to declare their full cargoes; this followed an extended Navigation Act of eleven years previously which required all British ships of more than fifteen tons, including those in the Empire, to register.

But although the Navigation Acts were still in force, the effects of the war on merchant manpower had its effect. By 1794 a change in the law meant that up to three-quarters of the crew of a British ship could be foreign. As time went on, British ships would carry many foreign crew, from all over the world. Goanese would specialise as stewards, some, like the Somalis, would find their forte in the stoke-holds. The Chinese would come, and Indians, Africans from all over that continent; sea-going islanders from all over the world. As the British Empire expanded, so British ships would undertake an immense re-distribution of seafaring people; although many would eventually return home, many others would fetch up in foreign ports, and settle there: Liverpool and Tiger Bay (in Cardiff), to name just two. As an indication of the continued growth of trade, there was an expansion of the London docks from 1800: the West India dock opened in 1802, the East India in 1806, whilst the Greenland Dock was improved in 1807. London kept its position as the largest port, although Liverpool was rapidly catching her up. The west-coast ports benefited from the French wars as ships entering and leaving did not have to run the gauntlet of the English Channel. Liverpool owed much of its good fortune around the turn of the century to the slave trade, now entering its last phase. Although abolition was agreed in 1792, to come into force in 1796, Liverpool repeatedly petitioned against; the war ensured a reprieve and the last slaver, the *Kitty Amelia*, finally left Liverpool on a final slave trip in July 1807.

The coming of the steamship, along with the increasing use of iron in ship construction, then the replacement of the paddle wheel by the propellor, transformed the way ships moved, as well as their reliability and their size. But the struggle between sail and steam was not easily resolved. The early steam engines needed immense quantities of coal and often they broke down. Sail was to enjoy another hundred years of oceanic use.

One prize for steam was the Atlantic crossing. It was in 1838 when two steamships left Britain for the United States, the *Sirius*, an Irish Channel ship of 703 tons, and Brunel's *Great Western*, of 1320 tons.

The *Sirius* left London on 28 March, and Cork on 4 April, arriving in New York with just fifteen tons of coal left on 23 April. The *Great Western* left Bristol on 8 April and arrived just after the *Sirius*; she had over 200 tons of coal left. The North Atlantic run had been breached; a triumph which would lead a hundred years on to the superb liners of the 1930s, including the *Queens*.

Later that year Samuel Cunard crossed back to England. He had already formed the British and North American Mail Packet Company, later the Cunard Line, and he secured the mail contract for the North Atlantic, setting up a regular run using steamships. Only shortly before the service started it had been pronounced as impossible. The Royal Mail contracts were often the saviours of these early steamship companies, as they had been for sailing ships before. At the very moment the British were espousing free trade and were soon to abandon the last of the Navigation Acts, they were continuing to subsidise shipping through the mail. As a proportion of a shipping company's revenue these contracts could be substantial.

The Peninsula and Oriental (P&O) set up to trade between Spain, Portugal and Britain, but rapidly moving its services eastwards, recouped up to 40 per cent of its operating costs through the Royal Mail contract throughout most of the nineteenth century; more generally the Mail contract could amount to a quarter. Royal Mail contracts brought prestige as well, the ship's name being prefixed by RMS instead of the less glamourous SS. At the time of the first serious steamship crossings of the Atlantic, Britain had around 26,000 registered ships, totalling nearly three million tons. Of this, 20 per cent was registered with the colonies. Of the home total by far the greatest was engaged in moving coal – over a thousand coasters in the trade between Newcastle and London.

The importance of this humble bulk trade cannot be over-estimated. For instance, because coal could be shipped out to foreign ports, British shipping rates were lower than those of other countries. Coal was the lifeblood of the steam technology which the British were by the middle of the century busily introducing to the rest of the world. It fired the boilers of pumping engines, railway engines, traction engines and marine steam engines. It was dumped in coaling stations all over the world (the Falklands being a good example of how remote islands could be fitted into the picture). The Royal Navy needed coal from locations between Nova Scotia and Australia, China to the Cape of Good Hope.

By 1850 coal exports were worth £46 million. Ships would carry it outward to all parts of the world, bringing home other raw materials. Ironically, it was carried at this time almost exclusively in sailing ships, the time taken to get it to its destinations unimportant. 'King Coal' was to continue to make fortunes well into the twentieth century.

The decade between 1850 and 1860 saw more great upheavals for shipping. By 1850 it had been flung into the arena of free trade, the culmination of a process which had been going on for some time. Now, even the coastal trade was open to all-comers (a source, as late as 1991, of bitter anger by British seafarers). Tonnage had risen to 4.3 million and over 200,000 sailors were employed. In 1854 came the first of a number of significant Merchant Shipping Acts, giving the Board of Trade increased powers to regulate shipping. From this Act also came the first schools for navigation, as did codified signal books for use at sea, adopted by the rest of the world, as a matter of course, as was English for communication at sea. New shipping lines were beginning; this was a time when joint stock companies were being formed, when capital was easy to get and when enterprise was still strongly running in British veins. Many of the great names of twentieth-century shipping were gathering: Cunard we have met already, Ismay, Holt, Harrison, Baines, Shaw and Savill, Elder, Bibby and many others, now lost to time, joined him. There were hundreds and hundreds of small owners of a few ships – sometimes increasing their fleets at great speed, then reducing them as times hardened – speculators all. Their memory has been enshrined latterly in the television series, the *Onedin Line*. It was a hard and brutal business. Two things were happening during this period. One was that tonnage was increasing in response to the basic trades: the export by Britain to the rest of the world of cheap cloth, cheap iron, cheap machinery and, most of all, cheap coal; and the exchange for the raw materials, and food, that fuelled manufacturing industries and their employees.

The extent to which the Empire held back the expansion of trade in other, more competitive, areas has already been examined. Britain traded with the whole world. What can be said is that the Empire remained as a potential burden – political and military but also economic. One day the cheque would be cashed. As one writer – Paul Kennedy – has pointed out, up until 1815 much of what subsequently became the British Empire was on the receiving end of British Naval fire-power, or might be.[1] After that date the reverse was true. Sooner or later other countries would be bound to challenge us. It did not

start with military action. In the years of the *Pax Britannica* it was
in few European nations' interests to fight the British. Most of those
nations with any trading ambitions lay open to the Royal Navy – or
at least believed in its reputation. The main thrust of competition
became *copying* and then over-taking the British in industrial ingen-
uity. The Germans, once unified, the French, the Americans and,
above all, the Japanese, came to erode Britain's industrial lead from
the mid-century on. In the second Industrial Revolution – the rise of
chemicals and of electricity – we ran poorly, innovating slowly, if at
all, and relying on our innate and solid base to see us through. Iron
and steam had made Britain; chemicals and electricity (and latterly,
electronics) were to undo her.

But there came a moment when, for the merchant service, the
summit was reached. Never before, or since, in the known history of
the world, had a single nation carried half the world's trade; never
had a nation owned over half the world's shipping. By 1870 that
heady state had been achieved by the British. Most of that shipping
was still sail. Already, though, others were creeping up. American
shipping had doubled between 1849 and 1859; fortunately, the bulk
of American ships were coastal or plied the Great Lakes. Then the
American Civil War intervened, to Britain's great advantage.

For a while it got better. One estimate is that by 1890 the British
Empire owned over 60 per cent of tonnage. One writer justifiably
calls these decades between 1870 and 1890 the 'crest of the wave',[2]
further pointing out that even when the tonnage figures began to
decline, the *quality* of the British fleet ensured that she would remain
pre-eminent. It would be the First World War that would, finally,
shake that position once and for all.

'Talk about your flash packets'
Song: *The Dreadnought*

As long as there had been ships there had been passengers. But during
the long age of sail most passengers endured rather than enjoyed their
travel at sea. Sailing ships are slow and frightening, full of the creaks
and groans of a thousand strange, dangerous pieces of canvas and
rope, and shouting men heaving at violent pieces of cloth. Sailing
ships heel in a wind. Their lack of reliability had to be faced for those
who would cross the Atlantic. It is a measure of the desperation (and,
no doubt, ignorance) many people felt that they chose to emigrate
across that vast and gale-torn ocean. It was in the emigration trade

that the modern passenger liner was borne. The nineteenth century saw a huge increase in emigration, as the stories and even sometimes the truths about the United States filtered back to Europe.

The first steamships, early on in the nineteenth century, encouraged passengers by their ability to arrive more or less on time. It was the short channel crossings, and coastal waters, that saw the first serious increase in passenger traffic. Passengers, like the mail, were high-cost items; the early steamships had little room for bulk cargoes as so much space was taken up by machinery and fuel.

But by the time the Atlantic was beginning to be crossed regularly by steamship in the 1840s, passengers were valuable as revenue. Many were still carried in sailing ships and endured weeks of misery. Even steamships could not yet provide – nor thought to – much in the way of comfort. Sailors had endured centuries of privation; passengers had to fend as best they might. For British shipping the twin sources of hard-cash passenger routes came from the emigrant trade, first across the Atlantic and thereafter to the farther flung outposts of Empire, like Australia and New Zealand; and from the constant need to replenish the Empire itself with people, largely in India.

The opening of the Suez Canal, in 1869, transformed all this, cutting the voyage to China by nearly a fortnight and the distance by 3,000 miles. Up to then passengers had had to trans-ship from Alexandria to Port Suez along the Nile, an unhealthy, dusty and exceedingly horrid journey. Emigration to the United States continued throughout the nineteenth century from all over Europe. The often oppressed peasants of Ireland, then central Europe, the Balkans and European Russia, joined with hundreds of thousands of urban poor from Britain, France, Germany, Italy, the Netherlands and Scandinavia, heading for what they fondly imagined to be a kind of earthly paradise. Between 1845 and 1855 2.5 million left British ports alone.

Gold fuelled the imagination of many would-be travellers – and not just Californian or Alaskan. In Australia gold was discovered in the early 1850s and in New Zealand in 1862. Between 1858 and 1882 Shaw Savill carried over 100,000 people to New Zealand alone, all in sailing ships, as the immense distance between the tip of Africa and Australia meant that no steamship of the time could have made the voyage. That changed slowly. As marine engines improved, sail could not compete. Cunard was using a fast steamer, the *Persia*, by 1855. Able to carry over 250 passengers she could cross the Atlantic in nine days (compared with the great *Queens* in the mid-twentieth century of around three to four days). This was progress indeed.

Travel, even at this speed, could still be mightily uncomfortable, though not perhaps as bad as it had been in 1838 when, not long after the *Sirius* and the *Great Western* had made their historic crossing, the *Royal William* followed them, so loaded with coal that her passengers were able to dip their hands in the sea from the deck. By the 1880s it had become apparent that money could be made by improving the conditions in which passengers were carried. Ismay's White Star line began to build a series of big (over 10,000 tons) ships which were to culminate in the *Olympic* and the *Titanic*. The golden age of Atlantic passenger travel had dawned.

For the Far East, too, the latter part of the century saw the rise of the steamship. Whereas not all that long ago servants of the British Empire would leave for India expecting to make perhaps one journey back – on retirement – if that, now regular passages could be planned. Wives might make the passage every couple of years, themselves first recruited by husbands returning from a first spell of duty after five years. In the early nineteenth century the Indian voyage could take four months; within fifty years it could be measured in weeks, then in days (seventeen by the 1890s, at a cost of £50.00). Terms associated with this trip have gone into the language: 'Port Out, Starboard Home,' the best cabins to ensure shade from the tropical sun, has been immortalised as 'posh'. The British dominated these passenger trades as they did freight. At any one time in the 1890s British ships could be carrying 200,000 passengers; between 1896 and 1897 a thousand ships were launched from British yards and, of every thousand tons passing through the Suez Canal, 700 tons were British (plus ninety-five German, sixty-three French – who had built it –, forty-three Dutch and only two American). The biggest shipping lines were P&O, Elder Dempster and British India, all of whom had made their fortunes out of the Empire. Shaw Savill ships traded people and goods to New Zealand, as did the New Zealand Shipping Company, the latter by the 1890s bringing in the first ship-loads of frozen lamb. Voyages to Australia were then taking around thirty-five days.

Ships might burn as much as 3,600 tons of coal each way. Average ship's bunkers would hold about 2,500 tons, so the importance of the land bases like Aden becomes clear. Singapore's own coaling stocks would be around 20,000 tons – all of which had to be shipped out from Britain. The Royal Mail Steam Packet Company took letters to Central and South America and the colonies in the Caribbean, the Ocean Steamship Blue Funnel Line traded in the Far East, basing many ships permanently out there. There were four shipping lines to Canada, two from Liverpool to West Africa and a weekly service to South Africa (one day to become the Union Castle Line, running until the late 1960s). Across the Atlantic ran the mightier and mightier ships of Cunard and White Star. On the North Atlantic run a ship, like the *Oregon*, would burn 330 tons of coal a day; her bunkers held 4,000 tons.

Launches of British Ships:

Yr:	Steamships:	Sailing ships:
1888:	458	81
1889:	595	95
1890:	651	92
1891:	641	181
1892:	512	169
1893:	438	98
1894:	549	65
1895:	526	53
1896:	628	68
1897:	545	46
1898:	744	17
1899:	714	12
1900:	664	28

To the Victorians, in the twilight years of both their Queen's reign and, did they but know it, their nation's greatness as well, it all seemed ordained. The British celebrated the destruction of these hitherto vast ocean distances, they marvelled at the speed of it all, at how the Royal Mail could penetrate India in just over a fortnight and Australia in six weeks. And all by steamship and steam train, all by dint of Britain's great leap forward – and through the efforts of her Navy (or so it was fondly imagined) and her brave sailors.

'All I ask is a merry yarn,
from a laughing fellow rover'
John Masefield, *Sea farer*

In 1800 there may have been as many as 300,000 seafarers in a population of twelve million (2.5 per cent) compared today with 18,000 in a population of fifty-six million (0.03 per cent). As many as one in six families may have been dependent on the sea in one way or another. The life of a seafarer remained harsh, and extremely hazardous. Accidents – other than falling overboard – were common; disease still killed thousands year on year, both tropical and more mundane. The ships were often badly run, with poor food and strict discipline from bad masters.

One long-time historian of Britain's seafarers, Ronald Hope, puts it thus, in discussing the time of the Napoleonic Wars:

> The price of victory at sea in the French Wars was 100,000 dead and the number of maimed seamen begging in the streets was a national scandal. No infectious disease other than smallpox could be controlled; scurvy was still rife since oranges and lemons were expensive ... casualties ... were frequent – deaths from drowning, falls from masts, suffocation from foul air in the holds, burns, wounds, poisoning and much more.[3]

In the rapidly industrialising towns and cities, such considerations were also apparent, but whilst the impetus for change gathered pace there, at sea out of sight was truly out of mind. Late into the twentieth century seamen have continued to suffer from poor conditions under extreme circumstances. No other industry has been worse served. Efforts were made on shore to alleviate a sailor's lot. The Marine Society had been started as early as 1756 (and is still going today). It was followed by other bodies concerned with the sea and its sailors. The Royal National Lifeboat Institution was founded in 1824 (and still receives more money than any other charity, which it idiosyncratically remains); the Destitute Sailors' Asylum in 1827.

By and large, though, land-based society did not recognise, other than in popular verse and song, the contribution seafarers were making – an exact parallel with today. As far as 'polite' society went, this was as much due to the nature of seafaring and those who chose it, as to do with any knowledge. Sailors down the ages have dined out, so to speak, on their reputation for drinking and whoring. Two hundred years ago the life set them apart for years at a time from home and family. The conditions they faced, much as in war, meant they had suffered more than many; but the nature of that suffering would be lost on those who had not been at sea in a storm or who had not travelled far. At the same time, all was not bad. Sailors could make a reasonable living, and might chance across a means to making a fortune, if not at sea through some encounter with foreign parts.

Some early shipping companies were well worth working for – the

East India Company for example was renowned for looking after its employees. As the nineteenth century wore on others would take 'John Company's' place in seafaring legend. The nature of the work, however, did not vary. Seamanship had remained much as it had been down the preceding centuries: hard, relentless, cold and dangerous. Men – and boys – still had to crawl up those towering spars as they swayed in high winds, hand themselves out along slippery yard-arms and wrestle with huge canvas sails being torn by the wind. Ships, while sail yet remained as the principal powerhouse, could be becalmed, as well as storm-tossed, held a few miles from land for days or weeks at a time. Voyages to and from the Far East might vary from a three-month passage to a year or more. Even in the lengthy sunset of sail, when the clippers sailed back from China with their holds stuffed with tea, or later wool or wheat from Australia, voyages depended entirely on the vagaries of wind. In one famous voyage from Australia, a clipper tried in vain for weeks to beat around Cape Horn only to fail. Her skipper turned her round and sailed non-stop back to Liverpool, back past Australia, round the Cape of Good Hope, and thence through the Atlantic. In conditions like this men had to be tough or go under.

'Familiar steamers, too, majestic steamers'
John Masefield, *Ships*

One class of seafarer never before seen was the engineer. Early on there were clashes between the practitioners of the new infernal arts and those of the old. Engineers began and remained a class of their own, keeping different watches, working in the bowels of the ships, making a dreadful stinking mess on deck and all over the billowing canvas. The first steamships were as potentially lethal to their servants below as sailing ships continued to be to sailors aloft. Not only that, they were prone to explosion and fire, those two most dreaded of maritime calamities. They were heavy on fuel and weak on power. But they got better, and given Britain's position as the only truly industrialised nation, with abundant supplies of coal, it was inevitable that they should.

The steam engine, as every schoolchild knows, was invented by James Watt in 1782. Its early development on land was relatively slow; on the water it was not until 1802 that the *Charlotte Dundas* made her first appearence on the Forth and Clyde Canal. Thereafter progress was steady. The problems for all ships, merchant and naval, was three-fold. The first was the space taken up by the machinery, particularly the boilers. This was made much worse for many years by the paddles and their associated gearings.

Secondly, the engines were very inefficient, developing low power. As a result, for some time steamship use was confined to use in port, as tugs, or in towing barges, or as an auxiliary to sail. This latter was important for any ships contemplating long trips as bunkering facilities in the early years were limited. The technological break-throughs were the invention of the compound engine – by John Elder, in 1854 – and then of the triple-expansion engine by Dr AC Kirk, in 1874. Although the first of these triple-expansion engines suffered from the problem of low boiler pressure, subsequent use of forced draught meant they became a standard form of marine engine for many merchant ships until displaced by the diesel this century.

The great leap in marine engine technology finally came in the last decade of the nineteenth century when Charles Parsons invented the steam turbine; for both large passenger and cargo liners, and for naval vessels, this method of turning propellors meant a huge increase in available power, and was used until the 1970s. The propellor, first used in the *Archimedes* in 1837, was immediately adopted by Brunel for the *Great Britain*, launched in 1845 and then the biggest ship afloat. For the Navy, too, the invention was critical as paddle wheels took up too much space otherwise usable for guns, and were also highly vulnerable to attack. But although the steam engine continued to be fitted to more and more new ships the old ways died hard. Many ships continued to be fitted with full sailing rigs, in part because using steam as the auxiliary power was extremely economic; in part because steam engines did break down and fuel did run out; in part because sailors – and shipbuilders – are traditionalists by nature.

Then, in the 1850s and 1860s, came the first of the greatest sailing ships ever built. They lasted, through the eccentricities of both owners and economies until the Second World War. They were built for the tea trade and they were the 'clippers'; later, larger 'windjammers' would be built and although beautiful beyond imagining under full sail at sea, it would be the early smaller clippers which would live longest in public memory.

> 'They mark our passage as a race of men,
> Earth will not see such ships as these agen.'

John Masefield's lament for the tea and wool clippers has been echoed by countless writers, poets, artists. Born of the American schooners of the Napoleonic Wars, which were designed to be blockade runners, the long sleek lines with a 'fast entry' of raked bow, the increasing height of mast, the overhanging 'counter' sterns, made these ships remarkably beautiful.

The golden age of the tea-clipper, when the yearly race from China to the Thames became an event of popular imagination, was between the 1860s and 1870s. The Suez Canal, opening in 1869, made steamship operation to the Far East a viable proposition, just as the Panama Canal, opening in 1912, put paid to the windjammers' nitrate trade around Cape Horn, where steamships dared not go. For a brief time, on these longest of voyages, sail ruled. The British shipbuilders had fought back against the Yankee clippers, helped by the American Civil War, to produce *Thermopylae, Ariel, Taeping, Fiery Cross* – and the *Cutty Sark*.

In 1866 there occurred the most famous of the tea-clipper races ever. The *Fiery Cross* left Foochow on 29 May, the *Serica, Taeping and Ariel* on 30 May, the *Taitsing* on 31 May. *Taeping* docked in London just before 10.00 hrs on 6 September, the *Ariel* half an hour later and the *Serica* at midday. The other two arrived two days later, all having covered the 16,000 miles in record time. The tea-clippers became woolships, in an effort to keep trading, but the bigger four- and five-masted steel-hulled windjammers drove them off. It was with these four- and five-thousand ton monsters with their mainmast over 200 feet above the deck, crewed by teenagers seeking adventure, that sail was finally to close as an ocean-crossing commercial venture. The limits of technology had long been reached, only to be superceded in the late 1970s and 1980s when sail again became, in part, a viable proposition. But the ugly circular computer-directed 'sails' tried out on various merchant ships could not have been further from the delicate whites and fawns of canvas lifted from deck to mast-truck, spread across three, four or five steel frameworks, of the last of the ocean-going merchant sailing ships.

> 'We looked toward the Admiral where high the
>   Peter flew,
> And all our hearts were dancing like the sea.'
>
> Henry Newbolt, *The Old Superb*

Nelson's Navy, in 1815, basked in a glory that has lasted down to today. It is the images of those times people conjure up still when they seek to set a modern naval action in context. It was the Nelson 'tradition' which the headline writers recalled in the Falklands War. Although the Royal Navy stood down from the Napoleonic Wars triumphant and proud, the following hundred years provided a mixed and often unhappy time. The *Pax Britannica* might rely on the strength and shield of the world's largest Navy but that shield was tarnished and tawdry in many of its parts.

The problems varied but the underlying one was two-fold. Firstly, the Board of Admiralty were aware that they had always to keep the goal of supremacy uppermost; that hog-tied them in many ways, terrorised them in others and forced agonies of indecision over fleet composition and size. Secondly, the 'traditions' handed down became a set of mill-stones which afflicted the Victorian Navy and created a pompous, ritual-obsessed hierarchy in which 'smartness aloft' intruded upon the business and conduct of war.

These issues were made worse by the extent of the British Empire the fleet had now to protect and the varied conditions in each part (China station river gunboats versus long-range Pacific Ocean cruisers). Finally, the Royal Navy had no major war to fight between 1815 and 1914 and the changes that it made to its fleet had to be based on a mixture of technological inspiration, guesswork, and the copying from others' experiences in battle.

The fact remained that the Royal Navy was the world's strongest and it kept that lead for more or less a hundred years. The two-fleet standard arose: the British naval capital ship register had to be at least twice as big as the next two naval powers. If France and America had twenty battleships each, the British had to have at least forty. The technological changes which affected merchant shipping were, on the whole, adopted rather faster by the Navy. Steam was used first in 1822 in the *Comet*, a coastal tug and survey vessel. By 1845 there were 145 steam vessels listed, although none yet in the battle fleet.

A year later the *Ajax* was launched, steam powered and screw driven. The propellor was a vital ingredient in naval acceptance of steam as it meant no awkward paddle box straddling the gun-deck, reducing fire-power as a result. As with the merchant ships, steam and sail sat alongside each other for many decades to come. The last sail-masted armoured ships built were the *Warspite* and the *Imperieuse* in 1881. They weighed so much that, under sail, they would not move at all; the two masts were replaced with a 'military' one between the funnels.

The world's first truly modern 'battleship' built was the *Warrior* in 1859. At least one naval historian has compared the advance made with this design as 'the biggest ever made [in naval warfare] until the building of the first nuclear submarine'. *Warrior* can still be seen – she is now alongside the *Victory* in Portsmouth Naval Dockyard, elegantly restored. The *Warrior* was built in response to the French warship *Gloire*, which had pioneered 'iron-clad' armour. *Warrior*, however, was entirely built of iron and the strength it gave her hull meant she could carry much heavier armour plate and more guns. Her cost, though, was enormous, nearly four times a conventional wooden hull of her time. Costs of warships were to dominate much thinking in the years that followed.

Warrior was nearly a modern 'battleship', and indeed, that name would become a generic term for the biggest and heaviest warships. But she did not have turreted guns, not least because with masts and rigging, guns in revolving turrets suffered from restricted firing angles. *Warrior*, then, still fired a 'broadside' and it was not until the problems of getting a powerful and reliable enough steam engine fitted, in the 1870s, that masts, rigging and sails could finally be dispensed with and the modern gun turret fitted.

HMS *Devastation* (launched in 1871) may be cited as the first Royal Naval battleship which looks as if it had not been an after-thought from Nelson's fleet. Broadside firing ships lingered on and the very last recorded action by one took place off Peru in 1877 between HMS *Amethyst* and a British-built armoured battleship, the *Huascar*. With the cruiser *Shah*, the *Amethyst* engaged the *Huascar*, which had been seized by Peruvian rebels and had been stopping British merchant ships.

It was the final act for a battery of muzzle-loading, truck-mounted guns; fortunately for the British the Peruvian ship did not score any really damaging hits with her 300-pounder rifle-barrelled guns. She actually fled the British warships, which included *Amethyst*, and finally surrendered to other Peruvian gunboats. Scenes like this fit a popular idea of gun-boat diplomacy, although strictly speaking, that term covered smaller conflicts up and down the numerous rivers of the British Empire and its environs, and involved the rather ugly flat-bottomed craft built specially for shallow waters.

The river gunboats were the cheap naval answer to controlling vast regions. Whenever local chiefs or tribes threatened – or were threatened – the British dispatched their little steam-fired flat-bottomed ships, with a detachment or two of soldiers. It usually worked.

The larger picture is of the Victorian Navy patrolling the world as of right. Merchant ships of all nations were grateful for that protection; but as so many were British in build and flag, the Navy's 'right' was a clear manifest.

By the time of the Spithead Review in 1897 the British Navy had reached a high-water mark in the worldwide effectiveness of ships in the projection of power and influence. The American naval theorist, Mahan, had celebrated all this in *The Influence of Sea Power on History*, published in 1890, really a hymn of praise to the British attitude toward all matters naval.

Even at this moment of glory, as the fleet lay at its Spithead anchorage awaiting Queen Victoria, the seeds of twentieth-century demise were sown. The twin angels of death, the torpedo and the submarine, were being married; both were thought of by British officers as underhand and unsporting. The fact that Rear-Admiral de Horsey off Peru had sent a torpedo after the *Huascar* when she slunk into harbour was a major cause of his decline in Admiralty standing.

The submarine was thought by many to be completely beyond the pale. In the later development of the U-boat they came to symbolise the tricks of an evil enemy who would resort to any tactic to win. Until the 1960s the Royal Navy remained unhappy about its own submarines and their use. So did the British public: the sinking of the *Belgrano* by HMS *Conqueror* in 1982 and the public reaction to it may be seen as a vestige of the feeling that it is simply 'not British' to do this kind of thing.

There were other straws in the wind after Spithead. The Navy was facing the upsurge of a number of foreign navies, notably the German, but also the French, the Italian, the American and the Japanese. Her own organisation was creaking and although, shortly, that was to change, the accretion of a century's traditions was to delay and to hobble what remained the biggest fleet in the world.

'Rule Britannia, Britannia Rule the Waves'
Rule Britannia

The old Queen's Jubilee is often used as a bench-mark, as a turning point, a pinnacle – or all three – in the fortunes of Great Britain and her Empire. It was all to no avail. By the turn of the century Britain was already in serious decline as an economic power of the first rank. For it was now to be the Empire that held Britain back – as some had always argued it would. As we have seen, most of her trade had always been with the rest of the world. Now the rest of the world was beginning to stir: France and Germany in Europe; the United States, and Japan further afield. All were already major industrial powers and would grow faster and more consistently than Britain for the next 100 years, despite two hugely costly defeats in war for Germany, and one for Japan.

Britain would decay, and use the Empire and its cheap markets as a prop, as the rest of the world turned away from British goods. Part of that turning away was due to the two wars: both Japan in the first conflict, and the United States in the second, benefited greatly from Britain's inability to keep trading and fighting as she once had done. The existence of the Empire gulled us into believing we remained a superpower. Only with its dismantling did we begin to see that it had held back the ugly truths about our ailing manufacturing industry, our poor record of competitive selling and our growing complacency.

For what was happening was that as markets closer to home got harder to penetrate with what were less and less competitive manufactured goods, the British turned more and more to the informal and the formal Empires, far away. In the 1860s capital exports, for instance, had been around 50 per cent to Europe and the United States; these had dropped to 25 per cent by the early 1900s. Meanwhile they had risen from 36 per cent to 46 per cent to the Empire and from 11 per cent to 22 per cent to Latin America. And whereas we had sold cotton, steel and machinery to the States and Europe in the mid-century, by the late 1800s these goods were now being exported to Australia, Brazil, India and Argentina.

There were worse statistics. Industrial production, growing at about 4 per cent between 1820 and 1840 had fallen to 3 per cent between 1840 and 1870; in the period 1875–95 it was only 1.5 per cent. British exports, which had expanded by 5 per cent between 1840 and 1870 fell to 2 per cent between 1870 and 1890 and 1 per cent between 1890 and 1900. This decline was disguised in two ways. First because the volume of world trade was expanding so fast these increases were substantial in their own right. Even in the slumps, which were frequent, Britain remained a very rich country, growing richer. Secondly, and crucially, it was growth in invisible earnings which kept the whole economy moving upwards. And a large part of invisibles were the carriage of the worlds' cargoes in British ships, insured in London.

At a more mundane level, few people in 1897 could have conceived that Britain was in trouble and getting in deeper. Just as today, almost exactly a hundred years on, it is almost impossible to imagine a time when we had not heard how badly we have been doing, so the late-Victorians *knew* they were living in the greatest, most powerful, richest country in the world. In a sense this burden of fame and fortune destroyed us; the trappings of power became increasingly a real burden, to be carried through to the end, even though the cost was destroying the wearer.

Even in shipping there were already ominous signs of our future prospects as a 1903 table of the world's biggest passenger liner companies reveals:

Company:	No. of ships:	Tonnage:
1. Hamburg-America (Ger)	202	541,000
2. Nord Deutscher (Lloyd) (Ger)	111	455,000
3. Elder Dempster (Brit)	120	383,000
4. British India (Brit)	120	379,000
5. P&O (Brit)	58	313,000
6. Messageries Maritimes (French)	62	246,000
7. F Leyland (Ger)	55	243,000
8. Union Castle (Brit)	41	223,000
9. Nippon Yusen Kaisha (Jap)	69	218,000
10. White Star (Brit)	25	212,000

The history of maritime Britain mirrored much of what took place on land. Twice, though, in the fifty years after that golden end to Victoria's reign, it would be maritime Britain that would save the nation from starvation, defeat and, in one case, from total surrender. If there can be any prescience in a table of passenger shipping companies we might note that the Germans had the biggest two passenger liner companies, the Japanese the ninth biggest and although British companies had five of the top ten places, they were slipping downwards. The British, though, could still point, as Edward VII wearily ascended the throne after his mother's interminable reign, to the quantity and quality of British shipping all over the world. To those issues, and to the lives of the seafarers, we must now turn.

2

TRANSITION: NINETEENTH INTO TWENTIETH CENTURY

'All day they loitered by the resting ships.'
John Masefield, *The Wanderer*

When Queen Victoria sailed between the lines of 165 warships at Spithead on 26 June 1897, she could rejoice in more than just the huge fleet assembled for her delectation. Her admirals would have pointed out to her that this mighty armada had necessitated the withdrawal from the stations of the Empire of not one ship. What she was reviewing was basically the *home*-waters fleet. Of that fleet, which included twenty-one battleships and fifty-four cruisers, only France could boast a close approximation in numbers. The Spithead Review triggered more than just a British burst of pride; the burgeoning European powers, the United States and Japan all looked with envious eyes at the British fleet, and made their plans accordingly. Though France was still perceived as the most likely adversary in war by the British, it was Queen Victoria's German grandson, Willy, a lifelong navalist, who left Spithead with a plan which would soon give the British the biggest military headache.

The defeat of France by Germany in 1872 had demonstrated some of the ambitions of the rising central European power that was Bismarck's Germany. When the new king succeeded to the throne in 1888, Germany's coastal navy was to get its biggest lift. Kaiser Wilhelm II had always loved warships. What he saw at Spithead convinced him that Germany had to have something as good – or better. In his Secretary of State for the German Marine, Admiral von Tirpitz, he found the man to implement a battleship-building programme which would throw the British into panic and confusion.

It was not just in Europe that Britain's naval might was being challenged. The bulk of her trade remained with the two Americas, North and South, a double continent in which she had least stakes, colonially. Canada was a liability with a huge open southern border. In South America there was only British Guiana, perched on the

north-east coast. As early as 1889 the Director of Naval Intelligence
in London was warning that because of the rise of the American,
Argentine and Chilean navies the Royal Navy was 'completely out-
classed'. In South Amercia, the irony was that it was often British-
built, or British-designed, battleships which now faced the Royal
Navy.

The point was that other powers, outside Europe, had learned the
Mahanian lesson that big-gun ships brought their own reward in
influence and power projection. There is an exact parallel with
modern missile systems and with nuclear weapons. The Soviet Union,
basically a very under-developed society as we now realise, retained
immense military power by having huge numbers of crude ballistic
missiles.

The end of the nineteenth century saw the last great scramble for
colonies. Since the Monroe Doctrine was first espoused by the nascent
United States, under-written by the Royal Navy, European powers
had been 'warned off' the western hemisphere. It was to be the United
States which colonised – or re-colonised – parts of the Caribbean,
after it dismembered the Spanish Empire in Cuba, Puerto Rico and,
further afield, in the Pacific and the Philippines.

European powers looked east and south. The British held India
and Hong Kong and many places in between. France, once she had
recovered from the Napoleonic débâcle, pushed south into North
Africa, starting with Algeria, and then on into the vast territories of
the north-west Sahara. She held Indo-China – modern Vietnam,
Cambodia and Laos – too and like Britain and Germany, various
treaty ports on the Chinese mainland.

Britain had just gone on indiscriminately adding bits of the globe
to her flag. In 1882, threatened by a revolt in Egypt, the British
had moved into the Canal Zone and effectively set up a colonial
government by proxy in Cairo. Much of the southern part of Africa
found itself governed from London by 1897. The last colonial scramble was in Africa and the Germans, although late in the game, also
managed to secure some prize colonies – in south-west Africa, in the
Cameroon, Togo, and East Africa. The last available parts of the Far
East also fell to hungry European powers.

All this had been closely watched from that same Far East by a
newly awakened island state – Japan – whose modern introduction
to the west in 1868, after a couple of centuries of isolation, had
led within just twenty or so years to a tremendous upsurge of
economic and military power. The Japanese displayed that same

ability to mimic and improve that they have shown in the past forty years. In particular, they seized quickly upon British ship-building techniques; and upon British naval armaments and the policies they enforced. In the late nineteenth century the British were only too pleased to help them, for the old enemy, Russia, was casting a covetous eye on the last great colonial prize of all, China, and the British believed that they had to have a powerful counter-weight in the region.

> *'Dirty British coaster with a salt-caked*
> *smoke stack ...'*
>
> John Masefield, *Cargoes*

All these great movements are the backcloth for the great events that were to be played out in the coming fifty years. Those five decades would prove to be critical for British maritime ambitions. To under-stand what happened, we need to appreciate the balance of forces ranged against this island and its far-flung Empire, along with the mis-placed energies and the failure to see that, even in the early 1900s, British maritime power was so threatened. The underlying problem – not perceived at the time – was that British shipping was by now increasingly strung out across the world. Forty per cent of its work was taken up in cross-trades and therefore reliant on the peace and goodwill of other nations.

Against all this has to be set the slow collapse of British industry as a competitive force in world markets. It would have taken a soothsayer of quite gargantuan power to have predicted much of this, a century ago. The British, and the world, believed the evidence of their eyes. In 1900 British ships were still employed in moving 60 per cent of world trade. Although the total number of British ships had fallen from its peak (in 1866 when there were over 26,000 sailing vessels and nearly 3,000 steamships) even by 1914 there were nearly 13,000 steamships and still over 8,000 sailing ships.

Those ships carried over 90 per cent of goods between countries in the Empire, nearly two-thirds of that between the Empire and the rest of the world; a third of the trade between countries outside the Empire entirely. By this stage textile exports had finally been ousted by coal and engineering goods. Food imports had become, sig-nificantly and dangerously, more and more evident: frozen meat, dairy produce, wheat and exotic fruit, of which the banana was the most popular. Another way of looking at the figures is to take the value of world trade. In 1912 it is thought that there were 250–300 million tons of goods being moved worldwide. Of this 150 million tons were being imported or exported into Britain. Exports of coal had reached 77 million tons and may have employed as much as two million tons of British tramp ships to do it. The British fleet was still carrying one half of world trade by *value*, rather less by weight.

The giant passenger liner had made its debut, first with the great ships of the White Star line on the Atlantic run, and then with ships from many European nations, again notably Germany, which by 1914 had the world's largest ships on its register. Of them all, sadly, the *Titanic* is the best remembered today, partly now because undersea technology and satellite positioning systems have enabled us to find her two miles down in the North Atlantic; mostly because of the savage indictment of the White Star line, who advertised her as unsinkable.

The hugely successful *Mauretania*, which was to hold the Blue Riband for twenty years and which was described by Kipling as a 'nine-decked city gone to sea', sailed in the shadow of this unnecessary tragedy. She was 790 feet long, eighty-eight feet wide and carried over 2,300 passengers and 800 crew at twenty-eight knots and weighed 32,000 tons. Her engines were, of course, turbines and they enabled ships of this size to be powered at what would have been thought, only a few years before, impossible speeds.

But the German liner *Imperator* was bigger at 52,000 tons. Whilst passenger liners were being built at this size, merchant ships remained much smaller – in 1912 around 7,500 tons as an average – but their crew, compared with today, was much larger, as many as eighty, half of whom would be engineers, stokers or trimmers. The numerous coasters were much smaller, ranging right down to a few hundred tons, with much smaller crews, too. The vast bulk of all mechanically driven ships still used coal and, other than the passenger liners, ran on the reciprocating steam engine. But oil, as a fuel, was beginning to make its mark in cars and lorries on land and by 1903 the marine diesel engine had made its first appearance – in a Russian ship. Its subsequent spread was rapid, but not so in British ships.

The 'traditions' of British shipping – which meant sticking to the old ways – were frequently to trap it, right up to the present; but nothing illustrates better the failure to keep technical innovation going than the oil-burning marine diesel engine which was to prove cheaper and more efficient more or less from the start. Oil-burning ships used less crew, too. There is a double irony here for it was the British who first invented the oil-tanker, back in the 1880s. Before then oil had been transported in barrels, awkward in shape and wasteful of space. But, having produced the world's first purpose-built tanker, neither the fuel it carried, nor its potential as a revenue earner, was grasped until far too late.

It was a gradual change on the whole, from sail through auxiliary steam and sail to all-steamships. All through the latter part of the nineteenth century merchant ships were becoming more soph-isticated. Sail – and not just in the clipper ships – held on for far longer than many might have predicted because it provided free power. Many of the cargoes were not perishable and time was not a problem. As we have seen, coal was one cargo carried by sail, for the bunkers of coal-burning ships. Steamships took longer than they might to oust sail partly because of the technical problems involved. But by the turn of the century steamships were using compound engines, 'Scotch' boilers, which meant higher working pressures. They were built more and more of steel. All this helped fuel economy. It was in 1880 that the first triple-expansion steam engine was fitted in a ship, the *Propontis*, but she suffered from a poor boiler design. Siemen steel (German, note, in origin) finally enabled the *Aberdeen* (1881) to improve fuel economy at a working pressure of 125psi (pounds per square inch).

By the middle of the 1890s a cargo ship might burn as little as half an ounce of coal per ton carried per hour – no more than the energy released from burning a couple of sheets of writing paper. It was the need for this kind of economy at relatively low speeds that precluded the fitting of turbines in cargo ships until much later than their introduction into passenger ships, where the emphasis was on speed. Eventually the *Cairnross* (1913), compared with a sister ship (the *Cairngowan*, fitted with triple-expansion engines) showed that geared turbines in a cargo ship could work out cheaper.

Some classes of cargo – like fruit and refrigerated meat – were vulnerable and in the specialised ships they needed the geared-turbine engine made an early appearance. Fuel oil, too, as a substitute for coal, also began to be used, first in oil tankers, then, slowly, in passenger ships and cargo ships. But the innate conservatism of ship owners, and the ease with which coal could be obtained, meant that it was not really until after the First World War that oil became more commonplace as a fuel. Meanwhile a positive army of

stokers, firemen and trimmers were employed in the engine rooms
and stoke-holds of these ships; coaling was the bane of many a seafarer's life.

As with fuel oil, so with the internal combustion engine. The
Danish ship *Selandia*, built in 1912, used diesel engines and could
make a round trip between Europe and the Far East without refuel-
ling; the lesson was not learned in Britain. Long after marine diesels
had been adopted by European shipping, British ships continued with
steam. The other great innovation of the late nineteenth century was
in the specialisation of ships. The bulk carrier, the oil tanker, the
refrigerated ship, all made an appearence, as did the large, fast
passenger and mail liner

'I march across great waters like a queen'
John Masefield, *The Ship*

The modern world was born somewhere between 1870 and 1900.
That is to say the centuries-old patterns of national development in
which countries were basically self-sufficient was being undermined
by a new need for inter-dependence. Britain, as the world's foremost
trading nation, had perhaps appreciated this more than most. By
the end of the nineteenth century most developed nations could be
measured by the degree to which they, too, had joined this much
more complex, much more vulnerable form of intercourse.

While world trade continued to grow at a rapid rate, between 1890
and 1910 Britain's share was beginning to decline. For instance, world
commodity trade rose by 66 per cent between 1904 and 1912;
Britain's gain was only 46 per cent. In merchant shipping that was
reflected by a 4 per cent decline in tonnage – not a lot but the first
indication of what was to come. In contrast in this period, Germany's
shipping fleet increased by 180 per cent, the Netherlands, our old
Dutch rivals, by 168 per cent.

Japan's, though, rose by a staggering 1,161 per cent, making her
the world's third maritime nation by tonnage. This rise was in parallel
with her emergence by the early twentieth century as a modern
industrial power, the fastest industrialisation recorded in history.
From her isolation in 1868 to her defeat of Russia in the Russo–
Japanese War was under forty years and it presaged Japan's position
as a major world power in this century. The model she used in all
things was Great Britain.

'Stand by to reckon up your battleships'
Henry Newbolt, *The Little Admiral*

Although it was to be the submarine, the torpedo and the mine which inflicted the most damage in the First World War at sea, navies were reluctant to admit that these deadly new weapons had made redundant the huge capital ships. The greatest kudos came from surface fleets; of them the battleship reigned supreme. The battleship seemed invulnerable to anything other than battleships and nothing bore this out more than the greatest sea battle since Trafalgar, Tsushima, fought in 1905. An aged and ill-led Russian fleet, which had struggled around the world from the Baltic, in an attempt to relieve Port Arthur in Manchuria, besieged by the Japanese in their war with Russia, met Admiral Togo's warships and was annihilated: the entire Russian fleet, including four modern battleships, was sunk.

European naval attachés, observing the battle from Japanese ships, telegraphed messages home which stunned their recipients. A hitherto little-known upstart *Asian* country had wiped out a major European battle fleet. It is by no means far-fetched to say that Tsushima led both to the Russian Revolution and farther off to Pearl Harbour. In the short term it meant a hasty alliance between Britain and Japan and an urgent re-thinking of naval warfare for, after a hundred years of indecision in naval encounters, the Japanese had shown it was possible, with a big enough fleet of battleships, to inflict devastating defeats on an enemy.

Or so, at the time, it seemed. The British, as it happened, were already engaged in upgrading the battleship weapon; Tsushima simply re-inforced Admiral Jacky Fisher's belief in the all-big-gun battleship. What he almost certainly knew was that the Japanese had been building one, too. The *Aki* was delayed from being launched ahead of the British *Dreadnought* only by economic problems and the failure of the guns to arrive on time. The Russians and the Americans were also studying plans for such ships.

The Royal Navy got there first and it was after their class-ship that this type of warship was named. When HMS *Dreadnought* first was launched, in 1906, she carried all before her. The concept was simple: her armament was basically all twelve-inch guns, carried in five twin turrets. She could bring eight of them to bear in firing a broadside at any one time. A trend was started which, thirty years later, would culminate in the largest battleship ever built, the Japanese eighteen-inch-gun, 65,000 ton *Yamato*.

The *Dreadnought* was the first shot in the undeclared naval war between Germany and Britain, as much as anything brought on by Tirpitz' ambitions for a deep-water fleet, the visible surface of Germany's increasingly aggressive colonial policy. In Britain a panic ensued in 1908 after it was discovered how many big-gun ships the Germans had, or had planned, and for nearly a decade both countries vied to supercede the other in numbers and fire-power of battleships.

One result of the gathering storm in Europe was the withdrawal of the Royal Navy from many parts of the world and a concentration of forces in and around Europe. Two countries, the United States and Japan, were to take note of this ending of *Pax Britannica*. Conflict in Europe might have been inevitable; it sealed Britain's fate as a global naval power.

> '*When we got round the Horn, my boys,*
> *We had some glorious days.*'
>
> Song: *Rounding the Horn*

Edwardian Britain, which succeeded the great reign of Queen Victoria in 1902, was Imperial Britain, brash jingoistic Britain, centre of the greatest Empire the world had ever seen. Its ships were everywhere, its commerce supreme, its people triumphant and noisy in their acclamation of free trade and the British way. The period between the start of Edward's short reign and the First World War is a fascinating one in every respect. We should all learn from it: whilst the veneer of supremity was all around, the rot had set deep into the fabric underneath. The economy was immensely strong but immensely vulnerable. Few looked to the long-term future, even to the continent where France, Germany and Italy were making great economic strides. Britain's future depended entirely on a peaceful world.

The *Daily Mail*'s famous headline, around 1912, 'Fog in Channel, Continent isolated' captured the mood and the attitude perfectly. It was all to change, horribly, between 1914 and 1918, And whilst the machine gun swept away so many millions of young men on land, the world's proudest Navy was to suffer humiliation after humiliation at sea, unable to bring its huge surface weaponry to bear against the torpedo, the submarine and the mine.

Before that story begins we can make a journey to a lost world. Seafarers at the turn of the century were as bullish as their landlubberly brothers and sisters. They espoused, too, the last truly great romantic view of the sea that could be believed in. In those few years, when sail sat alongside the newest innovation in steam, when it was possible to find a British ship in just about every known port on this earth, true stories mingled with fiction.

The golden age of a maritime culture spewed forth an age which had Joseph Conrad writing with John Masefield, Ralph Vaughan Williams writing a *Sea Symphony*, and when every young sprog who ever wanted to go to sea wanted, one day, to write it all down. Fortunately, for us, quite a few did.

3

A WORLD AWAY

Sailors love yarning; it comes with the job. One reason, often missed by landsiders, is that the return to the land provides the opportunity for a wide audience, interested in the exotic. Another, for the yarner, is a chance to speak to more than the closed circle of ship-mates, within which he has, perforce, been confined throughout the long voyage. Sailors' tales do speak of the sea; but more, they always tell of the foreign ports and places visited. In truth, the sea has frequently been the dull interval between the clash of sailor with the land.

To go to sea in the not too distant past was the means by which the ordinary youngster could see the world. More than that it provided a career in which the relatively poor could become rich either by the usually rare means of making a fortune 'over there' or, more commonly, by sticking with the job and rising to be ship's master, or beyond. The sea was, therefore, all things to many men: escape from the mundane, a means to travel, a means to fame and fortune.

Merchant shipping was, in truth, a dangerous career, one beset by the hazard of the sea itself, those one might sail with, and by the no less real chance that it would result in moral decay abroad or at home. Sailors have never been entirely popular: they have too often been the bearers of bad tidings, disease perhaps coming top of the list. At the turn of the century Britain had the largest number of merchant seamen she was ever to have in peacetime. From around 170,000 in 1891, the number rose to 209,000 in 1912. Yet of this huge number, nearly 50,000 were lascars, the number of other foreigners, 30,000. Overall, the quality remained poor. The reason for that was money.

For example, the master of an average (4,000-ton) cargo vessel was paid £22.00 a month, his first mate £12.50. The chief engineer might get £20.00, whilst the able-bodied seamen only got £4.00 (£3.00 if in a sailing ship). This was the period in which the National Union of Seamen was struggling to life; sailors remained hard to organise until very recently when only the short-sea trades were left. Legal questions over the right to strike, or take any industrial action, kept early trade-union activity low.

Just before the First World War a typical cargo ship might carry a crew of seventy, forty-three on deck and thirty-four in the engine room. A steamship of this kind would burn up to seventy tons of coal a day, all shovelled into the furnaces by hand. A fireman would throw as much as two tons onto the grates in a four-hour watch; he would stand two watches a day. One has to remember that this was coal handling unlike that of the aristocrat of firemen, the steam railway engine man. There the activity might go in spurts, there was a view to appreciate and a home to return to each night, after a day's work where admiring onlookers could boost an ego mightily.

On board ship the heat in the engine room would be intense, the ship's motion often violent. Everything got covered in coal dust, including the food these men ate, and the bunks they slept in. Voyages – especially in tramp ships – would last for years. One writer describes these men thus: 'those human salamanders emerge from time to time glistening with perspiration from the Hades of the furnace room, and lie with nothing but a scanty loincloth around their middle, cooling their black bodies in the wet refreshment of the suppers'.[1] 'Deckies' lived with these blackened souls in the cramped and hellhole space of the forecastle, or f'o'csle: seamen to starboard, firemen to port. This same space would include the lamp room, the paint locker and crew lavatory. The legal space for each sailor – 120 cubic feet – was half that required for prisoners. Deck officers had cabins but usually pretty sparse ones. The bridge would be open, protected only by a 'canvas dodger'. Given all these circumstances one might reasonably ask why on earth did anyone ever go to, or stay at, sea? Ridiculous as it may seem to a late-twentieth-century ear, attuned so finely to the general irony attached to terms like 'romance', and suffering a degree of *fin de siècle* ennui, it was largely a mixture of hope triumphing over experience, mixed with the harsh economic realities of the time. Whilst the largely middle-class, or lower middle-class, voices which follow concentrate on the romance, one may be utterly sure that, for most of them, the incentive was financial.

It is worth bearing in mind, too, that for the first half of the twentieth century landsiders also suffered pretty dreadful working conditions. It has only been since the onset of the Welfare State, that nanny to us all, that conditions have improved to the point where we can throw up our collective hands in horror at what our grandparents or great-grandparents were prepared to endure, in war as well as peace, in factory and mine – or at sea.

One problem in trying to get to the root of what motivated seafarers in this not-too-distant past is that, almost to a man, they did not keep diaries. We are left with the gloss of reminiscence which, para-doxically, may well overload the hardship ('look how tough I was') and ignore the more usual periods of intense boredom which all seafarers know. There is, understandably, a concentration on shore-side yarns, too: the girl-in-every-port myth made up for the awful truth of lonely drunken evenings in the back of beyond. Of the accounts we have, all recall that first ship in graphic detail, embroi-dered or not. One seafarer, who is pleased to call himself a modern Sinbad (who wove fiction, remember, in his 'facts') remembers like this. (All the following accounts relate to ships sailing at the turn of the last, or in the first decade of this, century.)

> Father put me on the London train at Oxford, and gave me 30 shillings with which to buy my outfit when I reached Town. A brother of the owner met me, gave me some lunch, and at once took me down to the East India Docks. I had never seen the sea or set eyes on a real ship before. The dock was full of vessels, and to my eyes that was Paradise. I felt that each splendid ship must be mine, and as we passed along I read: *Macquarie, Hesperus, Tukarina, Pericles, Orestes, Aristides*. What names! I gazed through a mist with a choke in my throat. Still we walked along. If these were not to be mine what magnificent lady of the sea was I destined for?
>
> We turned sharply beneath the jib-boom of the barque. I had my eyes glued to the gangway of the *Hesperides* but my arm was seized and I was dragged a bit farther on to the gangway of a stubby, dirty, iron-decked atrocity of a cargo steamer. Before I had digested the hard fact I was on her unlovely deck and I saw her name on a lifebuoy – *Godiva*.[2]

Later he is 'treated' to a fine cabin, the watchman having mistaken him for a guest of the owner. All too soon he is flung, unceremoniously, into the stinking pit of the f'o'csle and forced to buy his own set of sea-going kit. Apprentice seamen had to find their own clothes and kit. They also had to sign articles. Bill Adams recalls the articles signed thus:

> The said apprentice to furnish all sea bedding and wearing apparel, and faithfully to serve his said Master, his executors, administrators and

assigns; to obey his and their lawful commands, and to keep his and their secrets; and not absent himself from their service without leave; nor frequent taverns nor ale houses unless upon their business; nor play unlawful games. In consideration whereof the said Master covenants to teach the said apprentice, or cause him to be taught, the business of a seaman and provide him with sufficient meat, drink and lodging and medical and surgical assistance and to pay said apprentice the sum of £30.00 [a *year*].[3]

The teaching could be crude, as another recalls:

My first lesson in learning the names of the numerous ropes must have been funny to watch but was anything but funny to me. The Second Mate took me along to the mast rigging and grasping the end of the first rope, he asked me what its name was. I said I didn't know. 'Oh,' he said, 'you don't know?', grabbing me by the neck and belting me across the stern with the rope's end. 'That, me lad, is the Main Clewgarnet; you won't forget it, will you?' The same procedure went on at every rope, and needless to say I did not forget them, but I was unable to sit down comfortably for many days.[4]

Seafaring tales of the times are full of this; as they are of the use of terms like 'stern' for backside, as if the reader expects a sailor to use his own peculiar language as proof of the veracity of it. But many of the stories are full, too, of the immense effort put into *sailing*: this was the end, remember, of centuries of a system of transport, and there was a pride in those sailors who went to sea first on one of the great sailing barques, by now huge in weight, in length and in size of spars.

It was dark when I went aboard again, a porter carrying my sea chest, I with my canvas sea bag on my shoulders. In it my oilskins, sea boots, blankets, tin plate, tin pannikin, tin knife and spoon. I entered a tiny alleyway whence on each side a door opened into a tiny room. The apprentices' half deck, just behind the mainmast. Four lads each side. In each side just room enough for four narrow bunks and four sea chests set about a tiny table hinged onto the other bulkhead.

We moved the ship to the dock nearest the river, to be ready to go out at dawn. No machinery of any sort to help us; we eight lads, with the carpenter and the two mates dragged on great ropes till nigh midnight. The ship, 300 feet long, by some 50 feet wide, by 23 feet deep in the water, 3,000 tons of cargo in her holds. We were almost done when the crew came aboard. Singing, shouting, cursing, they rolled drunkenly into their quarters in the forecastle; a deckhouse just behind the foremast.

Ships like these sailed across the world to the Far East and beyond.
The life on board could defy description. With sail, time was not the
issue. Neither, in any sense, was comfort.

> The half deck where we lived had three feet of water in it, and our sea
> chests were floating around, mixed up with canvas bags and straw
> mattresses. We no sooner got some of the water bailed out, than over
> came another sea and filled up the half-deck again; so we gave it up as
> a bad job.

In conditions like these, attitudes hardened considerably. It might
seem astonishing that stowaways would contemplate joining this life;
perhaps they were blissfully ignorant of what they were to miss. If
so, in this case, they got some taste:

> The tug came as close as she dared in the tossed sea, maybe 50 or 60
> feet from the ship's side. MacDonald tied a rope around a stowaway,
> hove its other end aboard the tug, shouted 'haul in' and lifted and
> dropped the screaming stowaway to the cold winter sea. The other
> struggled, too scared to do any screaming. But in a minute the tug boat
> men were hauling him in too. The tug turned on her heel, tooted her
> whistle thrice in farewell and was gone. We were free, before us 14,000
> miles of unfenced salt meadows . . .
>   I was aware of something: aware of a strong majesty in my ship,
> throwing the sprays high, seeming to challenge the long rolling ocean
> swells. No ragged robin now, no meadowsweets, no wood anemone,
> nor bluebell. But bronze bells clanging, sonorous across a sullen sea.
> And, as a sail went threshing and flapping to its masthead, a deep voice
> singing; and a roar of windy voices coming in on the chorus of my first
> sea chantey.

Little need be added to that last paragraph for anyone seeking the
reason why the sea held such sway over the young. The last sailing
ships lasted, as we shall see, into the start of the Second World War.
Experience in a sailing ship was a requirement well into the 1930s
for those who sought a master's ticket, so many thousands of sailors
were able to pass down this road, hard though it was.

The formal training of officers took place also on recognised training ships. Old hulks like HMS *Worcester* or HMS *Conway* were
home to generations of schoolboys whose parents could afford to
send them to these establishments, run much like the public schools.

> The *Worcester* of those days was an old four-decker, the ex-*Frederick
> William*, a genuine original wooden ship, late of Her Victorian Majesty's

fleet, and at first the thrill and the novelty of living on board such a vessel prevented my spirits from sinking too low.

Looking back from the end of an active sea career, I am more than ever convinced that a spell in a training ship is of incalculable value to a cadet in that, unlike a shore establishment, it accustoms him to much that he will find afloat.

But Donald Baillie, despite acknowledging he had elected to join 'one of the toughest professions, condemned ... voluntarily to a life notorious for its hardships', found HMS *Worcester* harsh in the extreme.

The food was atrocious, as were the washing facilities:

> Right up in the bows on this deck (the Lower) were the wash places, and every morning on turning out each boy had to run forward, even if it were the whole length of the ship, wearing nothing but his pyjama trousers, and wash in cold water. The proceeding was a Spartan one in winter; the half-ports in the wash place were unglazed, the bitter winds straight off the North Sea and the Essex marshes whistled through them, and it was no uncommon thing for snow, sleet and rain to blow in over our bare torsos.

It hardly need be said that caning – by the cadet petty officers – was frequent. But it was the shortage of food – good or bad – that stuck in the memory. In fact food, as the most obvious relief from the general monotony of life at sea, is one topic on which all seafarers, from all ages, can agree. Long after other details of a voyage have faded, the quality or, more usually, the lack of it, of the food is what sailors can unerringly recall. One shipping line, now gone, is still tagged 'Hungry Harrisons' by many today.

Baillie went onto his first ship: a P&O steamer, which provided him with the luxury of a shared cabin. Best of all:

> We ate all our meals in the cabin, being waited upon by a Goanese steward, who made us feel comparatively grand. We were fed on a more modest scale than the officers in the saloon, but even so the food seemed to us amazingly good and the menus extraordinarily varied after the appalling diet in the *Worcester*.

Yet, he recalls, life at sea, whilst providing the great exhilaration of freedom, retained, even on a first trip, the dull sameness of all ocean crossings.

The voyage would have been monotonous in the extreme if it had not held the interest of novelty so far as I was concerned, for the *Pera* ran direct from London to Adelaide, via the Cape. We actually sighted Cape Town but steamed relentlessly past it and on to the Leeuwin [the southernmost cape in Western Australia]. We set a trysail and a staysail to help us on our way on the long haul down to Australia; and, just as I had read many a time in the storybooks, our chicken coops – the only livestock we carried – were nearly washed over the side in heavy weather running our easting down. Atkinson and I, as we struggled to secure them and rescue the terrified ducks, geese and hens from the scuppers of the hurricane-deck, imagined that we must be experiencing a phenomenal gale.

Without the distraction of any ports of call, it was a long and gruelling initiation into life at sea. We led a simple and restricted existence, composed almost entirely of work, sleep and meals. My private log book, laconic in the extreme, contains the same entries over and over again.

And yet all the time this reality is overlaid with what we might call the other side of life at sea. Edgar Britten, who rose to be Commodore of the Cunard fleet in the 1930s, says this:

Enough has been written of the terrible hardships experienced in windjammer days, and I do not intend to stress this point. I do not think I would, even if I could, for strangely enough I remember all that was best in this phase of my career.

Long lazy days of unending sunshine, sailing along with flapping sails, and scarcely a breeze to ruffle the placid seas. It was during these enchanting spells that the ship's orchestra came into its own. A comb wrapped round with paper, a sea-kettle, and a frying pan can produce an enchanting rhythm when blended with the soft hiss of flying spindrift, and the hum of straining cordage.

Sometimes in the dog-watches, Micky would bring out his concertina and squat in the starlight, ringing out the old sea-chanties, wild, ferocious, triumphant, then of a sudden ghastly with despair. My pleasantest memory of him belonged to those night watches when, the music over, he would tell stories of the sea, the saga of windjammer days.[5]

Too soft a picture, no doubt, and one tempered by his subsequent career and fame, for in the 1920s and 1930s, certainly, the great passenger-liner masters were well-known names. Would that, today, we knew or cared for the names of the captains of jumbo jets. But Britten's rise was not that uncommon; James Bisset was another who came up through the ranks, sail to steam, then onto fame and fortune in Cunard.

> In February, 1905, at the age of twenty-one years and seven months, I passed the Board of Trade examination for First Mate at Liverpool, England, and decided to look for a job in a steamer. As old shellbacks used to put it, I had made up my mind to 'knock off going to sea and go into steamboats'.

Bisset had made four voyages in sailing ships, via Cape Horn, in the previous six years. His youth and his experience are typical of the time. Seafaring was a young man's way, and although many were forced to stay on, many others 'swallowed the anchor', married, and went ashore. Bisset was deemed to be inexperienced in steam and he spent months wandering the dockside offices in Liverpool, looking for a steamship post. He knew that sail was doomed although 'there were still many hundreds of sailing vessels under the British flag, and hundreds more under the American, French, German, Scandinavian and other national flags'.

But steamships were offering a better set of conditions: more money, shorter voyages, better accommodation. Eventually Bisset got lucky and joined the SS *Rembrandt*. His description of her and her crew stands as a single expression of the typical ship, the typical crew, in the British merchant fleet of the pre-First World War years.

> ... the SS *Rembrandt*, a single-screw steamer, 4,279 tons gross with steel hull and steel decks, had been built at Glasgow by D. and W. Henderson Ltd., and launched in 1899. She was 380 feet long, 45 feet beam, and had an average speed of 12 knots. She could carry 4,000 tons of cargo and 12 passengers. She was on the regular run from Liverpool to ports in Argentina, Uruguay, Brazil and the Canary Islands, making on average four voyages a year.
>
> The loading of the cargo had been completed on the preceeding day, and the hatchways covered with their hatches and tarpaulins, and battened down. This was the carpenter's work, and the Mate [Bisset had joined as 'Third'] had left it to me to supervise. That day, too, the bunkers [surrounding the stoke-hold] had been filled with 1,000 tons of coal, from railway waggons run alongside and hoisted bodily from the bogies with a crane.
>
> The ship's tanks had been filled with many thousands of gallons of fresh water for the boilers, and for the personal needs of the passengers and crew – and the animals – on the outward voyage to our first port of call, Buenos Aires, some 6,000 miles, which we were scheduled to cover in three weeks.

The old traditions of sail were continued in steamers, to a certain extent, in that crews signed on and signed off in their home ports for each voyage but as the stay in port was so short, the ship's complement very often signed off and signed on again immediately on arriving home and were given instructions to rejoin ... that would be 8.00am on the day of sailing.

Under this system, most of the AB seamen, firemen and trimmers in the SS *Rembrandt* had had continuity of seagoing employment in her for many voyages previously. The firemen and trimmers were all 'Liverpool Irish'. They were tough-looking characters, who worked in the stokehold in dungeree trousers, hobnailed boots and flannel shirts with a 'sweat-rag' round their necks, and came up on deck, clambering out of the fiddley like demons out of hell, grimy and sweaty, for an occasional breath of fresh air, or to go forrard off watch.

He describes the seamen as 'old salts' who knew their work. But, he noted sadly, as the ship put to sea, none of them sang.

My heart sank as I realised that men in steamers do not sing at their work. Never again, perhaps, would I hear and join a chantey chorus as a crowd of toughened men tailed on to the main topsail halyards or to heave up the anchor. 'Rolling home', working in unison and rhythm with songs on their lips – the songs of seafarers for centuries, doomed to disuse in a mechanized world.[6]

More than that was changing of course. The old ways would be more violently affected by the war which was coming, a war which as it broke out many welcomed, though the more thoughtful feared.

That war had been fuelled by a huge arms race in warships, the first modern arms race, because it was based on the belief that technology could overcome will-power. 'We want eight and we won't wait' was one cry for more of the *Dreadnoughts* which Britain was hastily building as James Bisset sailed on his voyages.

We are blessed with far more accounts of life in the pre-First World War Royal Navy, than that of the merchant fleet. The insights are revealing.

4

WEAPONS OF WAR

*'One by one the great ships are
stirring from their sleep'*
Henry Newbolt, *Sailing at Dawn*

The Royal Navy of the years before 1914 was a huge organisation, wrappt in its own glorious past. The pomp and ceremony of the Victorian years lingered on, despite the valiant efforts of men like Jacky Fisher, the great reforming First Sea Lord, to change, well, everything. It was Fisher who introduced the *Dreadnoughts*, the world's first twentieth century battleships. It was Fisher, too, who brought in the 'nucleus' crew system, a means by which the fleet reserve ships were maintained by up to a two-fifths complement in order that they would be ready for action if needed.

The Navy of these years had enormous responsibilities; its brief was truly worldwide, and in that respect it was stretched to the limit. The size of the British merchant marine meant that its protective role extended to every ocean. The Navy took this literally, as it did its huge programme of flag-showing. Meanwhile, for the first time in a century, it faced the growing threat from a major European power, determined to play to win the navalist game. Life, however, went on:

> January 1st, 1906. I saw the old year out sitting in Morrells Hotel with Aunt Rosie. I also toasted the New Year with a glass of port. I then came on board and found all the snotties [Midshipmen] drinking in the wardroom. When they came down into the flat there was a general scrap. After all this I kept the morning watch. I took an artificial horizon in the forenoon but could not work it out as there were no 1906 Almanacks. Hardy looked at our notebooks in the afternoon and gave orders that notes were to be finished by the end of the week or there would be a row. Stayed on board and wrote up work.

Hugh Eastwood wrote this diary on board HMS *Bulwark*, a 15,000-ton pre-*Dreadnought* class battleship. 1906 passed by with the usual round of battle practices and a cruise in the Mediterranean. There, much partying took place, along with sightseeing. There were ships' boat races (our diarist is much bothered over the weight of his crew), and shooting competitions, in one of which the ladies who took part outshot the men. Women travelled on board on this cruise – at least the privileged sisters of one of the officers did. Life, from all one reads, was very relaxed, interpersed with work towards exams in seamanship and other arcane pursuits.

Five years later Eastwood was in HMS *Royal Arthur* (a cruiser, those archetypal warships of the Empire) on his way to China.

We sailed at 9.00am today from under the Sheer Jetty at Portsmouth. The ship was commissioned last Friday. An enormous amount of work has been got through since then. The ship was provisioned and stores innumerable for HMS *Kent* and others in China were taken on board.

The best part of the day I spent stowing gear in the flat – aft – and securing it. We are proceeding at six knots to Plymouth. I was very fortunate in getting all my gear on board last night being very doubtful whether I should get it in time. Unfortunately I have not got a gun or a camera both of which are extremely necessary articles for a station like China.

We arrived at Plymouth at about 7.00am and anchored inside the Sound. During the morning quantities of wine for WR of HMS *Kent* were received in addition to hosts of other gear. At 10.30 the new draft for HMS *Kent* arrived alongside in SS *Traveller* and the forenoon was spent in redisposing the ship's company and stowing bags and hammocks etc.. After lunch the Commander exercised fire stations and collision stations, my station being C pump with the QD [quarterdeck] men.

The ship sailed for China and, as with so many voyages, time passed in a mixture of trivial and not so trivial pursuits.

November 6. Cape St Vincent was passed about 4.00am The sea is much smoother now and the weather already quite warm and delightful. After lunch we exercised General Quarters and the casement gun ports were opened to give more air to the mess deck which by now had become very stuffy. They were quite difficult to remove having remained shut for several months previous. After evening quarters we started our clay-pigeon shooting. Surgeon Joy kindly lent me his gun and some cartridges and I hit nothing which was amusing.

When we were about twenty miles from Gibraltar TB93 overtook us with orders for us to transfer all ratings and gear for Malta to her and then to proceed direct to Port Said. This is due to the Cholera which is present at Malta. Transferred the men by sea-boats; dined with captain; danced on the quarterdeck.

By now routine was set: there was clay-pigeon shooting most days, along with a bridge tournament, cricket (under versus over thirties), dancing. The voyage to China was a long one. On 15 November the ship arrived at Port Said:

> At 7.00 we entered the channel to Port Said and at 7.50 after passing the Canal offices we dropped an anchor and swung our stern in and secured it to the Dutch House jetty. The lighters came alongside soon after 8.00 and coaling commenced at 9.00. Arabs do the coaling here in 2cwt buckets but our stokers have to stow it. We were fortunate in having the wind blowing from aft. Coaling was finished about 3.00.

Coaling ship features a great deal in the accounts of the time. Until oil began to replace coal as the fuel for the furnaces, this operation had to be undertaken in regular back-breaking bouts. Not only that, the coal dust spread everywhere, covering precious brass-work. All on board knew that after any form of coaling they would be busily at work cleaning up the mess, for many hours, or even days.

> Within a few hours of anchoring we were all wallowing in clouds of coal-dust – coaling ship, an evolution of beastliness common to all ships then, and which, with the advent of oil fuel, happily passed from the lives of seamen. All day long we laboured feverishly and as darkness came down we cast off the colliers and proceeded again to sea, with heaps of coal still on our decks for shovelling down into the bunkers.

This was how Herbert Edwards, on the cruiser *Drake* for that coaling, remembered it in the 1930s.[1]

Keeping a ship of any size spotless was a full-time job for many of the crew. But a warship also had to fight and the same crew had to learn about the weapons on board, how to use them, how to maintain them. Although by modern standards guns were relatively simple things, they were at the forefront of technology for their time. Moreover, the officers and men were expected to be able to maintain them without benefit of specialists. The Edwardian Navy was the last in which a ship's crew could be expected to learn and cope with all that went on in a warship. Even so, the engineers were a race apart. Soon wireless would arrive, and then more and more complex gun direction equipment.

Meanwhile midshipmen, the officer cadets, were taught a vast range of subjects: seamanship, navigation, warfare, mechanics, fire-fighting, collision regulations, engineering, weaponry, flag etiquette, manners.

In the forenoon all midshipmen went to the naval instructor. In the afternoon I was attached to the commander and went round the ship [HMS *Indomitable*, an *Invincible*-class battlecruiser]. The other midshipmen were told off for duties with the gunnery torpedo and engineering Lieutenants. At 6.30 the midshipmen's whaler crew went away. Seamanship – general instruction – in the forenoon. In the after-noon midshipmen stripped a four-inch gun.

Friday: The forenoon was occupied in general drill. The first evolution was out sheet anchor. The launch, the pinnace and our first and second sea cutters were required. The first cutter took the kedge and the second cutter towed the launch and the pinnace. The launch took the sheet anchor and the pinnace the wire. The sheet anchor was then got in again. The second evolution was out nets and in nets [anti-torpedo netting around the ship], twice. This was done without any hitch and our time was best in each case. The morning was concluded by all boats pulling round the fleet. In the afternoon the midshipmen had a pilotage lecture. At 3.30 Admiral Bayley inspected the ship.

Sunday. Ship prepared for sea – all boats got ready for hoisting in. Steam ordered for 14 knots by 6.00am on Monday.

Monday. We intended to start early and fire torpedoes. A thick fog set in however and we did not proceed until 1.30. Midshipmen took sights and did school in the morning. In the afternoon we had battle practice stations and I went to a turret and worked a Dumaresque [an early gunnery range 'computer']. The torpedoes were not very successful, only three going off well, the others only going about 30 yards. *Bellerophon* collided with *Inflexible* – tore a large hole.

Midshipmen are a rich source of diary items: they had to keep spotlessly clean and scrupulously accurate journals for inspection. Apart from the endless entries on training in one of the shipboard classrooms, and of 'evolutions' like anchoring or torpedo-netting practice, these journals frequently contain the most exquisite draw-ings of parts of the ships, not just of the guns, but of complex systems, like the drainage systems which ensured waste water found its way into the bilge, whence it could be pumped out. Ship manoeuvres, too, are recorded, and the long voyages a ship might make during the course of a year. Sometimes a whole year's travel would be encom-passed between the major south coast naval ports.

In 1896 HMS *Imperieuse*, an 8,500-ton armoured cruiser, sailed to Madeira: 'Hands employed cleaning ship as requisite. Preparing for sea. Lifebuoys tested and found correct. Slipped and proceeded out of harbour in charge of pilot,' John Casement, another 'middie' tells his diary.

> Sighted Portland. Put clocks back 17 minutes. Divisions, prayers. Both watches employed cleaning paintwork. Exercised watch at disconnecting steam steering gear.
>
> Exercised closed WT [watertight] doors. Mustered sea boats crew and examined uncontrollable lights (sic). Put clock back 14 minutes. Read fire stations. Watch securing guns and boats.

And on and on across the Bay of Biscay and south. Routine, routine, and all for the day when they might have to fight. To the reader of the late twentieth century two things stand out: first that there was a great emphasis on the right way to do things – everything down to polishing buttons. This is the traditional view of the Royal Navy at this time.

Secondly, it is quite clear that the Navy was having to come to terms with a rapidly changing technology, not just in the engine room, but in armaments, in navigation, in communications, and on deck as well. And there is, too, a sense in which fighting, perhaps for the first time in decades, was beginning to be real in the lives of some, if not yet all, of these men. What is never stated in the diaries, because it would have been so obvious, was the underlying assumption that the Royal Navy was the arbiter of all that was right and good in navies, worldwide. The RN was supreme, its ways the only ways. This mixture of pride and prejudice was to create a near disaster in the two world wars, when a ruthless enemy simply would not play by RN – or any – rules.

In 1906 – a year from which we seem to have many accounts – a young merchant officer joined the Royal Navy for a year's attachment. He was a rather stuffy young man, we may surmise of lower middle-class origins, much exercised by his health and over the state of his relationship with a young woman he had left behind in south London. But his extensively written – if a little self-conscious – journal of that year in the *Canopus*-class battleship, *Goliath*, is well worth study. It provides a deep insight into the ways of men on board naval vessels before the holocaust which was to engulf them. Sub-Lieutenant Simmonds did not have a happy beginning to his year, which began in September 1906.

The place [the gun-room] was unbearably stuffy and full of tobacco smoke and there were three fellows playing cards in their shirt sleeves. I stood there feeling very uncomfortable as nobody vouchsafed a word and I had no idea what I was supposed to do. Finally I addressed one of them and he asked me if I had a chest as there is absolutely no accommodation for clothes. I was again asked to drink and before going any further I should like to say how excessive the drinking appears to be. They are all younger men than I down here, some of them I should say are not yet 20 but they are continually having drinks.

After dinner – which he found he had no appetite for,

I was still quite in the dark as to where or how I should sleep and nobody seemed inclined to help me at all. The messman brought me all my boxes into the gun-room and after a time the senior engineering sub interested himself and sent for a man to sling a hammock for me.

The next day:

At 7.00am I was called and I turned out. I went into the bathroom which was ankle deep in water and there were no proper baths and I also had to hunt through my boxes for soap and towels, which I luckily found, and looking glass and shaved in the gun-room. After breakfast I put on my frock coat and wandered about until divisions at 9.30. During divisions the officers wear swords and if, in my case, having no divisions, simply stand on the quarter deck. I took note of all that happened and the officers duty seems simple enough, simply to examine the men's clothing ready for the captain's inspection. At 10.30 we had church on deck, both the litany and communion being read but no sermon. The paymaster played the hymns on a small harmonium.

Later that same morning Simmonds got to see the captain who put him at ease until:

He also asked me what arrangements I had made about my gear and seemed rather annoyed when I suggested I might have a cabin, telling me it was unusual for sub-lieutenants to be so provided and suggesting that I should hire a chest.

I now began to feel quite down-hearted after all the good times I have been having at home. It's a very lonely feeling, nobody wants to talk to one, and I feel quite an outsider. A marine came to me and offered himself as my servant, so that difficulty is overcome.

Although Simmonds felt excluded in these first days, gradually he began to take more part in the operations of the warship. One thing was that, whilst *Goliath* remained in harbour, she was visited by day-trippers, who poured on board from little steamers from Weymouth. Mail came at least twice a day too, on board.

> I have not yet said anything about the meals. The food itself is not so bad but it is not served very nicely. The plates, knives, tableclothes would be better for a little cleaning and there is absolutely nothing in the way of decoration to the table. Our meals are as a rule after the style: breakfast at 8.00am – porridge, fish eggs; lunch at 12.00 – a heated up dish and cold meat, cheese; dinner at 7.30 – soup, fish, entrée, joint, cheese, dessert by paying extra, coffee. Everything is of the plainest. Afternoon tea can be had if payed for. Fellows often bring books and papers to read at meals. We are waited on by two domestics which is barely sufficient considering that there are twenty in the mess. The conversation is not by any means intellectual, and a great deal of mild horse play goes on.

But he was settling to it:

> I shall quite get to like this life. The time does not drag at all. There always seems to be something going on. I am officer of the day today ... It is not necessary to stay on deck the whole time so long as you tell the quartermaster where you are going ... This afternoon the men were piped to bathe and when this happens every precaution is taken to guard against an accident, such as lowering a boat and keeping a lifeline handy.

In this tiny cameo we can see the contrast between officers and men. Sailors – ratings – got to clean up by being allowed to jump into the sea; Simmonds got a bathroom, however wet and messy. His meals, plain or not, were eaten in a civilised order, well clear of the mess decks and the rowdy crowded life to be found there. Lack of space for the large crews carried by warships was no less a problem in this period than it had been in Nelson's day.

Warships had evolved enormously, mostly in sheer size, but accommodation for the crew (not, generally, however their officers) was primitive. Conditions for RN sailors were even worse than on merchant ships. The key problem was privacy: there was absolutely none, other than in one's hammock, but these were slung only at night. There were lockers but everything was visible to everyone else.

Meanwhile, Simmonds had now settled entirely into a routine. He visited Weymouth frequently, and walked in the countryside around it. He met girlfriends from London, down for a holiday, and took them to a hotel for tea. He watched a man building elaborate sand-castles and begging the tourists for a few pennies for his efforts.

His shipboard duties were, as he had guessed, simple:

> I work with Phillimore in everything except target and battle practice when I go in the fore turret with Baddeley. Today I go on watch from 8.30 till 12.45; again from 4.00 to 6.00pm and then from 8.00 to 12.00. [These watch times varied each day, to ensure each man got to work every twenty-four hours in any one cycle.] It is really unneccesary to turn out for the night watches in port, unless anything happens. So, as regards watch-keeping there is not much to do. As for the other duties, at 9.00 divisions and prayers, afterwards various duties such as general quarters, inspecting bags, drill etc. In port there is rarely anything doing in the afternoon. At 4.15 evening quarters, perhaps an evolution [like nets out] afterwards. So there are a good many idle hours.

Goliath appears to have had a relaxed captain. On the *Hampshire*, a *Devonshire*-class cruiser in Portland with them, the captain was not above sending for his officers' ties to check they were regulation width. Simmonds had to play along with some of these rules, of course. He also had to pay his mess bills (for one month: £2.12 shillings–£2.60), and to help with that frightful job of coaling: the ship managed sixty-six tons an hour.

When they put to sea it was for a local trip into the bay for firing practice. It is interesting to compare this activity with the furore which would be created today were the RN to practice its gunnery so close to shore, and so frequently. One should bear in mind, as well, the number of warships taking part in these exercises, day by day, week by week.

> It has been quite a strenuous day. We got under weigh at 7.00 this morning and proceeded to our firing position. After divisions the decks were cleared for action, all the sails, davits and anything moveable was taken away, and when the firing is going on hardly a soul is visible on deck.
>
> The commander had told me I had better go into one of the turrets as it was all new to me, so I got down into the foremost one. There is hardly room to move inside, there is so much machinery attached to the two huge 12-inch guns mounted in it.
>
> Everything is worked by hydraulic and the loading is a wonderful sight. The projectile comes up on a tray to the level of the breech which is also opened and closed by hydraulic. An hydraulic rammer then

thrusts the projectile home and the charge, which comes up with the projectile, is put in by hand, the whole proceeding taking about thirty seconds. The projectile weighs about 850 pounds.

Inside the turret there are only four men actually working each gun, the remainder of the gun crew are in the shell room underneath. Both guns are fired by the same gun layer who can train and elevate either gun by a slight pressure on the pistol grip.

When the gun fires the din is so loud that one does not notice the actual noise but the terrific blast gives one rather a sickly feeling, in my case this evening it has resulted in a headache.

In fact this might have equally been caused by the chemicals used in the charges. Later, Simmonds was told to put a little cotton wool in each ear, something he seems not to have thought of himself.

The firing of these broadsides vibrated through the whole ship:

All the pictures are taken down from the walls and anything breakable carefully stowed away in the cabins as the concussion of firing shakes the whole ship. We first fired four 3/4 charges from every gun.

The big guns of the Royal Navy were its pride and joy: it had been to this end that the all-big-gun *Dreadnoughts* had been built, the equivalent change on land of artillery to guided missile in our day. But as soon as they had been invented they were obsolete. Already the torpedo and the mine could destroy the huge platforms needed to carry such weapons to sea. The onset of the submarine and the aircraft would finish the job. Over their entire lifetime, and across the globe, only 170 were ever built of these great 'battleships'. Half never saw conflict of any kind. Fifty-five were sunk: 17 per cent by accident, 44 per cent by aircraft, 38 per cent by torpedoes (ship and air launched), 10 per cent from torpedoes launched from submarines or surface ships. Just 9 per cent were sunk by shells fired from another battleship, the adversary which they were designed to fight.

To those who inhabited these huge steel monsters, their power must have seemed – before 1914 – invincible. They travelled faster than any large warship in the history of naval conflict, they were armoured, they threw wagon-sized shells for thousands of yards. The only issue was how many you could put to sea, compared with your foe. Battleships were popular on land, too. They were the highly visible projection of Britain's might, the enthronement of her achievements. They were, too, romantic objects, vessels which held, like the Holy Grail, Godlike mysteries, in this case of technology.

PART TWO

Breaking Strain:
The Two World Wars

5

THE MIRROR CRACKS:
1914–18

> *'Mother, with unbowed head*
> *Hear thou across the sea*
> *The farewell of the dead'*
>
> Henry Newbolt, *Farewell*

That year before the First World War, 1913–14, was a wonderful experience for a young man in one of His Majesty's ships. Everywhere we went we were welcomed warmly and hospitably. We played a lot of games against the locals and kept fit.

In those days the South American republics were largely staffed by Englishmen; as there was a revolution every time the bell struck, someone had to run the country. So it was that the railways, the trams, the power, the water, the banks and the trans-ocean cables were partly financed and largely controlled by Britishers.[1]

Harold Hickling was a sub-lieutenant on the light cruiser *Glasgow*, later to take part in the Battle of Coronel, when he was lucky to escape with his life. But in these last days of peace, life was still a precious, capricious thing. Hickling remembered being in Rosario in Argentina and being told he had to see the 'Round Table'. Innocently, he and his fellows imagined it to be a nightclub. What they discovered was a brothel, complete with revolving 'table' on which the nude working girls displayed themselves for the customers.

Later, the *Glasgow* called at the Falkland Islands, an important coaling station for ships coming from or leaving for Cape Horn. 'Stanley, the capital of the Falkland Islands, with a population of under a thousand, consisted of a Government House, a cathedral, two pubs, the Falkland Island company store, and a huddle of houses on the hill-side above the southern side of the harbour; it was barely a mile from end to end,' he recalled.

Then, in August 1914, the war came.

We had had a long hard winter in that bleak waste of Northern Waters, with fog, snow, gales of wind, and all the unpleasant weather there is to be met with. In the higher latitudes we frequently had only an hour or two of daylight in 24 hours. Most of the time the hatches were battened down. There was no such thing as air conditioning below decks. Sweat ran down the ship's bulkheads in rivulets. Everything was wet. We gave up trying to use sheets. Blankets are warmer when damp.[2]

That description of convoys crossing the Atlantic by Herbert Edwards could have come from either of the two world wars. In fact, he was writing of the first. The war at sea between 1914 and 1918 was dominated, as much as the later conflict, by the menace of the submarine and its chief weapon, the torpedo. Yet, on the surface at least, the huge capital ships of the British Grand Fleet, and the German High Seas Fleet, continued to display, like roosters at a cock fight, that enormous talent among early twentieth-century navalists for self-deception.

By the start of the war the submarine was a viable weapon; its torpedoes feared by all. The Grand Fleet, that mighty arsenal of heavy guns, had withdrawn from the south- and east-coast ports to the bleak wastes of the Orkneys in order to ensure German U-boats could not threaten it. Yet the purpose of this armada had been to deny the Germans the use of the sea, by its constant presence in the North Sea and Channel. Herein lay the paradox of both world wars for the Royal Navy in home waters. Simply put, technology had by the turn of the century begun to outstrip all the tried and tested methods of naval warfare. From now on, it was to get psychological – although it took the scientifically devised technological battles of the Second World War anti-submarine warfare to demonstrate this underlying truth.

The Royal Navy had evolved its main battle fleet enormously in the decade and half since Queen Victoria's Jubilee in 1897. For one thing there were the *Dreadnoughts*, and super-*Dreadnoughts*, with their all-big-gun fire-power and turbines for speed. Even so, these ships were the final manifestation of a principal going back beyond Nelson. They were still to fight in a line, now hurling in total hundreds of tons of high explosive thousands of yards to fall onto a similarly placed enemy fleet.

Meanwhile an increasingly expanding number of escort ships were to be found ahead of this great fleet, sweeping the seas for mines, submarines and torpedo boats. In harbour these capital ships now had to surround themselves with huge nets, in case a submarine should sneak in and attack. It was the coming of aircraft – particularly naval aircraft – which finally demonstrated how easily battleships could be overcome.

The naval arms race of the years before 1914 had been all about battleships and it was to be the desire of the Royal Navy to engage the German High Seas Fleet which dominated early tactics in the war. No one doubted the Navy's ability to flatten the German fleet, given the chance, including the Germans themselves. The German resort to submarine warfare, conducted in the early months chiefly against British warships, was seen as a typically Hunnish underhand way of not coming out to fight, rather than as the future of naval warfare.

In 1914 Britain remained the world's main naval power. As such she was able to impose her strategy on the French, her principal ally. As generals (and admirals) cannot help but fight the current war as if it were the last, the underlying concept was Napoleonic in design: blockade Germany and starve her out. France had become an ally for the first time in 600 years. Britain, of course, dominated the geography of the approaches to the North Sea. With Italy as an ally in the Mediterranean, and Russia containing Germany on land to the east, it all looked horribly easy. But, as with the trench war in France, the Allies at sea became bogged down.

The Germans, for their part, had hoped that the British – following the Napoleonic method – would come in close, easy targets for mines and torpedoes. But the Admiralty in London had been well aware of the German desire for the fight to be carried on at their door and opted for a distant blockade, aimed more at the gap between the north of Scotland and Norway than the coastline of the North Sea. The Channel they had no fears over although, as it turned out, there developed a fierce battle throughout the war between submarines and the 'Dover patrol' of largely fast destroyers.

The overall strategy led, inevitably, to the capital ships remaining largely in harbour whilst smaller, faster and lighter ships patrolled endlessly back and forth. The British armed many merchantmen to reduce the strain on the Navy (whose writ continued to run worldwide). The Germans used U-boats and, early on, commerce raiders. Even so, in the first year or so of the war only 2 per cent of the merchant navy was lost. These ships continued to sail singly at this time, and were all picked off one by one.

In 1915 the Germans, growing desperate, instituted an unrestricted U-boat campaign, sinking any allied ship on sight and with no warning. It was at this point that the *Lusitania* was sunk off Ireland, on her way from New York. German sources in that city had warned that she would be a target. Controversy on all sides still surrounds the sinking. She had not been told by the British Admiralty of German

U-boat activity until 6 May (she left New York on 1 May). At the time of the U-boat attack, she was not zigzagging and she was close to land. The 1,198 people who died in the attack were not helped by the speed with which she went down – only twenty minutes – nor by the angle of her bows, which prevented many lifeboats from being launched.

The *Lusitania* was carrying 124 US citizens and their deaths undoubtedly led to the United States eventually joining the war on the side of the Allies in 1917. It has been suggested that both Winston Churchill, as First Lord of the Admiralty, and Jacky Fisher, First Sea Lord, deliberately had her steered into the path of submarines in order to outrage US public opinion but this seems unlikely. The Germans claimed she was an armed merchant cruiser and, therefore, subject to instant attack, but this was untrue.

Like many other future incidents involving submarines (including the sinking of the *Belgrano*) the attack on the *Lusitania* would live on as an outrage against humanity. The submarine has never been perceived as anything other than an underhand weapon, whoever choses to use it. The unrestricted U-boat campaign of 1915 was abandoned by the Germans because public opinion in neutral countries, especially the USA, was so violently turning against them, and the British meanwhile tried to fight back by a policy of patrolling. Patrolling was, above all else, dull.

> 4 May 1915: 09.10, proceeded to sea and all went well till 06.45 when we sighted a four-masted bark in a sinking condition, which turned out to be the *William T. Lewis* and the oil steamer *Balakani* had her in tow. It appears that she was stopped by a hostile submarine, the crew ordered to take to the boats, then the submarine opened fire on her but having a cargo of logs, she did not sink.
>
> 9 May: Met the old lady coming out of harbour so we have to put on our good manners when we see ma [HMS *Adventure*, the admiral's ship in charge of all the sloops]. So we went into harbour and secured to No. 3 buoy and coaled ship. Ma returned, she mustn't stay out too long she may catch cold.

This sailor exhibits a nice turn of sarcasm, beloved of all tars down the ages, when it comes to discussing 'superior' ranks. Based in Northern Ireland, so they could cover the approaches to the Clyde and to Liverpool, he got plenty of coaling ship and patrolling in down the year. He called the German U-boats 'Jack-in-the-boxes' but they saw very few. Mostly the work consisted of examining ships for contraband, cargoes which appeared to be one thing and turned out to be another. Finally, though, the sloop was transferred to the Mediterranean where, in company with others, she ran a U-boat to earth, somewhere on the Libyan coast.

'... off we went on nearing shore, to draw their fire. In we went and opened fire on a large buoy for we had an idea the submarines were getting their fuel by this means. But no sooner had we started than they let rip. It was a good fight till the gun which I was at came crashing to the deck, so that left us with one gun and to make matters worse our steering gear broke down again so I had to go aft and steer by hand.

We went out and reported to *Mimosa* and I'm blowed if he didn't have the cheek to send us in again in that state and he wouldn't go in himself. Well, it got too warm in there for us and couldn't sink buoy so we came out. No sooner had we come out when *Mimosa* made a signal to say she had had two torpedoes fired at her, and one missed and the other struck but failed to explode.

This problem of dud torpedo fuses was to plague the Germans in this war and the next; but many torpedoes did find their mark. The firefight described here ended when the Navy sloops silenced the shore batteries and the U-boats escaped. Stephen Baker, the able seaman who wrote this diary, was on board HMS *Mallow* for just over two years.

Here we go again [he wrote at the start of 1917]. What will this one bring forth? I am wondering if this terrible war will finish this year or if not I will be relieved to get a chance to see how things are at home, but I must not talk of home now so let us get on with today ...

Well, it is very dirty indeed, the ship is standing on end at times and we have our work cut out to hang on to ourselves or we would soon be down the lee scuppers. We are having our meals where we can as there is not a table shipped in the proper place.

HMS *Mallow* was a converted trawler, a precursor of those magnificent but horribly wet corvette designs of the late 1930s and early 1940s. The long arduous work ships like her did in both wars was only belatedly recognised. At the time it was out of sight out of mind for a public desperate for a big naval battle. The lives of sailors constantly on patrol was dull by and large, but at least they were at sea. For the sailors on the capital ships, crammed together for weeks at a time, anchored in remote Scottish lochs, it was just dull. Like their superiors, they longed for the Germans to come out and fight.

There had been skirmishes. In late August 1914, Commodore Roger Keyes had sailed his cruisers into the Heligoland Bight with high hopes that he would intercept one of the destroyer patrols he knew were sent there. When this engagement was under way, German light cruisers arrived in support, only to be engaged in their turn by five battle cruisers over the horizon. The result was predictable: the Germans eventually lost three light cruisers and a destroyer, although the cruiser *Arethusa* had had a lucky escape.

The British operation had been a hastily planned affair but, as with so many naval actions, fortune favoured the bold. This single hard-fought battle had a long-term effect: the German high command changed its plans for an offensive policy in the North Sea, horrified that the Royal Navy could so easily operate in its own arena, apparently with impunity.

It did not all go the Royal Navy's way, however. A month later three British cruisers, the *Aboukir*, the *Cressy* and the *Hogue* were lost to a single U-boat (U-9); in October the new battleship *Audacious* was sunk by a mine, and the pre-*Dreadnought*, *Formidable* was sunk by another U-boat (U-24) in December.

These losses had to be set against a tremendous success in the South Atlantic, in the Battle of the Falkland Islands. The Royal Navy's problem, aside from any new weapons the enemy might deploy, was as always the sheer size of its operation. The German threat was sufficient to ensure a withdrawal of all but the lightest forces back to home waters. This meant that what was left had largely to guard the fixed bases and coaling stations. As we have already noted, the awful truth for the British in a global conflict was that all those bases, all those colonies, were chains binding the Royal Navy to a fixed defence. An enemy merely had to bide his time and strike.

The Germans had had a Far Eastern Squadron and although the potential danger of this had been largely removed by Japan's entry into the war on the Allied side, the cruisers of this force had escaped, heading east and arriving off Chile in October 1914. There they had coaled. The British then arrived and at the Battle of Coronel they suffered a major defeat.

The British force, two armoured cruisers, a light cruiser, an armed merchant cruiser and a battleship, appeared on paper to outgun the two armoured and three light cruisers of Admiral von Spee, but the British battleship, *Canopus*, was too slow to keep up and the big British cruisers were weakly armed. As a result the two armoured cruisers, the *Good Hope* and the *Monmouth*, were sunk.

'The news of the Navy's defeat at Coronel shook the country to the very bunt,' says Harold Hickling, 'indeed the whole Empire was profoundly shocked ... Coronel came like a thunderbolt from a blue sky.'

The humiliation of this battle was too much for the Admiralty in London: they ordered two battlecruisers, the *Inflexible* and the *Invincible*, south. (It is a curiosity of history that another *Invincible* was to take part in another battle of the Falkland Islands sixty-eight years later.)

Von Spee, meanwhile, had decided to attack the Falkland Islands coaling station, unaware of the Navy's mad dash across the Atlantic. He arrived off Port Stanley on 8 December 1914, but the battlecruisers had arrived on 6 December. The Germans sailed into the trap; only the *Dresden* escaped, the other four ships being sunk. Eventually the *Dresden* was tracked down to Chilean waters (the British casually breaking Chilean neutrality, as had the Germans). The British sailed in and she was scuttled, the whole episode having been for the Royal Navy a satisfying example of their ability still to police the world at will.

Clement Woodland was assistant pay-master on board the *Invincible* when she was sent to the Falklands. His account starts with a list of the provisions they had aboard when the ship sailed. These included 13,388 pints of spirits, 134,396 pounds of flour, 2,749 pounds of biscuit, 15,251 pounds of fresh vegetables, 37,875 pounds of sugar, 4,253 pounds of chocolate and 9,388 pounds of salt pork, among a huge list. Then came the arrival at Port Stanley and the fleet action.

December 8: A memorable day! I overslept myself and was awakened by the flag lieutenant coming into the cabin and saying to Captain Malden [a marine wireless officer] 'you had better get up, a four-funnel ship has been sighted'. At this time we were busy coaling from a collier alongside and I was going to take part in the coaling.

As it was I jumped up and dressed with all speed. I went to the ward room and had a good breakfast then up on deck. I found that the coaling was stopped and steam was being raised. I heard that five cruisers had been sighted and that they had stopped as the *Canopus* had fired four rounds at them, but the range was too great. Also, it was reported that two of the enemies' supply ships or colliers had been sighted.

About 11 o'clock we steamed out of harbour. I think the order was *Bristol, Glasgow, Kent, Carnarvon, Cornwall, Inflexible, Invincible*.

The *Bristol* was subsequently sent with the *Macedonia* to capture the supply ships. We were soon out of the harbour and I could see the smoke of five cruisers in the distance. We were sent to action stations but soon came on deck again.

After a time we again went to action stations and I went with McEwan to the magazine below 'A' turret. About 11.30 we came up and went to the ward room. I had a good lunch of tongue, bread, butter and jam. Afterwards on deck again. We were rapidly overhauling the enemy and everyone was in great spirits. About 12.30 we went to action stations again so I went to the magazine. At five minutes to one *Inflexible* opened fire. At one we commenced firing.

'A' turret was hard at it. Apparently the enemies' three light cruisers went off together pursued by *Kent, Cornwall* and *Glasgow* while *Invincible, Inflexible* and *Canopus* chased the *Scharnhorst* and the *Gneisenau*. It was strange sitting in the magazine while one watched the ammunition sent up to the turret by a lift.

We were firing Lyddite common shell and armour piercing shell. I never had the slightest feeling of nervousness but I was a little annoyed that I could not see what was going on. The firing was continuous. About three the *Scharnhorst* sank; then we pursued the *Gneisenau*. After more firing there was a lull while we got to closer range. During the action we felt the occasional shock which told us we were hit. About 4.45 cease-firing was given.

I soon went up on deck. The *Gneisenau* was sunk. It was an awful sight. The *Invincible, Inflexible* and *Canopus* were standing by while the sea was dotted with struggling men, swimming or clinging to any wreckage. We launched our boats, threw down any ropes we could. I cannot describe the scene; it was awful. However, we picked up all we could. The water was so cold it killed many poor fellows before we could reach them ...'

The *Invincible* was a bit of a wreck. The ward room was completely smashed, the piano in bits, the table and chairs smashed up, in fact nothing was left. Another smashed up the pantry and the cabin next to it. Another hit a four-inch gun and cut it in two, passed downwards through the conning tower, upper and main deck, into the Admiral's stores and there lay unexploded. The after conning tower had a big hole in the base. 'A' turret was hit but little damage done.

This was Nelsonian; back home the Admiralty rejoiced and the public shouted in the streets. Looking forward a moment to 1982, it is possible to discern the same kind of passions among many British people over the battle for the Falkland Islands in our own time. The popular history of the Royal Navy is written in this way – small actions in distant places, where individual commanders show initiative and panache. On the East coast of Africa in 1915 Donovan Roe was on board HMS *Hyacinth* rooting out another German raider, the *Königsberg*. Kenya was a German colony then and they finally tracked her down in a river delta.

> At about 4.15 the monitors [big gun coastal bombardment vessels] came out engaging the guns on the banks all the way down. The whole squadron proceeded to Koma Island and anchored for the night, the monitors being cheered by all the ships as they came in and went alongside *Trent*. It transpired that fire had been opened on them immediately it was light enough, and as soon as they arrived at their position and opened fire the *Königsberg* also opened fire on them – they discovered a spotting tower on the island which they destroyed.
>
> The *Mersey* was hit on the forecastle, the six inch gun being put out of action, four men killed and four wounded (the only casualties sustained) The spotting from the aeroplanes was not very satisfactory but a good number of hits were obtained. When the second aeroplane had to retire the monitors moved up until they could see the *Königsberg*'s topmasts. The latter's firing which had been rapid and accurate died down and at 2.00pm ceased altogether, the ship apparently being badly on fire forward. It was not possible, however, to tell whether the cease firing was due to lack of ammunition or the guns being put out of action. The captain of *Severn* reported that he considered her not totally destroyed but so badly damaged as to be unable to take any further part in the War or come out of the river.

This incident, suitably beefed up, was much later made into the feature film, *Shout at the Devil*, starring Roger Moore. In 1915 *Hyacinth* steamed 30,417 miles and was at sea for 244 days.

The key naval battles of the First World War (aside from the slow attrition of the U-boats) were just two: the Dogger Bank and Jutland. Before we can understand them we have to make a journey a little back in time, to the pre-war naval arms race, and to the shipyards of Germany and Britain, to look at the battleship and the battle cruiser and, as well, to the men who sailed in them.

The apotheosis of power: the battleships of the First World War

The evolution of the battleship had been a continuous, if generally slow, progression throughout the nineteenth century. Nelson's First

Raters fired broadsides: that is on both port and starboard sides of
the ship, up to fifty cannon would empty as much shot as possible at
another ship close alongside. Wooden ships being almost impossible
to sink, unless a lucky shot hit a magazine, the idea was to bring
down all the masts and spars, maim or kill as many of the enemy
crew as possible, then to board and overwhelm.

The development of the explosive shell and increasingly larger
calibre guns changed all that; now ships could be sunk and at a much
greater distance. Armoured-plated sides were brought in, then iron
and steel hulled ships, propelled by steam. Armaments were cen-
tralised in citadels and given primitive barbettes which could rotate,
thus ensuring only half the guns previously needed were carried. This
was important because by now weight was becoming a crucial factor.

Gradually, it became clear to major warship designers that what
was needed was a deck cleared of all but the minimum in order that
the main armament got the widest arc of fire; that armour on the
sides and, eventually on decks as well, to protect against plunging
shells, had to be as thick as possible and that speed was of the essence.
By 1906, when HMS *Dreadnought* was launched, all these concepts
were to meet in what turned out to be the template for all the final
battleship designs.

At that time – the first decade of this century – improved gunnery
fire controls and a reduction of secondary armament was reinforcing
the battleship as a single-purpose war machine. The impetus towards
a ship which could concentrate a massive salvo of high explosive was
at odds with the equal desire to have high-speed ships. Even the use
of turbines could not overcome the huge weight penalties. In Britain
this led to a split in design between the battleship proper, with massive
armoured protection, and the battle cruiser, which had much less
armour but a greater speed. The battle cruiser turned out to be a
fatally flawed idea.

The large questions of speed versus guns versus armour were never
resolved; the re-introduction of five-inch and six-inch guns, along
with masses of light anti-aircraft quick-firing guns, was a belated
partial answer to combat the constant menaces to these ships of
lightly protected but very fast destroyers, torpedo boats and, finally,
aircraft, all these notwithstanding the constant threat of the submarine.

The battleship by the start of the First World War represented the
end of a line (although one was still being used in anger in 1991 in
the Gulf War). One reason for its longevity in the age of the submarine,

let alone aircraft, was its physical presence. Admiralties the world over found it impossible to resist as a symbol of naval power. Battleships are menacing like no other big warship.

The British had been modernising their battleship fleet from the turn of the century. At a stroke, *Dreadnought* made all these ships potentially redundant. Able to bring to bear eight twelve-inch guns, or up to six firing forward, and with a top speed of nearly twenty-two knots, she was, on launching, the most powerful warship the world had ever seen. Her commissioning occasioned a period of worldwide *Dreadnought* fever, extending as far as South America. The USA, France and Japan all rushed to catch up.

It was, however, Germany to which British eyes turned with alarm. The German Navy had been racing to catch the Royal Navy for more than a decade. Yet in 1897 she had only eight battleships to Britain's sixty-two. It was the arrival of Tirpitz, as Secretary of State for the Navy, which transformed its fortunes. Tirpitz was a proponent of a 'risk theory', by which he meant that a German Navy had only to threaten the Royal Navy in such a way that its ability to confront France or the USA, say, was compromised. Under such conditions, he argued, the Royal Navy would back off, thereby conceding the German Navy the freedom of action it desired.

Thus did the Germans enter the costly naval arms race preceding the First World War. Initially Tirpitz was cautious, hoping in part to fool the outside world by building capital ships in ever larger size but not in sudden jumps. It involved a programme of adding about 2,000 tons displacement to each successive class of ship. Unfortunately, he reckoned without British hypersensitivity to any form of naval challenge (comparable to the US/USSR arms races over ballistic missiles of the 1960s and 1970s).

When Admiral Fisher took over as First Sea Lord in 1904, he immediately began a programme of drastic change to Royal Naval operations and staffing. The old two-power standard (which meant the Royal Navy had to be at least as strong as the next two naval powers) was revised to be a two-power standard plus 10 per cent. The Navy's foreign stations were drastically cut back: China, Australia and the East Indies became the Eastern Fleet, now based in Singapore; the South Atlantic, North American and West Africa stations became the Cape Station (based on Simonstown). Over 150 units were scrapped. This meant that Fisher could now build up his home fleet to seventeen battleships.

The arrival of *Dreadnought* ensured that all Tirpitz's battleships had been made obsolescent overnight. Ironically, but inevitably, the ship Fisher had had built to forestall naval architects in other nations became the symbol of what to try to beat. The effect on the German naval high command was to encourage a second, much fiercer, arms race. The 'we want eight and we won't wait' slogan of the times encapsulates how far the general public joined in the scare. Another irony of the times was that both Churchill and Lloyd George were opposed on the British side to an upsurge of naval construction. At the start of the War the Royal Navy had achieved a bare margin of numbers.

Looking back, one might wonder, in view of the unrestricted submarine campaigns of 1915 and 1917 and the fears over the vulnerability of these battleships to those same submarines, what was the fuss all about? Much like the recent debate over a nuclear deterrent though, the arguments over battleship numbers in 1909 and subsequently were the same. Certainly battleships were not war-winning weapons but their absence from the British side meant that German warships would be able to roam the high seas and destroy British shipping at will. As it turned out, it was a close-run thing, closer by far than perhaps anyone realised at that time. German battleships carried smaller calibre guns (eleven- and twelve-inch) but they were better aimed, through gunnery direction systems, and had stronger armour.

In the early part of the First World War, the German Grand Fleet did not seek, after Heligoland, an outright fight. Rather, the commanders sought to break up the Grand Fleet by attacking east-coast ports. Yarmouth was shelled in November, Hartlepool in December. Admiral Beatty, as a result, moved his battle cruiser fleet down from Scapa Flow to Rosyth in the Firth of Forth.

In January, the Admiralty forewarned by their intelligence operation, which by this time had managed to break into German naval codes, had ordered Beatty south to the Dogger Bank, where it was to rendezvous with some of the Grand Fleet battleships. However, on 24 January 1915, before this had happened, a light cruiser had sighted German battle cruisers and a chase began. The British battle cruisers included *Lion, Princess Royal, Tiger, New Zealand* and *Indomitable*. The Germans had *Seydlitz, Moltke* and *Derfflinger* as well as the older *Blucher*.

It was the *Blucher* which caught the brunt of the British attack in the early stages but at the point where the British might have continued to chase and destroy Admiral Hipper's force, a signals mix-up intervened. Even as late in the day as this the Royal Navy was relying on flag hoists to relay messages, and these were often obscured by the dense quantities of smoke from the fully fired-up furnaces of the ships. At the Battle of Dogger Bank, though, it was the incompetence of the signals officer – a man who went on in the same capacity to confuse the battle fleet at Jutland.

Beatty already had had other problems. A shell from *Derfflinger* had caused severe flooding in *Lion's* port engine room, as a result of which she had to be taken in tow. More worrying, out of 243 shells fired by *Lion* only four had found any mark. Other battle cruisers of Beatty's squadron had done *worse*. On the other side, the Germans had learned a vital lesson, despite the loss of the *Blucher*.

The *Seydlitz* had suffered a major cordite fire in an after turret, a fire which had killed 160 sailors. The subsequent investigation of this fire had shown how vulnerable these large ships were to a fire developing at lightning speed down the turret trunks and ammunition hoists and straight into the magazines. The Germans brought in new procedures for handling ammunition; the British continued as they had throughout. One result was that three British battle cruisers at Jutland were to be lost through catastrophic magazine fires.

As one of the shells fired by the German battle cruisers had started a fire in *Lion's* forward turret, it is worth comparing the different attitudes of the two Navies. The Germans, after the *Seydlitz* incident, fitted extra anti-flash shutters and the quantity of flammable material held in and around the turrets was greatly reduced. The British, by contrast, surveyed the damage on *Lion* and concluded all was well. Only one man had been killed and twenty wounded in the turret fire. The fire in the top part had been put out quickly. Yet, as events were to demonstrate all too dreadfully, this was sheer luck.

No attempt was made to limit the amount of cordite (the shell propellant) held in the turret 'lobby' nor were anti-flash measures enforced. It can be surmised, in part, that this inability to foresee what might happen was a result of lack of battle experience. At the start of the War many serving senior officers had cause to lament the poor quality of their juniors, especially the ship's captains who, whilst they might have lots of sea experience, were not versed in war, or the arts of survival.

The bitter truth about the Royal Navy in 1914 was that although its ships had been transformed since Nelson's time, its attitudes had not. Nelson's sailors would, for example have recognised many of the routines of the Royal Navy a hundred years on. Sailors still 'messed' in small groups of eight or ten, slung their hammocks below decks when the mess table was cleared away and suffered similar cramped conditions to Nelson's men. Modern battleships like *Dreadnought* needed a huge space for engines, for the complex turret machinery and the attendant magazines. Fuel took up the biggest space, *Dreadnought* for example burning 2,000 tons of coal in five days when steaming at full speed.

In all this the ordinary seaman, whatever his particular job, was just a cog in a machine – this was the great change from Nelson's Navy. By 1914 warships required engineers, stokers (a third of a coal-burning battleship's complement of a thousand men), ammunition crews, turret crews, telephonists, clerks, surgeons and medical teams, signallers and mechanics, electricians and range-takers. All of these specialist jobs, as they became more defined, had parallel officer ranks to direct them. But it was still a hybrid Navy, composed of the new 'classes' and the older hierarchies. Nothing had been fully tested, and certainly not in the massive all-out battle that had been contemplated.

That came in the one major clash of the battlefleets at Jutland, in May 1916. The German High Seas Fleet, finally under a bold leader, Admiral Sheer, sortied out on 31 May, met Beatty's battle cruisers and bruisingly punished them before being engaged by Jellicoe's Grand Fleet. This was turned by a torpedo attack by German light forces. Further skirmishes followed during the night after the main action but the result was that the High Seas Fleet never again ventured out, until they came and scuttled themselves in Scapa Flow in 1918. In that sense, Jutland was a British victory.

But the losses were far worse on the British side. Three battle cruisers and three armoured cruisers were lost by the Royal Navy, along with 6,097 sailors; the Germans lost one pre-*Dreadnought* and one battle cruiser, along with 2,551 men (in the main actions). They could claim a victory in this sense; strategically the Royal Navy could claim, too, that it had 'won'. Not since the Japanese – Russian clash at Tsushima, a battle which heralded the start of twentieth century naval warfare, had so many giant ships faced each other. It was the last time two great battle fleets were so to do.

For the sailors of both sides Jutland was a salutory experience, a taste of what modern naval guns could do to a ship, however well armoured. The *Invincible* (victor of the Battle of the Falklands) was blown to pieces when a German shell penetrated the roof of 'Q' turret, and the flash penetrated the magazine, down the turret trunk; there were six survivors out of a thousand men. So confident had the

British been of victory that, when the Grand Fleet passed the wreck of the *Invincible* sticking up in two halves out of the shallow North Sea, sailors cheered, convinced that it had to be a German battleship.

What 'defeated' the High Seas Fleet was the nerve of the British (and, no doubt, their reputation handed down from the century just past). The British Grand Fleet sailed across the top of Sheer's battle line; after only eight minutes he ordered his ships to execute a sharp turnaway. Almost as soon as they had been spotted by the British range-takers, the High Seas Fleet disappeared again. Thereafter the action degenerated into attacks between cruisers, destroyers and torpedo boats.

Many of those who came out of the battle had had little idea of what was happening, perhaps mercifully so. Unlike the wooden walls of Nelson's time, the modern battleship was an enclosed world. The best view was not even from the bridge, as it was in the midst of swirling gunsmoke, but from the fighting tops or the range-control towers above. What the individual range-takers could see, though, was not all that cheering.

When the *Queen Mary* blew up, another victim of a magazine explosion, one spotter saw what he thought was a cloud of coal dust immediately after the shells landed. Then the ship disappeared in a huge ball of yellow flame followed by a mass of black smoke. When one of the following ships, *Tiger*, came alongside the men on deck could see sailors crawling out of the after turret, only to have to endure their being blown to pieces by another explosion. The deaths of those below can only be imagined. One survivor of an earlier sinking has told of how men in the engine room were thrown about like so many bits of flotsam, into the still-whirling pistons and valves of the racing engines, there to be shredded, still in many cases alive, before being consigned to oblivion by the inrushing water.

Burns, scalds and flayed flesh were commonplace in the engine rooms when ships were sunk in this way. Other, even worse, burns could be found among the gun crews where turrets had been hit, even if the shells had not penetrated the casing. Anti-flash gear for the men was still not yet in full or enforced use.

Yet in the midst of this horrible destruction officers on the bridges of the ships could still observe with fascination the huge shells from the main armament of the enemy ships flying overhead, even picking out the markings. The ships were firing at each other from up to ten miles away and a great ripple of flame could be seen as the guns fired. The shells took up to half a minute to arrive; tons and tons of metal and high explosive always appearing to be headed straight for the observer. The noise of ricochets sounded like distant trains. It had became part of the art of the gunners to ricochet these huge shells off the surface of the water, increasing their velocity and trying to ensure they bounced over the armour plate and into the vulnerable super-structure. Yet, on the very largest of the ships, even a hit at one end could go unnoticed at the other. On *Lion* for instance Q turret (amidships) was hit yet those on the bridge remained unaware of what had happened until a marine arrived, burned, bloodstained and, as a contemporary noticed, hatless. When those on the bridge looked behind them they could see the remains of the turret folded back like an opened sardine can, smoke billowing up and the guns twisted into fantastic shapes.

Lion of course, like *Queen Mary* and *Invincible*, was a battle cruiser, a lightly armoured high-speed version of the *Dreadnought* type. If Jutland proved anything, it was that the concept behind these ships was a disaster. The true *Dreadnoughts* and super-*Dreadnoughts* involved in the battle came through intact. *Warspite* had been hit by fifteen heavy shells yet it suffered only fourteen killed and thirty-two wounded. This great battleship survived the First and the Second World Wars, being scrapped only in 1948. Of all the world's battleships, *Warspite* can be said to have taken more punishment than any other.

Jutland was a turning point. In many ways it was the Royal Navy's Somme, with frightful casualties, many of them avoidable had more thought gone into the protection of ships and crews. Few could have really imagined what a clash of battleships would be like. As with trench warfare, the results were shocking: over eight and a half thousand sailors killed in a few moments' indecisive action. At the same time the battle had proved the fears on both sides that cheap light ships, in this case the torpedo boat and the destroyer, could severely limit battleship tactics.

Certainly, the onset of these craft meant that secondary armament had to be re-incorporated into battleship designs, with a crucial weight penalty, to be added to that of the underwater armoured belts already in place as protection against torpedoes. The submarine, although not sufficiently developed by 1916 to menace the battle fleets as it would in the near future, was of course the other potent example of how much naval warfare was changing. But it was to be in economic warfare that the submarine excelled; the weapon striking through the back door at the war economy.

*

By 1916 the land war had deteriorated into a bitter slogging match on the Western Front, in which millions of soldiers fought each other for the gain and loss of a few hundred yards of blasted ground. The Germans were faced on both west and east fronts by the Allied powers and could look for little in the way of a breakthrough. Germany was in dire economic straits; the British naval blockade was working.

The Battle of Jutland forced the German High Command to conclude that the High Seas Fleet provided no easy way out. Thus, notwithstanding the unpopularity of the previous campaign, they turned once again to the submarine. For the four months between October 1916, and January 1917, a 'restricted' campaign was run, sinking nearly fifty ships (still unconvoyed). In January 1917 tonnage sunk reached just under 370,000 tons; over 2,000 British merchant ships had been lost since the start of the war. The U-boat fleet had lost only a couple of dozen boats to British anti-submarine patrols.

Given the success of these tactics Admiral Sheer finally persuaded the Kaiser to allow a sink-on-sight policy from the end of the 1916. It was thought that if 600,000 tons of Allied shipping could be sunk every month and if twice this tonnage of neutral shipping was frightened off trading with the British, it would all be over within five months; the British would be starved out. By March 1917 losses had risen to just under 600,000 tons for that month alone. This effort was achieved by just over a hundred U-boats, operating out of Germany, Flanders and the Mediterranean, with a few based elsewhere. By April one in four ships approaching the British coast was liable to be sunk; only six weeks of supplies separated the British from disaster (uncannily close to a similar number of weeks in 1943 when a later generation of U-boats were to try the same tactics again).

At this point few of the countermeasures used by the Allies were in any way effective. Hundreds of small vessels had been hastily converted as auxiliary patrol ships; many were Q ships, trying to ambush unwary submarines. The first depth charges had been tried in 1916 and a directional hydrophone in 1917; mines were laid in the entrances to the submarine bases. Finally, and most costly of all, the Passchendaele offensive in Flanders was designed to capture the U-boat bases in Flanders.

The answer came suddenly: the convoy system was introduced. Grouping ships together under Naval protection had been resisted by all and sundry. The merchant navy believed it would merely ensure more targets for the U-boats; the Navy thought it would not have enough ships to cope. In fact, of course, the escort ships now detailed

to protect convoys had spent years of fruitless hunting, literally in
the dark. By October 1917 only twenty-four ships out of 1,500 had
been sunk. The convoys continued to the end of the war, by which
time the German submarine fleet had lost 40 per cent of its men.
Further to the convoy system, an emergency ship-building programme
was instituted and many ships were salvaged. Finally, the Americans,
joining the war on the Allied side in April, seized half a million tons
of interned German shipping.

For the merchant sailors the threat from submarines was just a
further burden to pay for what remained a harsh life. Ship-owners
stopped pay once a ship had been torpedoed; there was no com-
pensation for lost belongings. It was only the ships chartered to the
British Government whose crews benefited from some continuance
of wages – providing they got themselves to a home port within
fifteen days of being sunk, a rare occurrence.

There were some improvements in conditions on war-built ships.
The crew accommodation was moved from the fo'c'scle aft and
wooden bunks were replaced by iron cots, clear of the ship's sides.
This reduced the risk of bedbugs, and of the 'sweat' which ran down
an iron ship's sides. There was more light through extra portholes
and skylights and better washing areas were provided (compared, it
should be said, with none in many pre-war ships). None of this could
compensate for the terrible results of being sunk at sea.

In all the British merchant fleet lost nine million tons in the First
World War, half its pre-war tonnage. Worse still than these losses,
which could be made good, was the impact of the War on trade and
trading patterns. British ships had been freely requisitioned when the
War started, at special 'Blue Book' rates. These had been set at a time
when freight charges were low; the War caused massive inflation. As
a result few British shipowners made the kind of profits foreign
competitors could make on the same routes. Some did, though
through fair means and foul. Some written-off ships, for instance,
were compensated for at full rates once lost through U-boat action.

Whatever antics ship-owners might try back home, it was foreign
competition which was able to exploit the situation to the full. French
shipping remained free of requisition; on top of this two million tons
of British requisitioned ships were lent to the French. Italian shipping,
too, remained outside controls until 1917; the British lent them half
a million tons.

The two biggest gainers were the USA and Japan. In 1914 only 10
per cent of American shipping was engaged in off-shore trading, the

vast bulk of US goods being carried in British ships. By 1918 this situation was transformed: the US merchant marine had grown from 2 to 9.8 million tons. In the same period the British fleet declined by 2.6 million tons. Overall, the British percentage of the world fleet had declined from around 40 per cent to 32.5 per cent, still huge but now in a decline which would not stop in its general downward drift for seventy-five years.

In the Pacific, the Japanese (on the Allied side) were able to squeeze out the British more or less completely. The effect of the War on the British cross-trades in the Far East was particularly severe; the distortion caused by the economic impact of the European war meant little could be supplied from Britain which was not compatible with her war needs. The Japanese, with abundant cheap labour, were able to go on building ships, helped by a government which off-set building costs and gave direct assistance to the shipping industry. By 1918 not only had Japan made a clean sweep of trading in the Far East, she was cash rich, the result of a general wartime inflation of freight rates.

In 1918, at the signing of the Armistice, it would have seemed that Britain had emerged from the bloodiest and most terrible armed struggle in her long life, with an increase in power and prestige. The cost had been horrific: nearly 10 per cent of her male population under forty-five had been killed (the lost generation); another 20 per cent were injured, many seriously. That Germany was in a worse plight hardly mattered and, indeed, given the seeds of bitterness sown at Versailles, this was to be a major contributory cause of the Second World War.

But the economic damage was worse even than the destruction of manpower. There had been a thirteen-fold increase in government expenditure during those four years and as taxation could not possibly meet this sum, huge borrowings were needed: the National Debt rose from £650 million to £7,435 million. Much of these enormous sums was covered by the equally large capital reserves and by invisible trades, but these were constantly to mask the declining traditional industries: coal, iron, cotton manufacturing and ship-building, to name just a few. British shipyards had increasingly been building warships; as a result their proportion of world merchant-ship launchings fell from 58.7 per cent in 1914 to 35 per cent in 1920.

The result was that sterling weakened against the dollar; Britain, from now on, would be vulnerable to changes in world trade (a situation we know all too well in the 1990s). Given her expanded

Empire (now to include a number of German colonies in Africa) and the burden this was now to become (in view of the commitment to defend it), and given the growing gap between the belief of the British in their world status and the realities crowding in, the future was bleak.

Beyond the horizon that bleak outlook was compounded by the growing strength of the USA, clearly set to become the world's leading power, and Japan, whose astonishing rise from obscure medievalism in the mid-nineteenth century, to regional superpower only sixty years on might have caused more of a sensation today that it occasioned at the time. Britain was now to become more and more dependant on both these nations for support, both economic and military.

For as Britain had been unable to defend her Far Eastern possessions with much effect, so the Japanese had moved to fill the vacuum, partly through the Anglo-Japanese alliance, maintained despite suspicions that the Japanese had been fermenting unrest in India. This Alliance, however, was viewed with great suspicion in the US where conflict in the Pacific with Japan at some future date was already contemplated. It led, as well, to the disaster (for the British) of the Washington Naval Conference.

Pax Britannica in coming to an end had set in train a series of rivalries, fought out over markets and market shares between a number of rising nations. Yet as they were to do after the Second World War, the British tended to see the War as an interruption, however ghastly. Now, they could return to trading. As the state of shipping shows in the 'long weekend' between the two world wars, everything was changing. It was changing for the Royal Navy, whose triumph at the surrender of the German High Seas Fleet was short-lived. The cost of modern warships, the expenses of foreign bases, the threat to the old capital ships of the submarine and the aircraft, along with American insistence that the British be cut down to size, meant that the period between 1918 and 1939 was to create a continuing nightmare for the RN, not to be relieved in any measure by the peace.

6

THE LONG WEEKEND

*'With a lame duck, lagging, lagging
all the way.'*

Henry Newbolt, *The Old Superb*

The writing had been on the wall for British shipping before the First World War began. The four years of struggle speeded up the painful process of decline in her world trading position. But the War years exposed seafarers to more cruelties than U-boats. For example, the entire British entrepôt trade (the re-export of goods coming through British ports) was lost between 1914 and 1918, wiped out at a stroke. Meanwhile, twenty-five foreign new liner services were started and the domination of the liner services (which controlled, through cartel-based 'conferences', the freight rates and apportionment of total goods carried per shipping line) by Britain was again being strongly challenged in many areas.

Nonetheless, there was a chance in 1919 to regain some of that lost trade, and to rebuild a merchant fleet, incorporating the technologies of the time – like marine diesel engines. That, in Britain, the opportunity was not seized meant that the slow agony of British shipping would continue for another two decades until a second, far more deadly, conflict would seal Britain's fate for ever as the world's leading maritime power. The relationship between the economic power of a nation, its trading through shipping and its naval forces is clear, at least at one level. In Britain's case at the end of the War this relationship was ignored, with ship-owners – and government – unwilling to reinvest.

Germany, of course, had not been defeated, merely subdued; she was about to be humiliated, not least because of the insistence by the Admiralty in London that the entire High Seas Fleet surrender, a pointless exercise not at all justified by the performance of the Royal Navy in the previous four years. That surrender would rankle, along with many other Armistice clauses. For the British Navy, however, any triumph they might have had at Scapa Flow, when the High Seas

Fleet sailed in, only to scuttle, was shortlived. The truth was, as Lloyd George later said, 'The trident was passing peacefully from Britain to the United States'. Yet the British insisted, to themselves at least, that they had a sacred duty to defend the Empire, however costly. With the growth of the European dictatorships in the late 1920s and early 1930s, she was faced with the impossible task of maintaining strong home forces and a worldwide set of bases. This burden fell, as it always had, on the Royal Navy. At the same time, the First World War had begun that process of economic ruin which would continue, decade by decade, until nearly the end of the century.

In 1919 the Royal Navy's strength was 438,000 men, fifty-eight battleships and cruisers, 103 cruisers, twelve aircraft carriers, 456 destroyers and 122 submarines. But Britain's proud Navy had effectively conceded the Pacific and much of the coast of the Americas. It was to concede much more before the next two years were through. The huge size of the Royal Navy in 1918 could not be maintained. The only question was how fast was it likely to be cut and what would be the long-term implications? In 1919 the RN was told to assume there would not be a major war for at least ten years, an accurate forecast but not one calculated to make the Admiralty happy. But by 1919 it was becoming apparent that a number of factors were conspiring to limit future provision for any armed service. Although it was not until 1929 that the great crash came in world trade, many of the older British industries were in deep trouble after the War. Textiles, which once provided 40 per cent of exports, were down by two-thirds, coal had dropped by 20 per cent. Steel production fell by 45 per cent between 1929 and 1932; iron by 53 per cent. But shipbuilding was to hit its own bitter nadir in 1933 when it was a mere 7 per cent of its pre-war level (and by which time three-fifths of the workforce were unemployed).

The problem was compounded by the collapse of the export trade and although home consumption made up some of the difference, Britain had grown strong by selling goods abroad; her population was too small to sustain the growth she needed. New industries did start – including plastics, cars, aircraft – but they were not enough. Before 1914 a quarter of Britain's production was exported; by 1939 this had dropped to not much more than 10 per cent. Britain's share of world trade fell from just over 14 per cent in 1914 to under 10 per cent in 1939. It was as a result of these kind of pressures that Britain returned, in the early 1930s to protectionism, and 'Empire

Preference'. This, along with the collapse of the world economy which made many raw materials cheaper, helped to keep the British economy afloat. From the mid-1930s rearmament helped as well, along with the new economic theories of Keynes, which engaged the national government in investing in ailing industries, and in infrastructure.

There was another, crucial, factor in determining the size of the armed forces in the decade after 1918. This was what crudely could be called the power of the people; there was considerable pressure on government not to 'invite' another war. The pacifism which grew out of the slaughter of the trenches lasted a long while and did much to influence the foreign policy of appeasement. The British simply did not want to contemplate war – any war. The backlash against the millions of deaths between 1914 and 1918 was compounded by a slogan used in the Great War of 'The War to end all Wars', and with a belief among many that the newly formed League of Nations would finally put a stop to large-scale conflict.

This pressure from below also meant that governments for the first time had to address more seriously the issues of health, education and social welfare and although, in comparison with the heights of post-Second World War welfarism, their efforts look lamentably weak, nonetheless the social budget was beginning to compete with the arms budget. In the period up to the great crash of 1929, the traditional economic view that governments had to minimise their spending and balance the books, added to the anti-war movement, and to social pressure, meant that in all respects the armed forces suffered.

In to this picture came, in 1921, the Washington Naval Conference. This Conference, and subsequent Treaty, affected Britain more than any other power, as the nation with the largest Navy. To say it was a disaster for Britain would not be exaggerating. Among other things, it led to a limitation on battleship tonnage, and a ten year 'holiday' from new designs. For the first time the Royal Navy was to be limited in size to that of another power. It was agreed there would be parity in tonnage of capital ships between Britain and the USA; Japan would have three-fifths of this figure, France and Italy just under two-fifths. An agreement was also reached on aircraft carriers.

But no agreement was reached on smaller ships including, most significantly, submarines. The Germans, of course, were not invited. By the provisions of this Treaty, the Royal Navy for the first time had to abide by an international ruling rather than with regard only to Britain's defence requirements. Hitler thought it meant a change from 'Britannia Rules the Waves' to 'the Seas of the Union' – meaning the

USA. But it was a fear that there would be an Anglo–American naval race, which the British could in no way afford, that determined that the Treaty would be signed.

America was the major gainer – again – because the battleship programme she already had was allowed under the Treaty to bring her to parity with the RN; her ships were all brand new as well. Even worse, the immediate result was a further blow to British ship-building and the skills associated with building big ships. A good deal of the effort by the United States was aimed at the Anglo–Japanese alliance. It was clear by the 1920s to anyone who cared to look that at least one future war would be to decide who had the dominant position in the Pacific and around its rim; Britain, by US dictat, was not being invited to take part. It is worth speculating what might have happened if the Anglo–Japanese naval co-operation had continued, and what that might have meant in 1941 for the Americans. Conflict in the Pacific between Japan and the USA was always likely but it might not have developed into quite the carnage it did.

To some extent, this argument over naval forces was a side-show, did the Admiralty in London but know it. The next ten years at least were going to be dominated by a much more urgent issue: Britain's economy and the gold standard.

Whilst the inter-War Navy was struggling to keep itself afloat, in every sense, merchant shipping was also suffering from the caprices of world trade, and of the impact of the war, whose chief effect was to deny for four years a number of the 'nice little earners' the tramp ships in particular had relied upon.

In the period between 1918 and 1921 there was a short-term boom in shipping. All that came to a sickening end in 1922 and British shipping did not recover until after the Second World War. Part of the problem was the dumping on the market of four million tons of wartime shipping by the British government. This competed with a host of new tonnage ordered by British companies since 1918.

Apart from that, the bitter truth was that the world had too many ships; trade was insufficient to fill them. From the late '20s the world recession made this problem harsher and harder to solve. Between 1913 and 1938 the volume of world trade was to increase by only a third; merchant fleets rose by a half and, because many ships went faster and were bigger, their effective carrying power was higher still.

In 1932, at the worst part of the world economic slump, a fifth of tonnage was laid up. In Britain the merchant fleet was the hardest hit of all, partly because it was still the biggest. But that was only part of the story. There was a huge reduction in passenger trade after the Great War, particularly the migrant trade to America; British passenger ships had relied heavily on this. The cotton industry collapsed, faced with greatly increased competition from Japan. Coal exports, the underpinning of so much tramping, fell from seventy-seven million tons in 1913 to thirty-eight million tons in 1938. National shipping lines began taking liner trades from the British. There were other changes, too. The motor ship, running on diesel, began to make inroads on the traditional steamship. Whereas the motor ship could run at 12–17 knots, the steamers strolled along at 8–10 knots. The British, with huge coal reserves, opted for steam, despite the growing cost advantage of oil. (The Navy had largely switched to oil by 1918.)

The growth of oil as a fuel was matched by a large increase in the world tanker fleet. Once again the British failed to capitalise. World oil production had been one million tons in 1870, forty-five million tons in 1914, and 276 million tons in 1937. Although it had been less than 5 per cent of trade by tonnage in 1913, by 1937 it had become 21 per cent. The world tanker fleet (of 1.5 million tons) had been half owned by Britain in 1914; by 1939, when world tonnage had risen to 11.4 million tons, only a quarter was British.

The Rochdale Report on shipping published in 1970 says: 'It would appear that during this period, whether due to the effects of low profitability or other causes, there was marked tendency for UK companies to fall behind rather than lead their overseas competitors in going after new types of business . . .'[1]

Most damning, it goes on: 'While Scandinavian owners were building diesel-engined tankers, fruit carriers and cargo ships suitable for charter to liner companies, UK tramp owners continued to favour the traditional 9–10 knot dry cargo steamships.' Exports were declining; imports were rising. The ships entering British ports were increasingly foreign: from 34 per cent in 1914 to 41 per cent in 1937. The value of world trade carried by British ships fell from 52 per cent in 1912 to 40 per cent in 1936.

Unlike many other governments, the British government showed a marked reluctance to help out either shipping owners or shipbuilders. Finally, when the weight of the recession was its heaviest, and when the rise of Nazi Germany was all too obvious, the British national government stepped in and began a rapid programme of warship building, and a scrap-and-build programme for merchant ships.

Most notably, the government underwrote the completion of the world's largest-ever passenger liners, the *Queen Mary* and the *Queen Elizabeth*. Both were to serve as troop carriers for six years before they were able to do the job for which they were built, carrying well over a million troops between them. On the eve of the second great war with Germany, Britain still had the world's biggest merchant fleet. It is a measure of the heights from which she was falling that this should be so, rather than from any positive action to maintain her position. In 1939 Britain owned a third of the world's deep-sea tonnage, a quarter of all tonnage; she possessed half the world's passenger ships, over half its refrigerated cargo vessels, a quarter of its tankers. Her Navy was still among the largest in the world, ranging worldwide, albeit in increasingly difficult circumstances. The Empire was still intact – in fact, at its greatest ever extent. This was now to prove the biggest burden of all.

The trappings of vast global power were still all there, and would have been impressive enough even to Queen Victoria. But Britain's reign as a world power was long since over. The true strength she once had – in her economy – was gone, fatally weakened by more than half a century of decline, and delivered a near-mortal blow by the First World War.

As many commentators have remarked, too, it was the relative *increase* in the economies of the USA, of Japan and of Germany, that mattered. Set against them, the slow and painful gains of the British were all too easily stripped naked. Now would come the flaying.

For merchant seafarers these inter-war years of the 'long weekend' were hard years to endure; after the world trading slump of 1929/30 it got worse. James Boyce joined his first ship in 1935.

There was no shortage of boys wanting to go to sea – and I was one of them. Many tramp ship owners were undoubtedly exploiting apprentices. Some ships had as many as eight on board, paying them the usual sixty pounds for the four-year period; namely twenty-eight pence a *week*.

For this they worked twelve hours a day, on the usual watch system of four hours on, four hours off, when the vessel was at sea. During this time they did exactly the same jobs as the seamen – steering, chipping, scraping, painting and the rest. Most pre-war tramps did not have refrigerators, so the only way food could be kept for a limited period was in an ice box. After a week or so at sea the ice melted and out came the salt meat – salt horse! When this happened the feeding was little better than the fare on the old sailing ships. In fact, on some ships it was worse.[2]

Eric Newby, working on one of the last great sailing barques, remembers salt horse only too well:

Salt pork, which appeared in various disguises at least once a day, was like theatrical property, produced to create an atmosphere and then whisked away uneaten. In its worst form it was fried and smothered with a metallic-flavoured bean stew ... Sometimes the pork arrived floating in a thick heroic kind of pea soup as solid as porridge, which was eaten laced with the same sulphurous-looking pickle which had been part of the night watchman's perquisites in Belfast.[3]

On some ships to have food at all was a luxury, though even recently ships in the North Sea waiting to load oil have been known to run out of food as they waited week on week to load oil from 'mono' buoys in bad weather. But, in the 1930s, running out of food was more to do with owner parsimony than with storms. Richard England, a crew member on one of the last of the trading schooners round the British coast, remembers just how bad it could get. The schooner, *Emma and Esther*, had run out of wind in sight of the coast:

We'd been at sea for three weeks and the food situation was becoming serious. Our salt beef, in a harness cask on deck, was tainted before we left the Mersey and the hot sun made it stink to high heaven. And there had been a blunder with our bread, though well-intentioned. Shore bakers were beginning to wrap bread, claiming it would keep indefinately. Our captain substituted it for the usual hard tack and we thoroughly enjoyed the luxury of soft bread for the first week at sea, then paid dearly for the pleasure when the loaves turned mouldy under their grease-proof paper wrappings.[4]

Food was one of the few 'pleasures' seafarers could look forward to on any kind of voyage; for the rest, barring bad weather, it was (and remains) terribly monotonous. One personal log from the 1930s describing a voyage from Britain to Australia on the MV *Limerick*, with no intermediate calls, simply lists the days like this:

Painting chartroom and captain's cabin; painting derricks; painting officers' deckhouse and bridge; painting derricks; painting port-hand rails; painting waterways and rails; scraping and oiling foredeck; sweeping alleyways, oiling decks – passed Cape Town; chipping decks and so on, endlessly, until they reached Fremantle.

James Boyce made a first trip to South America. The fascination
of the sea lay as much in the characters as in the hopes of arrival.

> There were two old sailing ship men in their seventies among the crew
> and both had the name of Roberts. One was a Scot and the other a
> Welshman and they were known as Jock and Taffy. Jock was a big man
> with a walrus moustache and had a pronounced American accent which
> had been acquired by sailing for many years in American sailing ships.
> 'Down Easters' he called them.
>
> Both of them chewed tobacco. Taffy was always seen with a dark
> trickle running out of the corner of his mouth. We thought it a disgusting
> habit but the men were not allowed to smoke whilst working. If the
> mate caught a man smoking he would be logged [fined] for disobeying
> an order. We heard that all the men were fined a day's pay for not being
> fit for duty on the day of sailing. As they were poorly paid anyway, this
> was a heavy punishment.

SS *Harmattan* was sailing with a cargo of coal from Cardiff to South
America; this was the kind of voyage that the merchant fleet had
grown strong on. It was 1936 and this kind of trade would not last
much longer. In South America, the crew went ashore.

> During the weekend, dressed in our shore-going clothes, we explored
> the town. We felt like fish out of water as we made our way towards
> the town. We had to walk quite a long way through what appeared to
> be the local playing fields. We made our way toward the town centre
> and down the main street we passed many bars from which we could
> see many of our sailors drinking. We sat for a while to watch the local
> people, we were fascinated by the way they dressed. Judging by the
> stares we received, they were equally interested in us.

Ships like the *Harmattan* unloaded and loaded their cargoes in tiny
ports up the great rivers of the world. The process took time –
sometimes weeks. This was the essence of the inter-war (and for a
while post-war) seafarers' world. In a way, it was the reason many
went for it represented a form of exploration, however tenuous. More
than anything, this is a way of life now gone for ever, replaced by the
harsh lighting and harsher timetables of the container ports, many
miles out from the nearest town or city, inaccessible, remote, bare.

Of all the seafarers, apprentices had the worst of it:

> Most of the coal-burning tramp ships in which I served my time carried
> four apprentices and we lived together in one room measuring eleven

feet by nine feet. This contained four bunks in two tiers, a wooden table and bench, a small settee, four drawers under the lower bunks and four lockers. We ate, slept and lived in this one room for as long as we were on the ship which could sometimes be for years, [recalls Captain McBrearty.] There was no space in the room to keep all your gear and your trunk, so this had to be stowed elsewhere like the forepeak store. Heavy clothing and spare gear was left there until needed.

Everything had to be done in *your* time, so eating, sleeping, washing etc., had to be done in your four hours off ... Even during your time off during the day it was hard to sleep because the general work of the ship still went on. Chipping and scraping of steel decks did not stop because you were trying to sleep.[5]

Watches were divided between two hours on the wheel and two hours on standby when an apprentice might be called upon to do anything. McBrearty remembers forever trimming ventilators on or off the wind, checking hatch tarpaulins, slackening awnings, checking the stern light. Sailors were called to the bridge by a whistle; there were no internal phones. On the bridge the ships had voice pipes with a whistle on each end. Time was kept by the striking of the ship's bell.

Work on deck was very hard and there were many jobs required to be done which are not needed on today's modern vessels. Things like cleaning bilges. This was a loathesome task particularly after a grain cargo when the smell would be foul. Preparing the holds for a grain cargo was a big operation involving all the deck crew and the officers. Shifting boards had to be put up and the limber boards covering the bilges had to be either caulked with oakum or covered with burlap and battened down. Despite this, grain somehow always managed to get into the bilges.

Ships would carry coal to Buenos Aires, then go up to Rosario to load grain which might be for anywhere. This meant a thorough washing out of the holds. Yet whilst the officers might work alongside the men in this regard, in other cases a different segregation applied.

It was accepted at sea in those days that if native seamen were carried, then the apprentices would not be set to work with them. You could do the same sort of work but not alongside each other.

Interestingly, this testimony is not borne out by others, where mixed crews, in the sense at least of many races, did work together. What did not happen was a white European sailor being asked to work with a mostly Chinese, other Asian, or black, crew.

Back home, the apprentice seafarer found his enterprise and his hardships had paid off:

> ... When you eventually did get home after a long voyage you felt you were looked upon by the young friends you had known as something different. A little isolated maybe, not knowing much about the political situation or who had won the cup; nevertheless, you had done all sorts of things that the others would have no idea about.[6]

John Cooper, now in his late seventies, and having spent fifty-eight years at sea, does not look all that tough – but he certainly once was. A sprightly, small man, with an extraordinary giggling laugh, he looks like a parson, a saintly, lovable elderly man. But John remains one of seafaring's firebrand legends: he was, from the start of his seafaring career, a Liverpool fireman.

> Me first trip was as a trimmer for me father – he was a fireman. You had to get into the bunker and get the coal out to about ten firemen. It was hard work. I had to wear gloves for three months after me first trip. When you were doing it, you had to pee on your hands, that was your medicine for your hands. You had to make sure the ship was trimmed – taking the coal from the bunkers in the right order. I was just turned eighteen, then.
>
> The biggest part of the job was clearing the ashes. Every watch you had all this ash and you had to carry it to the ventilators and haul it up and dump it over the side. Later there were self-dumpers – they were in the middle of the stoke-hold. The ash was blown out through the bottom of the ship – you had to be careful 'else you'd be swept away with it. They'd shout 'all ready' and you'd get out of the way. Sometimes it would all get blocked and then the sea would clear it and it would all come back on you. We'd shout out 'she's been sick' and we'd all be soaking wet.
>
> She was a Furness Holder ship, the *Baronessa*. You had to fetch your own gear – two Donkey's breakfasts (straw mattresses) included. To keep clean you had to use a bucket. On some shifts you had to go midships to get water out of a pump; at five o'clock that was locked up so we had to get the water from the condensed steam – we hung a bucket down the ventilators and then hauled it back up.
>
> We slept twenty to a room, if you don't mind, us to starboard, the deck crew to port. They were mostly all Liverpool; a great crowd. There was singing and dancing on the deck – you didn't worry about overtime then. We stoke-hold crew started a group – we called ourselves the Flying Ashpans.

The ship carried general cargo to South America, but a lot was cattle – for stud for Lord Vestey. They were on the deck. We used to go out at the most economical speed; coming back we used to go hell for leather. I stayed with the auld fellow [his father] for four years; then we had an argument over the allotments [the money he and his father gave his mother from his wages]. I didn't see him then for four years.

Looking back on a lifetime spent at sea, he says this: 'I'd do it all again. There were some smashing people I sailed with.'

For some pre-war sailors, life could be surprisingly soft at sea. Charles Walker went to sea first in 1937, on the *Manchester Brigade*:

In the *Manchester Brigade* two of us seemed to live in luxury for we had our quarters amidships, comprising a small messroom and another very small cabin with two bunks, one above the other. But we still had to go with a bucket to the bottom of the engine room to fill it from a tank which always had a thin film of oil floating on top – this for boiling water to wash our clothes and to bathe in. We had to do that in the crews' quarters.

In heavy weather it was very tricky for there were four sets of short ladders to climb with one hand holding on to the rail, and the other trying not to let too much water spill from the bucket.

The only thing wrong with our and the rest of the crew quarters was we were infested with cockroaches and everything had to be fumigated every few trips. It was a hard life but enjoyable. My wages as a deck boy was £3.12/6 a month; eight months on when I was made an ordinary seaman it rose to £4.16/4.

Merchant sailors prided themselves on their stamina and on the harshness of their lives when yarning. But some of their number, if not enjoying much better conditions, rubbed up against the other side of 'travel' in the 1930s. These were the men – and women – who sailed on the super luxury liners, especially the transatlantic routes.

Everyone on the *Berengaria*, even the dogs, were 'socially prominent'. There was Rin Tin Tin junior whose owner had a first class ticket, but lived with his dog on the third class deck ... There was Gertrude Lawrence's dog which she liked to exercise on deck each morning in defiance of regulations, and the melancholy incident when I caught her doing so and escorted her in grim silence back to the kennels. She sobbed all the way[7]

recalls Harry Grattidge, who went on to be a captain of the *Queens*. Many of the captains of these great liners have written their memoirs; during the 1930s they were as well known as pop stars are today. Their lifestyle was something every schoolboy could aspire to, for anyone could go to sea and rise to be a captain of a Cunarder. Because the captain ran his ship like a potentate, he *was* important and even the famous courted his company on the voyages across the Atlantic. His dining table was the one to covet, even for a first-class passenger and he could, over the course of a season, have every film star, every major politician from Europe, every rich steel or newspaper magnate at his table, a heady mixture of politics, business and hype, all discussing the issues of the day.

It is little wonder, then, that the memoirs of these men is larded more thickly than most autobiographies with names dropped as well as a thick helping of anecdotes about the rich and famous. Even they romanced, when given a chance. Edgar Britten was master of the *Berengaria* (seized from the Germans after the First World War.

> I have heard say that with the passing of the sailing ship so passed the romance of the sea. I wonder? Have a look at the *Berengaria* from the dizzy height of the bridge.
>
> Look back! See the black smoke belching from her three gigantic funnels. Down each two railway trains might easily pass. Look down! Down at her great broad decks gleaming white nearly a hundred feet below. Gaze on the massive hull of her, black as the night. Watch her razor-edged bows cleaving the mighty waters, an inspiring sight. See the white-capped waves racing along her 900 foot length, lashing the seas into white foam far behind in the wake. Feel the mighty power of her, this great hulk of steel and woodwork, crashing across the vast Atlantic at thirty land miles an hour; and although all alone on this great sea, with no vestige of land in sight, the whole world knows exactly where we are ... Is that not Romance?[8]

These ships were magic to their age; Kipling called one of their earlier number a floating city gone to sea. Ernest Diggle was the master of perhaps the greatest of all these beautiful ships, the *Aquitania*. On board, he says

> There lives a population of happy travellers who are staying for a brief period in this liner which is the most luxurious and efficient floating holiday resort and city in the world. That, in a word, accurately describes this wonderful liner. For she is nothing less than a self-contained city with her own reservoirs, oil-fuel and electricity plants, swimming pool, open-air baths, gymnasium, theatre, restaurants, dancing halls, inns, verandah gardens, shopping centre, main and

branch libraries, hospitals and dispensaries, cinemas, municipal offices, playgrounds, police force and fire brigade.[9]

The luxury of the settings and the sumptuousness of the food is what most remembered afterwards. Few even cared to think of the conditions in which armies of stokers and trimmers, or even stewards and stewardesses worked, the sheer effort which had to go into ensuring that the thousands of passengers who made the crossing were pampered at every moment. The floating cities of opulence which have never been equalled, even by today's cruise liners, were sustained on a rigid class system, not so much between first, second and third passengers, as between the workers and the players.

But those days have, thankfully, passed. What lingers is that indefinable beauty of the combination of good taste with the greatest of purposes – the crossing of a sea in style. This was the *Aquitania's* smoke room, styled on a late-seventeenth-century country house:

> The full length portrait of King James II hanging over the fireplace between carved drops gives, perhaps more than anything else, its true and huge scale. It is a room which reflects the prodigious energy, the masculine and massive hand of that eminent scientist turned architect, Sir Chistopher Wren. It is hardly to be equalled in the most important city or country home in America.'
>
> The *Aquitania* may have been the ultimate compendium of period styles, but she was also a ship with a bow, a stern, and a hull housing the power plant that would propel her 46,000 tons across the North Atlantic more than six hundred times. The last four-stacker ever to be built, she would eventually sail, tall and handsome, side by side with low-funnelled liners that could outrace her but never match her queenly serenity, or ruffle her dignity.[10]

Amen to that.

7

TWILIGHT OF
THE GRAND FLEET

*'We joined the Navy to see the world.
And what did we see?
We saw the sea!'*

Popular Song

Whilst the inter-war years saw first the rapid scrapping and laying up of many naval ships, followed by a period of almost no new building, then a scramble to re-arm, for the officers and men it was a period of business as usual. Ships of the Royal Navy continued to sail throughout the world, to distant stations, or on flag-showing missions. The home waters fleet continued to exercise as if the Battle of Jutland had never happened. There were new amusements: aircraft carriers had made their first appearance towards the end of the war; larger, more comfortable destroyers (compared with their earlier ancestors) and, finally, the last variants of the great eight-inch and six-inch gun cruisers, the archetypal ships of the Empire.

But it was the aircraft which excited many of the younger officer recruits to the service:

> Went with one of the senior Mids for the first PB [picket boat] coaling trip. Whilst inshore we noticed one of the *Vindictive*'s planes go up for practice and we were about to make fast again when we were sent back with instructions to pick up the plane as it had crashed. We found this had happened only just off the *Vindictive* and already numbers of boats were around the wreckage. Apparently the pilot who had only just made a very bad landing, and observer, both managed to get clear. . .

So confided Midshipman Lampen to his journal aboard HMS *Marlborough*. These early carrier planes were barely modified versions of landplanes. There was no arrester gear and they were stopped by a screen raised on the deck. But their airspeeds were slow; most survived the frequent crash landings in or out of the sea. So frequent were these survived crashes that Geoff Rotherham remembers that as an observer in training in the 1930s the air crew on his carrier had clubs for each kind of survivor.[1]

One was the 'Rats Club' for those who had jumped into the sea upon ditching; if you ended up in more than one you were called a 'man about town'. Once, he remembers, the observer of a plane which landed badly had jumped just as the pilot had opened the throttle in a last-minute attempt to do a 'go around'. The aircraft, possibly because of the reduced weight, managed to take off and the pilot then successfully landed only to nearly crash again when he noticed with astonishment his observer watching him from the flight deck. He, of course, had had no idea that the man had jumped out. Behind the fun and games – and occasional deaths – of these practices was a much more serious issue: who controlled the Fleet Air Arm. The Royal Naval Air Service had preceded the Royal Air Force but after the War, when Air Vice Marshall Trenchard was determined to set up a unified airforce, Admiral Beatty is reported to have given the RNAS away, saying aircraft on ships were a 'nuisance'. The result was that he spent years trying to undo this one moment's thoughtlessness to get back his carrier's planes. Not until 1939 did the Royal Navy 'own' its planes and pilots again.

On *Furious* in 1933, Midshipman Trelawny reflects on the chain of command problems:

> The air-arm is at present in the unfortunate position of having no defined head authority, no one in supreme command with the essential 'family tree' of organisation spreading out and de-centralising below him.

Trelawny was undergoing an air-experience course. The carrier, *Furious*, had been converted from a battle cruiser; despite her age she was eventually to survive well into the Second World War, being retired when her hull more or less gave out from age.

> The planes we carry are: a fighting squadron of Nimrods; a torpedo-bombing squadron of Ripons and a spotter plane squadron of Fairy 3Fs, which are shortly to be superceded by Fairy Seals.
>
> A carrier is a very vulnerable thing in wartime. Petrol is pumped up to the hangars by compressed air. There are few more explosive mixtures than petrol and compressed air. The flying deck is not armoured and a bomb would possibly penetrate to this fuel. The modern carriers have big anti-aircraft armaments but *Furious* has not had hers increased and it is inadequate.

Flying, for these young men, was an entirely novel experience, and one which they all relished.

We had already drawn gear, consisting of helmet, goggles and lifebelts. The latter were dispensed with when we were lent reed jackets, so that these were all the extra things we wore over our ordinary uniform. I was among the first two to go up, in No. 28 machine [wrote Midshipman Lampen].

We were shown how to stow away the slings after un-hooking, and how to hook on again and as I sat in the observer's cockpit I was the first to gain experience in this respect. The slings are on the wing centre section onto which one crawls. As soon as the plane is un-hooked the slings have to be stowed away, the four straps in four diagonal slots which were closed by patent fasteners, and the remainder of the slings in a box-like compartment which is closed by a flap. It was a wonderful sensation when the seaplane lifted off the water and we found ourselves in the air for the first time. We appeared to climb very rapidly and had soon gone some way up the Firth and over *Marlborough*.

We then turned to fly over the land on the south side of the Firth and we were about 900 feet up before we felt any bumps which were only very slight.

The midshipmen's journals from which accounts like these are taken are self-consciously pedantic in tone. All 'middies' had to keep one, as the fly sheet says, 'to train [them] in the power of observation, the power of expression, the power of orderliness'. As with those kept in the Edwardian RN, the post-war journals are often beautifully illustrated with indian ink drawings, coloured in; many have photographs pasted into the margins. Most describe the same kind of shipboard routines Victorian middies would have understood.

But the world was now changing all too fast. One post-war journal reflects that starkly. In 1920 HMS *Centurion*, with other ships, had sailed through the Dardenelles, recently the scene of the carnage of the Gallipoli Campaign, on into the Black Sea in a last effort to support the White Russians against the Communists. Midshipmen Townsend, aboard *Centurion*, had a glimpse of a society torn by civil war. Atrocity stories (what the Reds were doing to the Whites, needless to say) leaves his account a little breathless. But one entry, seventy years on, we recognise all too well:

From local information it appears that the Russians are incapable of organising: we sent them boots and the whole way up the line they would be sold to the inhabitants. We sent them uniforms and one regiment received the tunics, another the trousers and these men, having no boots, proceeded to cut up the accoutrements to wear on their feet.

The post-war Navy, though, was shrinking fast. Many of those who had served all through the First World War now found themselves washed up on an indifferent shore. Sea careers leave men detached from shore-life. Those fortunate enough to be able to plan out a future, after seafaring, may still suffer. But for those, like Commander Dearden, whose life *was* the Navy, the post-war cuts came as a bitter taste.

I had no illusions about the importance of HMS *Rival* as a unit of the British Navy; indeed my predecessor, a senior Lieutenant-Commander, did not even have the courtesy to remain aboard to 'hand over' to me. Nevertheless I did feel a thrill of satisfaction as I stepped aboard her, saw my pennant flying and made myself known to her officers and crew.

This, his only command, ended after two years.

My hopes sank to zero when I was appointed to the RN Barracks, Portsmouth, as a supernumerary Lieutenant Commander, a doer of odd jobs, most of which could have been equally well done by a midshipman of average ability and intelligence. I felt very bitter that my seafaring should have led to no more than this.

I loathed those weary months at Portsmouth; the dull uneventful duties as officer of the day, the superintending of the issue of soap and tobacco, the conducting of the weekly route-march through the streets, the nominal charge of working parties on the recreation grounds.

Once he had to get a thousand ratings from Portsmouth to Rosyth, through London; he only lost two. Much more distasteful was a round of pensioners lodgings in nearby Southampton, to check they were still alive, their pensions not being fraudulently claimed by relatives. They all knew why he had come, he recalls, and they resented it as much as he. Dearden's memories of the run-down of the service are parallel to those accounts of life after the Napoleonic Wars: men who had spent years fighting the French thrown suddenly into a void with no hope of promotion – or, in many cases, even prospects.

What they missed was that old black magic of being at sea, hard to convey to anyone who has not experienced it first-hand. Port larks – especially those in far away places – were always at the back of the sailor's mind; he yarned about them endlessly. But it was so often that ephemeral but compelling 'sea-drift' which kept a man spellbound.

After nine o'clock rounds that night I put on my greatcoat and went up to the bridge. The officer of the watch deferentially crossed over to the lee side, leaving me the small area to windward wherein to pace to and fro.

How wonderful it all was – yes! wonderful is the word. A fine clear night. Just a light breeze with a smooth sea. Overhead the dark canopy of heaven studded with myriads of bright stars. The half-moon shed a path of mystic light across the water. Overside the foam rushed past in soft fluffy rolls as our sharp bow cut through the sea, and but for the hissing it made there was complete silence about me.

Later that same night, Herbert Edwards saw a three-masted barque cross his ship's bows and his heaven was complete. He recalled, too, the prayer with which the Navy greeted each day:

O Eternal Lord God who alone spreadest out the heavens and rulest the raging of the sea. Preserve us from the dangers of the sea and from the violence of the enemy that we may be a safeguard unto our most Gracious Sovereign Lord King George and his Dominions and a security for such as pass on the seas upon their lawful occasions.[2]

This was the old Navy, the great world-roaming Navy which had lingered on from earlier even than Victorian times. Its fleets were still spread across the globe, but they were aging ships, now limited by international treaty and, far more significantly, by economic necessities back home. Yet, this mighty Navy could still put on a show. Geoff Rotherham, in Malta in the 1930s, recalls:

One of the great sights of the time was that of the fleet leaving port for a cruise. Out of the Grand Harbour under the ancient battlements of Valetta would come the Battle Squadron of six or eight ships, along with the aircraft carrier, *Glorious* and the cruisers. Out to meet them from Sliema and Lazaretto creeks would come *Coventry* leading as many as thirty-six destroyers [the size in 1992 of the entire RN frigate and destroyer active fleet], divided into four flotillas. The big ships moved majestically, each slipping its buoys in turn.

The destroyers scuttled out from their congested creeks to join the battleships, probably needing no more signal than the time-honoured 'follow father'. They would gather speed as they moved out to sea and form up in perfect order in their stations ahead of the battle fleet. What a spectacle this massive exhibition of power was when seen from the battlements of Valetta.[3]

But the cuts had bitten deep. They bit deeper still in 1931. The Invergordon Mutiny was part of the fallout, begun by basically decent and loyal sailors driven to complete despair by the news that the government was going to impose across-the-board cuts in naval pay. This had been precipitated by a letter from the Admiralty read to assembled ships' companies in which the economic state of the country was much emphasised but which did not say how big a cut was being ordered.

Bob Whinney was a junior officer on board HMS *Rodney*, a Washington Treaty-built battleship, when the letter was read.

How did it come about that a large part of the greatest and most prestigious Navy in the world found itself in this shameful impasse? In the first place, the Admiralty was a civil Ministry under a political Minister, the First Lord of the Admiralty, who had a Board of Sea Lords, Admirals. Complying with Government policy of economy, a system of reduction in naval pay was evolved and passed by the Board. Through the most remarkable error of judgment, the pay cuts imposed on junior ratings were not only harsh but unrealistic. Some families of junior ratings would have starved.[4]

He says this was made worse by the way in which rumours and press reports reached the men before any formal announcement. The shock waves were considerable although the 'mutiny' was pretty tame. The shock was more in the mere refusal by the 'men' to obey orders from officers.

On *Rodney's* forecastle that early morning, like the other officers I was horrified and deeply shocked. Of course, we knew there were to be cuts in naval pay; the Captain had cleared the lower deck the previous day to warn us all, to give a pep talk in sadly erudite terms. It thus became very clear very quickly that the men had two sources of information, namely their captain and the organisers of the mutiny.

They learned on *Rodney* that the whole fleet at Invergordon was 'infected':

... Despite the displays [of groups of mutineers hanging about and periodically cheering] ... the ceremonies of hoisting Colours in the morning and lowering them at sunset were observed with respect and the sixteen-inch gun magazine safety regulations were adhered to with a sentry smartly dressed on duty at the official keyboard. As Officers of the Watch, we, in turn, wore our frock coats and sword belts and carried telescopes, as was customary.

Herein lay the real problem. The gulf between officers and ratings was enormous. It would be entirely true to say that they lived completely separate lives, inhabiting not just different parts of the ships on which they served together, but different social and cultural universes. When a rating came to Whinney to try ask him to 'explain' to the men what the cuts would mean, the Captain's address having gone right over their heads, Whinney's attitude, though sympathetic, was to consider the approach 'verging on the impertinent'. He reflected how desperate the men must have been to try to communicate in this way.

Even so, Whinney's own career was seriously affected when he passed this message on to a superior, on the quite incredible grounds that it showed 'sympathy' with the 'mutineers'. These stark and, to a late-twentieth century audience, antediluvian, stiff-necked pomposities materially affected the way the Navy performed. Communication upwards between ranks was frowned upon. Ratings would watch whilst officers made complete and possibly dangerous hashes of tasks in the knowledge that to speak out would be to court reprimand. It took the near disaster of the early part of the Second World War finally to begin to sweep these archaic practices away. Herbert Messer was a middle-class youngster who, in a highly unusual move, joined the Royal Navy in 1937 through the RNVR as a rating. He could have opted for an officer's route but he chose, instead, to sample life on the lower deck. His account is one of the very few which describes the often appalling conditions he found with the insight of a middle-class education.[5] Worst of all, though, were the attitudes on both sides.

> The difference between the wardroom and the messdeck was startling. From the ambience to which one was used and, incidentally, which one took for granted, the messdeck was in stark contrast.

And of the officers:

> I cannot remember a Petty Officer who was not pleasant or able at his job. The same cannot be said of the officers, at least those with whom I was in contact. They were for the most part pompous fools aping the RN and, besides, being far from efficient.

He is describing *part-time* sailors here, larded, in the case of Petty Officers, with a few full-timers. Once in the Navy proper, though, he found very little was different.

> I cannot exaggerate the shock which I experienced on joining *Curlew* [an anti-aircraft-gun converted cruiser]. It was as if I had stepped off the parapet of time and fallen into the kitchens of some dark ages king.

I slung my hammock in a flat called the recreation space as there were no available billets on the messdeck ... Boots were hung from the clews and the remainder of one's clothes joined them or were used as a pillow. Hammocks are slung from hooks in the deck head and hang in rows, fore and aft; most men slept feet forward and so close to each other as to be almost touching. When one became used to it a hammock was a cosy ideal bed at sea for it stayed still as the ship rolled round it.

One's hammock had to be lashed in the manner laid down in the Seamanship Manual; it was a drill carried out by Nelson's sailors at the time when hammocks formed part of the defence of the ship – 'Distribute the bedding equally over the whole length of the hammock to prevent it appearing, when lashed up, more bulky in one part than another. Then pass the lashing, seven turns being taken, the first being a running eye and the remainder marline hitched. Stand with the right arm against the hammock, looking towards the head, and pass the end or whole coil of the lashing over the hammock with the left hand. Care should be taken that the turns are equidistant also, that the first and last turns are clear of the bedding. Twist the clews and tuck them under the lashing towards the centre.'

Messer found that the greatest two trials were the sheer overcrowding of the lower deck and what he calls 'brain atrophy'. It was, he says, a mental vacuum in which any question of the way things were done, however silly they looked, was a sin. Everything was reduced.

... There was no subtlety of any kind. Privacy was non-existent, ablutions, evacuations, reading, letter-writing, sleeping and eating were all conducted in a bedlam of halfnaked, singing, grumbling, swearing and seldom silent messmates ... The gulf between the messdeck and the wardroom was enormous; it was seldom that an officer spoke to a sailor other than to give him an order.

The messes were a series of tables, set across the ship's width. In the centre were the ratings' lockers. Over each of the tables was a cupboard which contained some food – bread, jam, sugar, tea and tinned milk. And, inevitably, an army of cockroaches. As Messer says, the only change from Nelson's day was the absence of the guns on the same deck. To make Navy tea two or more spoons of tea per head were put in the kettle together with a large dollop of tinned milk; in the galley this mixture was diluted with boiling water and allowed to stand until it had a 'viscosity unknown ashore'. This was then poured into cups piled high with sugar.

At sea under bad conditions tea made like this, perhaps with a slab
of cocoa thrown in, would sustain life itself. Little else would: bad
weather meant the galley might only be able to provide sandwiches
and no hot food at all. As in earlier accounts, ships as large as *Curlew*
suffered from condensation – the effect of hundreds of warm bodies
on the cold steel and iron of the hull.

In port it was a different tale. Ratings did their level best to enjoy
'a run ashore', returning in various conditions. The 'clinic' for doses
of venereal disease on board *Curlew* was called 'Rose Cottage'. This
was the time before penicillin; remedies were the older, cruder, more
painful kind. A lot of sexual activity was talk: a form of yarning
to break up the monotony of shipboard life under these closed-in
conditions.

Sailors wives, as ever, existed in their own forms of misery. Few
accounts are available from this or any other period. The history of
women is still being uncovered. One story remarkable for its candour
is that of Molly Passmore, married to an RN officer in the inter-war
period. Naval officer's wives were not recognised by the authorities
and, as a consequence, they had no allowances. Given that their
husband's pay was poor, the result was often great hardship as these
women tried as best they could to follow their husbands from port
to port. Given, too, the social mores of the time, these officers' wives
had to try to 'keep up appearances', as a rating's wife once remarked
to Molly Passmore. Ratings, on the whole, could not expect to see
their wives at all.

> I did not feel so depressed at parting from my husband this time as I
> knew I would be seeing him again in three months; also, spring in the
> Mediterranean is glorious and it was by now the end of April ...
> Sometimes at weekends, when all our young sub-lieutenants and mid-
> shipman friends could get off duty, we hired a Maltese bus and all piled
> in and went for the whole day to some other part of the island.[6]

Molly Passmore's candour shows in her frank admittance that whilst
her husband was away she enjoyed herself. The parties, the dances,
the bathing, though mixed, were circumscribed by convention – at
least on the surface. This code was broken, frequently, and both Navy
wives and their husbands had affairs. One, on the part of her husband,
finally broke Molly Passmore's marriage. But although life could be
fun at times, it could also be extremely harsh for the wife.

> I left for Plymouth the same day that Peter went north to Scotland. I

had never been to Plymouth before and when I arrived it was pouring with rain and I felt lonely and frightened. I was to experience this horrible sinking feling over and over again every time I arrived alone in a strange place.

Molly Passmore's story could have been repeated thousands of times. Had she but known it, when she married her dashing young officer the world was about to be changed for ever, and Britain's Navy with it.

By the late 1930s it was obvious that war was coming. The Navy, under-equipped and ill-prepared, had to face the worst of all scenarios it could have imagined: not one foe, as in the First World War, but three – Germany, certainly, Italy probably, and Japan, possibly. If nothing else had told them of the trial they would face, this list of adversaries would have said it all. After the interlude, would come the final act.

8

THE MIRROR SHATTERED: 1939–45

'How dread the storm to be, drifts up with ominous breath'

Henry Newbolt, *Ode for Trafalgar Day*

It is hard to accept, even today, that although Britain was eventually to be on the side of the victors in the Second World War, it was not her triumph. Too many emotions have been mixed up in this last great worldwide conflict for judgement – even now – to be unclouded. The British 'victory' was moral; she held out against a hostile Europe for a year entirely alone between the fall of France and the German attack on Russia. After that it was a question of waiting for the Americans and the Russians, who began to turn the war to the Allies' advantage from the start of 1942. From the summer of 1941 Hitler's main efforts were no longer against Britain. Britain's position was vital, though. She was the world's biggest aircraft carrier and her sustenance became a war aim in itself. Her efforts at sea in the west eventually reduced to this one: keeping the convoys going against an almost successful U-boat campaign. For the rest the successes were patchy. Once again, the Royal Navy was too stretched to affect any major victory even if there had been one to have. Control of the Channel was lost after the fall of France in 1940. Thereafter it was the RAF who battled for supremacy over that narrow and much-fought-over strip of sea.

The Navy had been shamefully neglected after the Washington Naval Treaty, as had the other forces. But the Navy still had the thankless task of protecting British shipping and the colonies world-wide. By the mid 1930s, when the Anglo–German Naval Treaty (1935) was hastily agreed, a last-ditch attempt to re-impose the two-power standard (now excluding the United States), it was almost too late. Apart from an ailing battleship fleet, the Navy had neglected the two crucial arenas of air-defence and anti-submarine warfare. This neglect extended to the bases scattered across the world. Both

Germany and Japan had begun to build up their submarine and torpedo bomber forces by this time.

Then, in the mid-1930s, a new and unexpected naval threat appeared: Italy. So seriously was the possibility of attack from the Italians taken that the Navy's main centre of operations in the Mediterranean was moved east from Malta to Alexandria, in Egypt. The Navy now faced three possible foes: Germany, Italy, Japan. With the Axis pacts in place by the late '30s the real horror of fighting them simultaneously loomed.

Although there were hopes that the French Navy could hold off the Italians, the threat from Germany was so great that the Far East was effectively abandoned, apart from the great naval base at Singapore. But that had a fatal weak spot – there was no protection from land attack.

In 1939, the fleets lined up as follows: the Germans had two battleships, three 'pocket' battleships, one heavy and five light cruisers, seventeen destroyers in its surface fleet, and a sizable, and expanding, number of U-boats. U-boats could be built at great speed, unlike large surface ships.

The Italian Navy had six battleships, seven heavy and twelve light cruisers, sixty-one fleet destroyers and 105 submarines – opposed by a French Navy of five battleships and battle cruisers, one carrier, fifteen cruisers, seventy-five destroyers and fifty-nine submarines.

The British had a bigger overall fleet but much of it was obsolete: twelve battleships and battle cruisers, six aircraft carriers, fifty-eight cruisers, 100 destroyers with 101 other escorts and thirty-eight submarines. It might have been enough – just – to contain the Axis powers in Europe, matched with the urgent extra building programme adding five new battleships, six fleet carriers and fifty new destroyers.

But on the other side of the world Japan had now ten battleships, ten aircraft carriers, eighteen heavy and eighteen light cruisers, 113 destroyers and sixty-three submarines. Two gigantic *Yamato*-class battleships with their eighteen-inch guns would soon join this formidable force. The Americans, of course, had the biggest navy of all: eighteen battleships, eight carriers, forty-five cruisers, 150 destroyers (fifty soon to come to Britain under the Lease-Lend Agreement), and fifty-six submarines. They also had 3,000 aircraft in their fleet air arm.

The game in a sense was already up for the Royal Navy. Relying for too long on the out-dated concept of capital ships, by 1939 the dinosaurs of a fleet, the Admiralty had begun only at the last moment to plan for a prolonged U-boat campaign. New classes of cheap escort, notably the *Flower* corvettes, were being hastily laid down by the late 1930s. Escort aircraft carriers would only come later – almost too late. In general the Navy's role would have to come second to that of the Royal Air Force. In 1939 this was inadequate, even if the air force of France was added, against the mighty *Luftwaffe*. It hardly needs to be said that Japan's air forces – especially its formidably well-trained and equipped naval arm, which was to lead at Pearl Harbour – was shortly to outmatch completely the RAF in the Far East.

The first hint of what was to come at sea arrived an hour after war was declared: the liner *Athenia* was sunk by a U-boat. In some ways this first sinking helped because it led the Admiralty to believe the Germans would immediately enforce a policy of unrestricted submarine warfare. In fact the U-boat commander, Lemp, had exceeded his orders, partly because he thought the *Athenia* to be an armed merchant-man, not as she was, a liner full of women and children evacuees, bound for Canada.

The lesson could hardly have been absorbed when, in October 1939, the aging battleship *Royal Oak* was sunk at the Navy's main base in Scapa Flow with the loss of hundreds of lives. The U-boat commander, Gunther Prien, had taken his submarine through a gap in the Scapa Flow defences, slipping past ancient blockships, long battered by winter gales and not reinforced. It was the kind of neglect, so common for the times, that the British were to rue. It was as a result of this attack that the home fleet was immediately dispersed to lochs on the west coast of Scotland – hardly a good position from which to blockade the northern exits to the North Sea. Yet the Navy did manage to do much better than it had done in 1914–18. Although there were some appalling naval losses: the sinking of the mighty *Hood* by a single salvo from the *Bismarck*, the loss of both the *Repulse* and the *Prince of Wales* to Japanese dive-bombers late in 1941, U-boats never quite managed to strangle the British transatlantic supply lines. Neither did they, in conjunction with bombers, stop the re-supply of Malta, although that was a dangerously close-run thing.

The Navy did have some signal victories: the Battle of the River Plate, and the scuttling of the *Graf Spee*, the 'miracle' of Dunkirk. But that latter 'victory' meant the Atlantic had been opened to Hitler's forces, and with Norway in German hands by the late spring of 1940, U-boats and long-range aircraft from the North Cape to the Spanish border could hunt out the merchant convoys coming in from the USA and Canada with relentless persistence.

John Cooper was in the first merchant ship to be sunk by the *Graf Spee*.

> She caught us in the Atlantic. But Langsdorf [the *Graf Spee* master who shot himself after his ship was scuttled] was a good skipper. He said 'I only want two – and no changing clothes'. He wanted the skipper and the chief engineer – it was a means of getting information and of hitting at shipping – it took seven years to train a skipper.
>
> We were ten days in the Atlantic then. You lose your nature – it's the first thing to go, with the fright. Sometimes you see the sharks coming round. I was nursed after in Rio.

John Cooper was torpedoed three times, a record matched by many others. Yet as with the First World War, pay was stopped the moment a ship was sunk. The sailor's discharge book, which remained with the shipping office, was endorsed 'discharged at sea'. If a seafarer survived the sinking, he was repatriated without pay. Once, after being torpedoed close to Liverpool, John was landed back at the pierhead and he made his way to the shipping office. When he asked the clerk for money to get home, the man looked at the records and announced that, because of the allotments, and the stoppages, at that moment John owed the company money.

'I hit him,' says John. Later he was arrested and when his wife found him in the police station she berated him for lying: 'You said you'd been torpedoed but all the time you'd just been arrested,' she said.

The U-boats were operating from the start of the war but their true impact did not begin until later. For the British, however, the early U-boat successes were bad enough, not least because the escorts available could not keep up with the German submarines if they chose to operate on the surface – as they frequently did. Charles 'Butch' Walker was a sailor aboard the *Sitala*, sunk off Ireland in October 1940.

> I was on lookout and the bosun came up and said, 'This is going to be rough.' As he said it I looked and there was this U-boat going right past us, so close I could have thrown a stone onto the conning tower. They could outrun the escorts, you see. They were all old destroyers or trawlers.

He came by us and then turned and Bang! A great sheet of flame. We went over and lowered the boats – the deck was slippery with oil. A trawler came – the *Lady Elsa* – and she picked 201 up. They took us into Belfast. I got a pair of striped trousers and a pullover. I don't remember going home – I was blind drunk. I was only 17.

This was the autumn of 1940, by which time the War had gone badly for Britain on land and at sea. The Norway campaign of 1940 is now recognised as having been a disaster forced on a reluctant Navy by Churchill's impatience that not enough was being done to take the fight to the Germans, however impracticable it might have been. The Norwegian campaign was also dogged by poor judgement about the changing balance of power in weapons, between the old capital ships and the new menace of aircraft. Admiral Sir Charles Forbes, who led a task force out of the Clyde on 8 April to engage the German forces now intent on invasion, was an old-style sailor, a man who was always dressed correctly on the bridge but a man who could order his one aircraft carrier not to follow his ships out to sea, until he was over-ridden by the Admiralty in London.

Forbes had in mind a battle between battleships; to cut a long and complex story short, the Germans successfully fooled the British into believing this was what they intended as well, thus keeping the British main forces well clear of their invasion. The *Renown*, an elderly battle cruiser from the First World War, was eventually to find the *Scharnhorst* and the *Gneisenau* and, against the odds, successfully engaged them, forcing the Germans to turn tail. All this was good Nelsonian stuff but it failed to prevent the Germans from landing in force along the coast of Norway.

One of the sailors who witnessed this invasion, and its aftermath, was Herbert Messer, still on the lower deck of HMS *Curlew*. As an anti-aircraft light cruiser, she was in the thick of the fighting. Just before that, the ship was involved in a near miss:

> ... our RDF picked up an echo from a large surface ship. We went to action stations and, for the first and only time in the whole commission, we heard the order 'all guns load with LA [low angle] ammunition'. It was pretty rough weather and the confused sea which slapped against the starboard quarter sent clouds of spray over the quarterdeck obscuring the vision of those of us on ten gun.
>
> Long before we saw the target our bridge had been winking out the challenge without any response. Soon, bearing green 15 degrees we saw the silhouette of a large battleship, travelling very fast on the opposite course to ours.[1]

Curlew had been completed in 1917 and she was basically a lightly armed ship, redesigned for action against aircraft. Her captain, believing he was looking at either the *Scharnhorst* or the *Gneisenau*, apparently had no hesitation in deciding what to do: once again, the Royal Navy's tradition of aggressively single-minded and insanely heroic action, whatever the odds, comes to mind.

> 'Prepare to ram, all guns' crews lie down' was the next order as we raced to intercept the huge ship which looked magnificent and menacing as she forged ahead with her turrets trained to starboard, her bow waves white against the dark background. All the time, as we closed, our signal lamp was repeating the challenge still with no reply from the other ship. Lying on the deck I thought that this was rather a tame way to die for should we ram that monster it was obviously us that would suffer the most ... Then at the last minute a lamp winked across the water, over to port went our wheel and, as we swung away, we recognised *Renown* perhaps just before or after her brief action with *Gneisenau*.

The *Curlew* stayed in Norwegian waters supporting the increasingly desperate efforts of the British to hold off the German Army, heavily supported by aircraft. As part of the British attempt to gain some parity with the *Luftwaffe* Spitfires and Hurricanes were sent to hastily constructed airfields in Norway; other aircraft operated from the carriers.

> One of our jobs, besides acting as an AA guardship, was to pick up the several airmen who crashed when landing on or taking off from the aircraft carriers. We lost one or two pilots and several equally valuable planes.
>
> On 7 May and for the next forty-eight hours we were at action stations repelling continuous and most persistent air attacks as we acted as the AA protection for the other ships in Ofotfjord which were not equipped to defend themselves against these conditions.

But the fight was already unequal and although Messer reports that *Curlew* led a charmed life with bombs falling all around, eventually, on 26 May, she was hit.

> I was taking a shell out of the magazine when the stick of four bombs hit us on the starboard side below the waterline and abreast of where I was standing, blowing the ship's bottom out. The shells bounced out of the magazine clocking me in the face and testicles in particular and everywhere in general; the blast from the explosion and the following

wave propelled me over the port guardrails and into the sea. Fortunately
I was still conscious and aware of what I was doing for which, perhaps,
the extreme cold was responsible, so I grabbed the guardrails from
outboard and hauled myself back on to the quarterdeck ...

'Abandon ship, every man for himself' had been piped but I couldn't
allow those Nazis to get away with it for they were still up there on a
bearing of green 25 degrees. All our guns were silent, a silence which
mortified me, so I picked up a shell from those sculling around on the
deck, fused it, loaded, trained and layed the gun and fired. This I
repeated several times until an order came from the bridge to stop. The
shells were just lobbing out of the gun and, due to the barrel being so
worn, were more danger to the ship than to the enemy.

Messer, though, still did not abandon ship but joined in a search for
anyone who might still be below; others had been pulling stokers out
of the gap formed where the ship's side had pulled away from the
deck. Many of them were burned or scalded and covered in fuel oil,
an extremely poisonous liquid to have on the skin or, worse, to
swallow, as many sailors were to discover. Messer's search was unsuc-
cessful but he by now was in a bad state, though he hardly knew it.

I went to help the blacksmith and his mate – a fellow RNVR and
messmate named Ryan – smash up the RDF equipment; I have a feeling
that the skipper was directing the operation. When that was completed,
suddenly I felt so very tired. The effects of my exertions after days
without proper sleep were beginning to tell. My tongue was practically
in two for I had almost bitten through it, my testicles were swollen and
pained me to the extreme while my body was sore from the shells which
were forced from the magazine by the explosion ... I was dressed in
matelot's trousers and an RNVR rugby jersey and was covered in fuel
oil from the soles of my boots to my chest besides being soaking wet
from head to toe and jolly cold.

Messer made his way back to his messdeck, shutting the watertight
doors behind him as he went. The water level was nearly up to the
table on which he rested his head and where, incredibly, he fell asleep.
If it had not been for Ryan, following him, he would have drowned,
but he was shaken awake and followed his mate.

On the port side, at the break of the fo'c'sle was the motor boat; so low
in the water was *Curlew* that ship and boat lay gunnel to gunnel. In the
boat was Captain Brooke, his cox'n, the blacksmith and Lt Hare; quite
gently the Skipper said 'Hurry Messer', as I followed Ryan into the
boat. I had my back to *Curlew* and didn't see her go as she slipped

below the water a few seconds after we had left her ... she was indeed a valiant ship.

How our parents – all parents of those serving – must have suffered.

The real naval battle had yet to come. It lay not in the chase of the *Bismarck* to final destruction in the Atlantic but in the much quicker recognition in this War that the whole edifice would crash down if the merchant ships could not get through. The convoy system was instituted quickly but U-boats were now faster, had longer ranges and were to prove far more ruthless in their pursuit of the single-minded goal of breaking the supply line. The only thing, Churchill later confessed, that he had ever really worried about, was the U-boat peril.

The really critical period in the European naval theatre came, as it surely must, in the early part of 1942. The Americans were in the War but being steadily defeated in the Far East where most of their attention lay. The Russians were holding the *Wehrmacht* – just – in Stalingrad. The British were holding on in the North African desert.

In the North Atlantic there was a critical gap between the air cover that could be maintained from the Canadian and Greenland side, and that possible from Scotland. Into this gap poured the U-boat packs, often hunting on the surface, generally still free from harassment.

The Germans were attacking US ships off the coast of the States at this time, too, the Americans eshewing the convoy system so close to home. By June 1942, 600,000 tons of American shipping had been sunk in this way.

The German U-boat commander, Admiral Donitz's orders were: 'Rescue no one and take no one with you. Have no care for the ship's boats ... We must be hard in this war.' Donitz now had 331 U-boats, of which about half were patrolling at any time. He could send many of these off easily from the hardened bunkers of St Nazaire, straight into the battle.

The packs were highly successful. Convoy SC94 was attacked by eighteen U-boats and lost twenty-six ships; SC107 lost fifteen. By the beginning of 1943 Donitz believed he was about to win the war for Germany. Nine millions tons of Allied shipping had been lost in 1942 alone (the total tonnage lost in the First World War).

The U-boats struck where they could in the Atlantic or the Mediterranean. Here are two accounts of sinking and their aftermaths. HMS *Chanticleer* was a *Black Swan* sloop, bigger than a *Flower*-class corvette, smaller than a destroyer, a later form of convoy escort.

In 1943 she was waiting to escort a huge floating dock to Malta, off the Scottish coast.

> The seas were so bad no one could turn for fear of broaching. The upper deck got smashed up, and depth charges broke loose on the quarterdeck. In securing them two men went over the side and were lost. No rescue or search was possible, not being able to turn, and it lowered our spirits.

Later, near the Azores, they made contact with a U-boat.

> Orders came a bit quicker now. 'Follow Director. Load, Load, Load.' All guns were loaded and the gunlayers and trainers followed their dial pointers. We started our run in on the submerged U-boat and we could plainly hear the echoes … At this point, with a tremendous roar the whole quarterdeck seemed to disintegrate upwards in a jumbled mass, and a wave of pressure hit me. The ship shuddered horribly and rolled to port … We have been well and truly fished, I thought. A helluva lot of people have just died.

Also in 1943 the steamship *Rhexenor* was attacked in the Atlantic by U-217. 'Butch' Walker was on board.

> We had been along the coast of Africa. We were two to a cabin – she was a good one. She was carrying cocoa beans and the deep tanks were filled with coconut oil, because the cook used to get a bucket down for it to cook chips. When we were torpedoed the ship stayed afloat. Then the U-boat surfaced and called us and said 'what ship?' so we said and he asked 'where bound' and we said 'St John's'. She shelled us after that.
> Next morning we were on our own – we had some really heavy weather. I thought, 'well, we are going to go now'. It started raining so we collected water using the lifeboat covers but what with their being left for months they were covered with salt. We drank the water anyway. Then, later, an Australian gave up.
> But if it hadn't been for the German navigator on the U-boat we would have died. As we were leaving he said 'have you enough food and water' and we said we didn't know. He said 'we can't give you any, we haven't enough' but he said 'steer south west' and we did. One boat landed in Guadaloupe, one in Antigua. We landed further south in the Virgin Islands. As I got ashore a big black woman gave me a tin cup full of soup. I got it down then it all came up. My belly was out here. I was black all over from sunburn – when I got in the bath I could scrub it off.

Only two died – in the lifeboats. She'd have lasted a good while but she came up and started shelling us. U-217 went out the next trip and was lost with all hands, sunk by American planes.[2]

Today, Charles Walker is in touch with many of the U-boat commanders and crew in Germany. 'I've forgiven them' he says. This extraordinary coming together of victims with perpetrators is probably the very last act of that War. Now, they swap stories and try to piece together what happened – who sank who and where. Walker is a regular visitor to the U-boat museum at Cuxhaven, where he stays with the ex-U-boat-serving curator.

Three weeks in a crowded lifeboat, sharing the meagre rations, can hardly be imagined but what Charle Walker endured was at least in warm water and with favourable winds. The agonies of life and death in the North Atlantic and in winter have been best written about in fiction in *The Cruel Sea*, a book which better than any other account, real or imagined, gives the reader the taste of those desperate days. In a world grown softer, it is hard to imagine, too, why sailors continued to serve, even given the wartime penalties, applicable to merchant seamen as well as RN, for desertion. But serve they did.

More than a quarter of the merchant service sailors died in the Second World War. This was a higher proportion of casualties than for any other of the services yet there was never any difficulty in recruiting when necessary, even in the worst period for U-boat sinkings. But the toll was high: over 50,000 British merchant sailors died. At the same time merchant sailors, torpedoed or not, remained second-class citizens in many ways. Ronald Hope, the historian of the merchant navy from ancient to modern times, quotes one ship's carpenter who survived a sinking as saying that aboard the *Queen of Bermuda*, which repatriated him, 'We were treated like criminals and our official reception in Liverpool was in no way welcoming.' Perhaps those concerned, in both cases, were feeling the guilt of the unscathed; perhaps not. Not all wartime voyages ended in sinkings. Captain Banner, now retired, gives this extended account of life as a youngster aboard a merchant ship in 1941, among the darkest times of the War for Britain.

I was born in Runcorn, Cheshire, a very old sea-port, even older than Liverpool, in 1923. I left school at the age of 14 years. I then started work in a local leather tannery, but my heart had always been with the sea, as all my family had been seafarers. I applied to join the RN as boy entrant but I failed the medical due to the fact I had had a mastoid operation as a youngster.

I then applied for a position as bell boy on the Canadian Pacific passenger liners but failed again as I did not know anyone in that company. When I was 15 I got a job, much to my delight, as a boy/cook on the sand dredger, *Sifter*, out of Canning Dock, Liverpool. This job only whetted my appetite to go further afield and see what was over the horizon.

In February 1941, I went to Manchester and saw Bert Furze in the Manchester Liners dock office in Salford docks and luckily for me he had known my late grandfather when he had been captain of the old MSC paddle tugs. He gave me a job as ordinary seaman on the *Dromore*. The ship belonged to Furness Johnson Warren Line. She was on the liners run across the North Atlantic to Philadelphia, Norfolk, Newport News and Halifax.

I joined immediately. The accommodation was spartan to say the least, the four ordinary seamen she carried were berthed in one room on the port side aft, in the poop. The vessel was a three island type, with a short well deck to Number One hatch, which made it very wet in any kind of weather. The deck crew consisted of six ABs, a bosun, chippy and us four. On joining I was issued with two wool blankets, a knife, fork, spoon, tin dinner plate, tin soup plate, tin half pint mug. We also got straw palliasses [donkey's breakfasts]. We were lucky in this respect as on other ships you had to buy these yourself [at 1/9d].

Soap for toiletry was supplied but for washing clothes you scrounged soda soap. All the items issued had to be returned at the end of the voyage or else they were deducted from your pay. Wages were £12 16/4d per calendar month, plus nine pence an hour overtime; this included your £10 a month war bonus. There was two days paid leave for every month served. The vessel had five hatches with two derricks per hatch; all the gear had to be completely stripped down before sailing. Wire runners, guys, preventers, topping gear, blocks, all removed to be serviced on the voyage. On top of that we had four lifeboats to swing out on radial davits, and to be secured to pudding spars, and bowsed in ready for instant launching. Everything was done in reverse order once we arrived in a port. This meant a long and tiring day so the first night in port was an early night.

The sanitary arrangements for the deck crew consisted of one outside washroom, with three ancient wash basins, no running water and a salt water shower which didn't work anyway. The toilets were two set like thrones on high but if you had any sense you did not close the door as it was made of plate steel and could jam tight if anything happened. To have a wash you took a bucket down the engine room and asked the duty engineer for some hot water out of the condenser hot well. If he was in a good mood he would let you have half a bucket but if he wasn't your trip had been in vain. The water was taken back up on deck and if you were lucky the fresh water pump wasn't locked, you cooled your water down and had your bath out of the bucket, saving some to put your dhobying [washing] in.

The food was quite good, the only problem was tranferring it from the galley amidships to aft over the hatches in bad weather, to the messroom. All food was put in open kits or trays for twelve men; can you imagine the condition it arrived in, especially the soup which was probably half full of salt water when you arrived, with the meat etc. very cool.

The special Board of Trade days were Sunday and Thursday. On these days you had a piece of bacon and one fried egg for breakfast – that is, if they didn't blow off the tray in transit. At lunch-time there was a boiled duff with custard for afters. You received a strict ration to last two weeks of tea, sugar, and one tin of condensed milk each, plus condiments like BoT pickles and jam in extra large tins. The crew had crew tea, the officers had better quality 'cabin' tea; ours had big stalks in it and it was brewed in a big black kettle. The messing arrangements were that the ABs, Bosun and chippy ate in the main messroom while the ordinary seamen ate in theirs. The tables and forms were of scrubbed wood, as was the deck and I can recall scrubbing them every Saturday morning ready for inspection.

When the long summer days came in the northern latitudes we would be on unpaid gun watches, sometimes up to midnight, until we reached 20 degrees west outward bound and the same inward bound. I did seven voyages in this lucky ship across the North Atlantic and I saw her after the war under the Greek flag in Birkenhead.

Captain Banner retired in 1985 but he says this: 'I miss it very much and if I had my life over again I would not change from sea-going; it's a great sense of belonging, being a seaman.'

By the beginning of 1943 Admiral Donitz had 400 U-boats, half at sea at any time. Before the War he had argued that he could destroy enough of the transatlantic ships that supplied Britain to starve her out with ninety. Why he lost is of great significance. In his book *The Price of Admiralty*, John Keegan believes there was one decisive 'battle' fought in early 1943 between the U-boat packs and two convoys, HX229 and SC122. In the course of a fight in the two-day 'air-gap', where Allied planes could not yet reach, forty U-boats, ninety merchant ships and twenty escorts, destroyers, frigates and corvettes were involved.

Twenty-two merchant ships were sunk and 372 seamen and passengers killed. Some of the events in that cold pitiless sea are heartrending, as most died from exposure in those waters. But Keegan points out that not one escort was lost to the ninety torpedoes fired; seven U-boats were damaged by the escorts, and seven by aircraft when they arrived overhead as the convoy sailed east. Aircraft also sank two U-boats. It was aircraft that eventually gave the Allies the extra edge – shore-based, or launched from escort carriers.

Still there remained those moments in the dark for the seafarers below, after a ship got hit. Says Les Walker sixty years on:

> To be honest, at the time you were the local hero, you didn't think about it. But on one ship I was only a cabin boy and I was asked to take the Chief's lifejacket down to the engineroom to him because he had forgotten it. He used to call me Manchester. I called to him and he said, 'leave it on the rail, Manchester, it'll be there when we get back'.
>
> Being a cheeky little bugger I said 'you Scottish sod, you'll never get back' and he was the only one we lost when the ship was sunk. That tormented me for ages. There were a lot of Indian firemen – they all got out, but not him.

Walker, like so many, was sunk more than once. On one occasion the ship survived being mined but was at such an angle that it was possible to walk forward into the sea. Miraculously, she made it back. On another occasion, Les Walker came ashore after being torpedoed to find a NAAFI mobile canteen dispensing tea and sympathy. 'When I asked for some tea, the women said "This is for the Navy, not you"', another example, among many, of the cruel distinction landsiders continued to make between the 'Grey Funnel Line' ratings and the merchant service. Even now this causes great bitterness among retired sailors. King George V determined they should be renamed the Merchant Navy, after the First World War. Few merchant sailors found it made any difference to public attitudes in the Second World War.

By the spring of 1943, long-range aircraft covered the Atlantic 'gap'; escort carriers were arriving to join the convoys, giving permanent air-cover. Other successful counter-measures, such as electronic on-board radar, the breaking of the U-boat code ciphers, and the increasingly sophisticated sonar on the escorts, all meant the day of the wolf packs was over. In May, convoy ONS5 was attacked by sixty U-boats; it lost twelve ships but the packs had lost seven

U-boats in one night and it was the turning point. In May 1943 the Germans lost thirty-four submarines. By May 1945 the U-boats had sunk 337 merchant ships since that fateful earlier May, but they had lost 534 submarines.

The battle did not end until the last moment. The Germans invented better torpedoes, like the acoustic which could follow a ship's pro-pellor noise. These sank many escorts, hitherto largely unscathed. There were torpedoes which zigzagged about inside a convoy, max-imising their chances of a hit. The Allies countered: there had been Asdic (Allied Submarine Detection Investigation Committee) equip-ment; then came better sets. Depth charges were replaced by 'Hedge-hog' which fired a pattern of twenty-four charges forward of the escort; it was replaced by 'Squid', a much more deadly weapon.

Only after the war did the Allies discover the 'Walther' U-boat, with hydrogen peroxide fuel (necessitating no surfacing) and a global range. Four were at the trial stage. The chief beneficiaries of this, as with other Nazi inventions for fifty years, was to be the Soviet Union. The rise of its Navy, and in particular its massive submarine fleet, can be seen as a direct extension of German naval tactics.

When the Soviet Union joined the war in 1941, Churchill decided to help it by placing convoy supplies around the terrible North Cape. The result was predictable and appalling. Battling against dreadful winter storms, the men in those ships knew that whenever the weather abated hordes of German planes would seek them out; when they failed U-boats were standing by to torpedo them; behind them lurked the capital ships, like the *Scharnhorst* or the *Hipper*.

Those manning the Russian convoys remember the weather more than anything else. It was the relentless nature of the winter storms which destroyed the will. Should any sailor be unfortunate enough to go overboard, he was almost certainly doomed. In December 1943 the escort destroyer *Wanderer* sailed with JW55B for Murmansk.

Unusually for that part of the world, it was a calm sunny, even quite pleasant day and the Hands were cheerfully cleaning guns when a young Ordinary Seaman took a needless risk, slipped and fell over the side . . . The Officer of the Watch, Sub-Lieutenant Foster was extremely quick to react to the cry 'man overboard'. He pressed the buzzer on the bridge to order the release of lifebuoys. The lifebuoy sentry aft was equally quick and the lifebuoys fell either side of and not more than ten yards from the man in the water. At the same time, the lifeboat's crew – always manned by those who got to the boat first, irrespective of who or what they were – got away very fast. They recovered the man and had him inboard in the doctor's hands within seven minutes of him going overboard. He was wearing a life belt and a lot of clothing, was known to be a strong swimmer and actually never went below the surface of the water at all. Despite this, the cold killed him at once.[3]

Bob Whinney, whose memory this is, also recalls how they dressed for these convoys like this:

The 'pussers', that is Naval Stores, dished us out with some extraordinary thick 'long johns' but there was no other special issue of clothing except perhaps gloves. However, there was our adopter town, Sutton Coldfield, and an unknown lady – a Canadian – known as Aunty May who used to knit – lots and lots of socks and balaclava helmets and scarves – enough for everyone we had. For myself, for the top half and working outwards, it was thick flannel pyjamas next to the skin; then a silk shirt, a Jaeger shirt and two thick woollen jerseys. For the bottom half, over the pyjamas were the pusser's long johns and flannel trousers; over the lot a kapok-lined suit plus mittens, a woolly hat and fur-lined leather boots.

At sea in *Wanderer* there was no enforcement of dress regulations; anyone could wear anything he liked except that officers had to be recognisable as such. Everyone had to wear something on his head so as to be able to salute when coming on the bridge to make a report, if for no other reason. Khaki, the soldier's colour, was not allowed on principle and red was forbidden as being too easily seen from the air.

The convoy on which Whinney's ship lost their able seaman was in fact on the edge of one of the more satisfying victories the Royal Navy had. A task force of destroyers and cruisers sank the *Sharnhorst* with the support of the battleship *Duke of York* in December 1943. None of the ships involved were ever in visual contact, the entire battle being fought by radar. This was revenge of a kind for the destruction of convoy PQ17, in July 1942. Twenty-seven ships out of thirty-nine, 99,000 tons in all, were sunk because of a mistake made by the Admiralty in London, who had believed the *Tirpitz* was at sea and ordered the convoy to scatter.

By this time the battle against the U-boat was being won. New tactics were all to tell: escort support groups, specifically set up to hunt submarines; escort carriers, of which a large number were produced, providing more and more convoys with their own air support; and better hunting techniques, using pattern searching statistical methods. Even so, the U-boats kept on fighting to the very end.

In the Far East, the Royal Navy's war was to be less successful. The great base of Singapore had been the last effort by the British to maintain anything like a full presence in the Far East. In 1941, just at the point when the Japanese planes were taking off for Pearl Harbour, it had been re-inforced with two capital ships: the *Repulse* and the *Prince of Wales*. These sailed from the base on 8 December to try to cut off the Japanese invasion force.

They had no air cover and, in any case, it was thought the Japanese would prove inferior as adversaries. Two days later both ships had been sunk by land-based Japanese fighter-bombers. Three months after that Singapore fell, attacked from the land side through what the British considered 'impenetrable' jungle.

The Pacific naval war was largely fought by aircraft. At the Battle of Midway, where five carriers in all were sunk, all fell to aircraft. The importance of getting – and keeping – air superiority was shown here at its most spectacular but it had been demonstrated in every theatre of the war. Ironically, it had been the Royal Navy's Fleet Air Arm which first sunk a German cruiser – the *Konigsberg* – during the Norwegian campaign in 1940, making it the first major warship in history ever sunk from the air.

But the British took a long time to absorb the lesson. The attack on Force Z off Malaya gave the game away, finally, and it was re-inforced by a Japanese carrier attack on Ceylon, early in 1942, which forced the Navy to withdraw to Africa. Of course, it had been aircraft which first spotted the *Bismarck* racing out through the Greenland gap and, then, ancient naval Swordfish bi-plane torpedo bombers who slowed her down enough for her to be caught and sunk but this lesson had not been fully learned.

The day of ship-to-ship warfare had passed if there was any aircraft – of even the humble spotter kind – nearby. In a turn-around of surprising speed, the Admiralty decided in 1942, that they needed to build between fifty-five and sixty-two carriers. The real problem in that decision may be seen in the fact that only a dozen had been built by 1945. The truth here, as with so much else, was that Britain did not have the physical capacity for the kind of ship-building programme it would have needed to win the war at sea. More and more it had to rely on the United States, whose yards were turning out the austerity 'Liberty' merchant ships at a rate of one every twelve *days* at their peak.

By 1945 the US merchant marine was greater than that of the rest of Europe. Britain, by contrast, had lost eleven and a half million tons, bringing the fleet to 70 per cent of what it had been in 1939.

In 1945 it has been estimated that two-thirds of the German economy and about the same of the British was engaged directly in the war effort. The USA had never devoted more than two-fifths of hers.

From now on the USA would command, from now on it would be her priorities which would dictate, right up until today, what the West's armed forces would do, even, mostly, where they would fight. Churchill knew this as early as 1941, when he said, on hearing that the Japanese had attacked Pearl Harbour: 'So we had won after all ... after seventeen months of lonely fighting ... we had won the war; Britain would live ...'

It was American economic power and Russian manhood that finally defeated the Axis. Although the British might strain to their utmost, the American economy was to supply to the British Empire 47 per cent of its tanks, 21 per cent of small arms, 38 per cent of landing craft and ships, 18 per cent of combat and 60 per cent of transport planes At the peak level of supply to Britain, the huge quantities of arms being sent amounted to only 11 per cent of the US war output.

In 1945 Europe was a shattered continent. In France, for example, there were three serviceable railway carriages. Germany had been laid waste, the Soviet Union was exhausted of the flower of its people (no one knows how many but, possibly, forty million were dead). All over Europe other, half-alive, millions were marching here and there, among the armies of the victors, looking for lost families, seeking out some kind of future. It took another forty years before a true peace in Europe returned – German reunification day on 3 October 1990.

For the British 1945 was a strange year. Much of the British economy lay in ruins, yet we had 'won'. Most damaging, though, was the state of our sterling reserves. The war, in effect, bankrupted us and it has taken until recent times for us to recover. The biggest obstacle, and one all politicians ducked, was to tell the truth to a people who had fought so hard and so long to win.

The British wanted – and got – a peacetime settlement which rewarded their effort. In the rest of Europe, folk could see the magnitude of what had to be done; it faced them in their immediate search for food and shelter. In Britain, we opted for the Welfare State, for benefits now, and for housing. Investment in the hard things – new manufacturing plant, new markets into which to sell – did not appeal at all.

The export trade had collapsed, from £471 million in 1938 to £258 million in 1945. Imports had risen from £858 million to £1,299 million and our overseas debts had rocketed to £3,355 million.

Capital assets worth £1,299 million had been liquidated. One estimate suggests a quarter of pre-war wealth had gone. All of which left us as the world's largest debtor nation at the moment of triumph.

The last hope – the Empire – had been lost, too, for the Japanese had shown all too clearly what an independent Asian power could achieve against the apparent wealth and might of a European power. But the nature of the collapse of Empire, and the shoring up of useless ties through the farce of the 'Commonwealth' would delay more critical decisions.

These were to prove costs of the highest kind. Two world wars and the impact these had had on British trade, her lifeblood, had accelerated the economic decline, manifest as long ago as the late nineteenth century. Progressively, and not always of her own making, Britain had thrown away, or lost, her advantages. Now, only the vestiges of world power remained and their maintenance was, of all the levies, the highest of all. If the 'finest hour' for the military was to be the Battle of Britain, for the merchant seamen it was the Battle of the Atlantic, more poignant than the former because the men who fought in it remained for so long on the defensive. Apart from the 50,000 seamen who died in the Second World War, many in freezing northern waters, over 2,500 merchant ships were sunk (eleven million tons). Those suffering the worst of the Blitz could never fully understand that distant war was the greatest battle of all. If our seamen had lost the will to carry on, Britain would have lost the war.

By the end 60 per cent of the pre-war merchant fleet had been lost, although much of it replaced by war-built 'Liberty' or 'Empire' ships. European nations had worse losses: Germany lost 90 per cent of her ships, Italy 91 per cent, France 56 per cent, Greece 70 per cent, Norway 40 per cent. The USA meanwhile had gained by 369 per cent, and even the Dominions (Canada and Australasia) had gained 72 per cent.

Once again, Britain's seafarers had paid a cruel price for war. Only the peace would tell whether they could hold on to what was left and then start to re-build for what was always bound to be a harsher, more competitive future.

PART THREE

The End of Seafaring?

9

THE EBBING TIDE

'Life's battle is a conquest for the strong;
The meaning shows in the defeated thing.'
                                    John Masefield, *The Wanderer*

British merchant shipping after the Second World War enjoyed an Indian Summer, from the late 1940s right through to the late 1960s. But even though it was a golden period, the underlying decline continued. This was an evening, not a morning song.

The attitudes of successive governments has been that British shipping can take care of itself. Within the shipping industry, as with the period after 1918, there was too much chasing after old markets which were either lost or changed. In not investing in new ships and in failing to see what changes in the patterns of trade and travel would take place, ship owners placed themselves and seafarers more and more at risk.

The great revolution inside merchant shipping came in the late 1960s, and it was technologically based. Meanwhile seafarers went on much as they had before although conditions now underwent, in general, a marked improvement. Indeed, many seafarers identify the 1950s and early 1960s as the greatest period for merchant sailors, in so far as the old system still prevailed in cargo handling, whilst conditions on board most ships had improved beyond measure. Even in the 1960s, Britain retained a very large general cargo fleet, which continued to trade worldwide.

Although British shipping had been sunk with alarming regularity all through the War – eleven million tons of it, 60 per cent of the 1939 total – much had been replaced through the crash-building programme. American 'Liberty' and British standardised 'Empire' ships more than made up the total losses. American yards managed to build a staggering twelve millions tons in each of the peak years, 1943 and 1944.

After the War some of this huge tonnage was put into the US

reserve fleet; much was sold on the open market – over seven million tons, of which British owners bought over one million tons. In 1948 Britain still had 27 per cent of world tonnage (if the US reserve fleet is excluded). The world fleet was about what it had been ten years before. Despite the generally favourable position of British shipping, the slide (in tonnage terms) was to continue, albeit at first more slowly. Part of the overall problem was the replacement of British ships on the old routes by those of other nations through the years of the War. In South America, the traditionally strong British shipping market, both US ships, and those of countries like Brazil and Argentina, had moved in.

Further afield, and much more damaging, once India became independent she applied cabotage – the reserving to her own ships of her coastal trade. This had previously, of course, been effectively a British monopoly. Although it was to take a long time – twenty years – the ending of the huge coastal Indian market for British ships was now inevitable. The loss of India did not just affect British coasters trading there. Many of the major British companies had traded to India; their rationale was now to be challenged. The line of communication that ran between Britain and India, past Gibraltar, Malta, Cyprus, through the Suez Canal, past Aden, all British in 1948, ended now in an independent state. As time passed, its own merchant marine would burgeon. (In 1990 India had a merchant marine only 240,000 tons smaller than Britain's mainland register.)

One of the traditional companies trading to and from India, as well as around its coasts, was British India. Arthur Dawson was an engineer on BI ships in the 1950s.

> I had an interest in ships from when I was about twelve years old. There was no merchant navy connection in my family. I served my time on the buses as an apprentice fitter. I applied to Lamport and Holt, but when I got my ONC their interest evaporated. Then, because of National Service, it was either shouldering a musket or the Merchant Navy – that was an alternative. But rather than two years in the services, it was five or six years.
>
> I still thought it was a better option – see the world and all that. I saw this ad in the local paper and I wrote and lo and behold it turned out to be the British India Steam Navigation Company. I went for an interview with an old chief in Southport. I joined in 1954.
>
> The Indian merchant marine was just starting. At the time, I still felt it was the day of the British Raj – perhaps a little foolishly. I thought of making it my career but my wife to be didn't fancy going out to

India. So I swallowed the anchor and came home and came ashore.

Conditions were good. We had an all-Indian crew on deck, Pakistanis in the engine room, Goanese 'boys', although we had all sorts or people on board from time to time. We were running ships mostly with diesel engines, though there was a mix. Cargoes were mixed; we carried passengers. We had the *Uganda* and the *Kenya*, they were pure passenger.

There were two types of service, the home service and the coast line. Those last were based in Calcutta, Bombay, even one in Mombasa, serving the East coast of Africa. A couple based on Karachi sailed with passengers up the Persian Gulf. Others sailed to Hong Kong and Singapore – Bangkok – some went to Australia, and even New Zealand.

On board we had our own mess; the deck officers messed separately. On one ship we had a skipper who insisted that all officers, irrespective of being deck or engineers, if they were not on watch, had to get changed and to go for their meals in the main lounge. A lot of engineers, not through idleness, just tended to put a clean boiler suit on and go into the engineers mess. I was one of them.

We had to work. You had your four on, eight off, but that was a bit of a misnomer because you had to do a meal relief. It was work, eat, sleep. In the main there was that split between deck and engine room – oil and water don't mix. But it really depended on the individuals. We had no air-conditioning, just fans. It got very hot.

Towards the end of my service there were more Indian and Singalese officers coming in. They mixed with us. On one ship, though, we had a couple of South Africans – of British ancestry – and they said 'we can't go out with this lad, he's black, he's inferior,' all this sort of bull. It was a formative time: I had never been away from home, when I went. I used to get very depressed at home on £3 a week. When I went to sea I found my lifestyle transformed. It was £11 a week and I had a 'boy' to look after me and all my food was paid for, along with my accommodation.

It opened my outlook on life, changed my opinions. I had always been brought up to believe that the British were God's chosen children – until I went to Calcutta. I remember being at a Christmas party with these Eurasian girls and I said to them how much we'd given them. They told me that we'd screwed India. I began to realise that we were no angels.

Elsewhere, other countries would gain independence and want their own shipping lines. Much as with airlines later, a national merchant marine was a source of national pride, a sign of development. Apart from that, it brought in valuable revenue. All this worked against the

British, those pioneer and hitherto first-ranking cross-traders. Indeed, the growth in the post-war world of bilateral shipping agreements was a constant source of British government complaint; in the 1950s, seventy-four formal complaints were made to thirty-one different countries.

None of this cut deep – yet. In the period up to 1960 British shipping continued much as it had before the War; ships were repainted in their old colours. New ships were ordered from British yards, built, then launched in style. Conditions on board ships had improved no end, helped perhaps by the post-war welfarist philosophy.

'I had just finished a five-month trip and after twenty-seven days leave with pay I reported to the Pool to ship out again,' recalls one seafarer, quoted by Hope. He found a berth in a new tanker and was put on pay more or less at once. 'We looked to see what we were joining. Bathing pool, smoke-room, library, recreation room, showers, single rooms for everyone on board ... Here was something I had dreamed of. Back in the old days, I washed in the heads, three to a bucket ...' That was in 1954.

On the other hand, life could still be very rough indeed. Ricky Calderley joined his first ship in the 1950s, like Arthur Dawson.

> This was in Fleetwood and the ship, *Sea Tern*, was a coaster owned by James Fisher of Barrow. I was a boy who just walked on board a ship and asked the skipper if there were any jobs going. His reply was that he needed a greaser and that it was a man's job [Ricky was only fifteen]. If I could do a man's job then he would give me a man's wage – £5 a week and, as she was under a certain tonnage he would give me another £2.50 to feed myself.

The ship used to call in at an Irish port for weekends as the crew were all Irish; the skipper let them go ashore. At fifteen, Ricky found himself acting as the ship's watchman, all alone on the anchored coaster with a Tilley lamp. He moved on eventually to a tramp called the *Lord Codrington*, a London–Greek-owned ship. He went to Albania on this ship, as the cook, and from there to China.

> I never sailed twice with the same company – I even did a few trips out of Lowestoft on fishing boats. On the *Codrington* there were all sorts on board. Chinese down below, Arab fireman, some Maltese, a Greek chief steward, a German ex-submarine commander was the mate. The skipper were British. We all messed together except the Arabs who used their cabins for prayers and so on. We were two to a cabin so the accommodation was good.

But the ship was alive with cockroaches. She had never been home –
typical tramp. You couldn't turn your bunk light off, you'd be covered
in them. I'd open the galley in the morning and as soon as you'd put
the light on – millions. I'd made some jellies for the officers once, and
I put them in the veg locker to cool off. I took them up at tea-time and
a shout came, 'come upstairs, cook', so I went and it was one of the
engineers and he'd dipped his spoon in the jelly and a cockroach had
run out. I said 'here have another' and the same thing happened.

On that ship – I was on it for eighteen months – we'd not one bandage
or sticking plaster in the medical kit, just a bottle of camomile lotion.
The crew were good but the company were right under the arm. But I
wouldn't have missed the seafaring for anything.

The Korean War, between 1950 and 1952, and the closure of the Suez
Canal between 1956 and 1957, heightened the boom for shipping. Oil
was now a huge industry and tanker fleets grew, both in number and
overall size. But here, as in many shipping markets, the British were
slow off the mark. P&O only ordered a substantial tanker fleet in
1955 – too late, as it turned out, to reap the benefits of the early '50s
oil boom. British shipping companies, most still family owned, stayed
highly traditional in outlook, unwilling to seek out young and qualified managers, hanging on to the same old techniques for judging
their business. Most telling, perhaps, no shipping company listed on
the Stock Exchange raised new capital between 1945 and 1960.

Meanwhile, the British coastal trade was being eroded by both rail
and road. The total tonnage declined by 47 per cent between 1938
and 1957 (when the M1 opened). More ominously, coal exports –
the backbone of the old deep-sea tramp trade – had declined from
thirty-eight million tons in 1938 to seven million tons in 1960 (down
82 per cent). By 1991 we were importing coal and the domestic coal
industry was effectively being run down to nothing.

British ports remained old-fashioned in buildings and working
practices; they were heavily unionised. Their failure to modernise
quickly enough, if at all, meant that the size of ships entering and
leaving were restricted to older, smaller, slower vessels – an increasing
proportion of which, within the European fleets, were British. Yet by
the 1960s port handling costs had become 40 per cent of shipping
costs.

There were other dangerous trends. The phenomenon of the late
1940s, and thereafter, was the growth of the new 'Flags of Con-
venience', notably Panama, Honduras and Liberia, in the early years.
These had existed before the Second World War but only rose to

prominence after it. American ship-owners had been driven to 'flag out' by the increasingly high costs of registering ships in the USA. Domestic shipping laws, along with union muscle and high taxation, meant that running costs became too high. The US reserve fleet came into existence to cover this; in a national emergency these ships would be taken out of mothballs and would provide the US-flagged emergency merchant fleet.

Countries like Panama offered an 'open' register at almost no cost. Regulations on crewing levels, their safety and comfort, were minimal; other rules might not exist at all. Taxation was more or less non-existent. Greek shipping magnates like Niarchos and Onassis were attracted to these flags in the post-war world not least because Greece was in the throes of a civil war. Others joined later. One result was that by 1959 Liberia had the world's third largest, Panama the fourth largest, registered fleets.

Other countries had by then begun to challenge the British. America's fleet was the biggest by tonnage but the figures included in the total her large reserve fleet and a big tonnage operating on the Great Lakes. By 1960 Japan had crept back into the list with over six million tons (Britain had over twenty million tons); so had Norway with over ten million tons (her fleet doubled between 1947 and 1958). Japan was then the world's biggest ship-builder. Like many countries, but unlike Britain, her government subsidised ship-building heavily, seeing the link with shipping – and thus trade – and also appreciating them both as nationally vital assets. The modernisation of Japanese shipyards had been greatly assisted by the United States; the USA had also aided German and Italian shipping.

British shipping lines were giving away trade by the end of the 1950s; Shaw Savill stopped a service between South and East Africa and Australia and New Zealand in 1956; the Orient Line, shortly to be taken over by P&O, stopped cruising in 1957 because of heavy demand on its passenger liner services. Perhaps the saddest of all the losses in British shipping have been those of the great passenger liners, killed off completely by cheap, fast, jet-air travel. The end came relatively quickly; it is easy to forget that the *QEII*, launched in 1968, was built for regular transatlantic crossings, as well as for cruising. The true destroyer of these ships, the Boeing 747 Jumbo Jet, made its first commercial flights eighteen months after the *QEII* launch.

In the 1950s these huge ships seemed immutable, a permanence of real beauty. It was not just the great *Queens*, either. Ships of many countries crossed the Atlantic, ran down the trade routes to South

America, crossed through the Panama Canal, sailed across the Pacific, and from that far-flung ocean travelled back to Europe. Regular, leisurely luxury travel was available everywhere. Other liners passed to and fro in the Mediterranean, on past Alexandria and Suez to the Far East and Australia. They carried passengers to these exotic places as they had done for more than a century. The size of ship changed little after the massive early giants like the *Mauretania*.

Ships travelling through the Suez Canal were smaller than many, limited by the ruling depth of the canal. Their designers vied to make them more and more elegant; their post-war interiors matched once more those of the earlier days. These passenger ships had signalled the first great age of long-distance travel. You knew it would take so long to get between Southampton and New York, so long to South Africa, or to India from the London River, or on to Singapore, to Bangkok, Hong Kong and Sydney (give or take a little). Life on board was geared to fill time; even the four days transatlantic voyage could seem an age for small child or a businessman but that was the way you went. These ships were designed – in their final manifestation – to take care of all that. They were stuffed with staff, as well as crew; they contained the same swimming pools, promenade decks, libraries, gyms, cinemas, restaurants, bars and night clubs as their pre-war sisters. Some were the same ships.

Eating, of course, could fill much of the day, and did. But much time could be spent on the sundeck lolling in a deckchair, reading a good novel. The passenger ships espoused a way of life we have lost for ever; ship-board romances, long evenings in the near tropics, the slow change of weather from cold to warm to hot, and back again. Winter crossings in the North Atlantic when even the great *Queens* had plates buckled and stanchions bent by the fury of the waves.

Within twenty short years it had all gone, replaced by the faintest of echoes in the cruise liners which have ever since tried artificially to re-create the past. The purpose has gone out of it all; today passengers crowd together in stuffy Jumbo Jets, riding faster than ever before, but to a man or woman longing for the whole thing to be over as quickly as possible. The loss of enjoyment of travel between faraway places has been total. It was always going to cost British shipping more than that of other nations. British passenger ships dominated the major routes as much as their humbler cargo counterparts dominated the freight routes. Even on the immensely crowded and competitive run between Europe and the USA, the British liners were supreme.

Further afield, to India, the Far East and to Australia and New Zealand, the British ruled. In the post-war world, the passenger ships to Australia were crowded with emigrants, as their North Atlantic counterparts had been a century before. The number of people travelling from Europe – especially to the USA – continued to rise. Post-war passenger shipping enjoyed a boom, re-inforced as post-war controls on foreign exchange and travel were rescinded. Americans, meanwhile, poured into Europe as the '50s rolled on.

Air travel across the Atlantic had been firmly established after the war but it was slow and expensive. The early Boeing Stratocruisers, lined up at the nascent Heathrow, contained rows of bunks. They had very limited capacity. Even more or a problem, travellers were very afraid of flying. There was no comparison with the luxury – in all classes – of the passenger ships. But the airlines were there; the first jet airliner, the British designed 'Comet', was promising a huge reduction in transatlantic crossing time. The early problems – including a number of fatal crashes – only delayed the inevitable. In 1958, for the first time, the numbers crossing the Atlantic by air exceeded those crossing by sea. Only ten years before, there had been a waiting list of passengers trying to make the crossing. In 1946 only seven companies were offering the passage; a year later the number had risen to fifty-nine as wartime requisitioned tonnage was refurbished and pressed back into service.

In that year just short of a million passengers made the crossing, only 100,000 short of the pre-war total. A third of that million went by Cunard White Star in the *Queens* or in the old *Brittanic* or the new *Parthia*. In competition with these ships were those like the *Washington* and the *America* of the United States Line, the *Stockholm* of the Swedish–America Line, and many others. As with todays' airlines, this route was the premier run. Ships were still being designed and built exclusively for it. In 1948 Cunard White Star (the White Star title was only dropped in 1950) launched the *Caronia* for the dual roles of North Atlantic liner runs and cruising. But the biggest post-war launch was in the USA – of the *United States*. On her maiden voyage, in July 1952, she captured the Blue Riband trophy from the *Queens* by a comfortable ten hours.

The *United States* was 30,000 tons *smaller* than either of the *Queens* yet she had roughly similar engine size. She was 916 feet long and 101 feet wide (the *Queen Mary* was 975 feet long and 118 feet wide). She had been built extensively of aluminium (including 1,200,000 aluminium rivets) which made her much lighter; she was given smaller dimensions to enable her to pass through the Panama Canal. She had cost what was then the enormous sum of £27 million (compared with £5.5 million for the *Queen Mary*) making her the most expensive merchant ship ever built. Significantly, of her cost, the United States government put up £15 million.

For many Americans, though, the only way to cross was in one of the *Queens*. The *Queen Mary*, now a tourist attraction in Long Beach, California, remained the favourite on both sides of the 'pond' in many peoples' affections. Slightly smaller than the '*Lizzie*', she was big enough. I remember seeing her off on her final regular transatlantic voyage in 1968 and then again, in Long Beach, in 1979. She seemed to have grown smaller in the intervening years. The *Queen Elizabeth* had a sadder end, burning up in Hong Kong harbour after being bought for conversion to a floating university. She, like all these last great liners, was opulence gone mad. An account of her final west-to-east crossing appeared in the December 1990 issue of *Ships Monthly*. Trevor Verner booked a first-class stateroom for £201.00, knowing he was watching history pass.

Like many before him, it was the food that really impressed:

> ... You could have your meals sent to your cabin or, at a small surcharge, you could dine in the lovely Verandah Grill. Morning tea, coffee, juice, rolls, etc., would be delivered to your cabin, then breakfast, then morning coffee was usually served in the Smoke Room or *Queen Elizabeth* Lounge. Tea, a really traditional tea, was served with grand style in the lounge. After dinner you could have supper virtually anywhere ... For those worried about their waistline there was a gymnasium, squash court, turkish bath, and two swimming pools, plus acres of deck space.[1]

Even the great *Queens*, though, could feel the power of the North Atlantic in late autumn.

> By dinner on Thursday evening I felt that the *Elizabeth* was an old friend but on Friday the *Queen Elizabeth* and the North Atlantic did not see eye to eye – her 83,000 tons felt like a tug boat and one could hardly believe that this huge liner could roll so much. I remember some of us sitting in the Midships Bar counting to ten during her rolling. She would seem to hang before coming back.

The North Atlantic route was not just between Europe and New York. A large passenger tonnage ran to Canada. In 1954, Cunard launched a ship for this run, the *Saxonia*, replacing the *Empress of*

Canada. Many passenger ships made this regular run in the days before the St Lawrence Seaway had been built. As new passenger ships continued to join the pre-war tonnage, much more space and many more facilities were made available for the 'tourist' class, acknowledging a reality that more and more of those travelling were not rich. This market, made up initially of emigrants, was changing as the real age of mass tourism began.

Once the shift to air had begun on the North Atlantic route, it was only a matter of time before it happened elsewhere. The closure of the Suez Canal in 1967 hastened the end of passenger services to the East; by 1968, most people were going by plane. To South Africa, that had been happening in 1965.

Gradually it seemed, then like a flood tide roaring up a narrow creek, the airlines seized the initiative. The last British troopship, the *Oxfordshire*, commissioned in 1957, became redundant in 1962 when the government announced all future troop movements would be by air (the Falklands can hardly be said to have changed that). The *Oxfordshire*, owned by P&O today, is now a cruise liner, renamed the *Fairstar*. There were other changes in sea-going passenger travel, just over the horizon. One was the discontinuation by many cargo liners of carrying a limited number of passengers. Normally restricted to twelve (the maximum number allowed before a doctor had to be employed on the ship), many cargo liner companies were able to offer a cheap means to travel all over the world. The cargo ships went slower, they offered few, if any, facilities, but they were cheap and they called at hundreds of ports the passenger ships never went near. Many people used them. Today, while it is still possible to find ships which have room for a few passengers, the cost is staggering. The ships tend to go to far fewer places, and to off-load in grim new container ports, often many miles away from civilisation.

By 1967, 90 per cent of long-distance passenger travel was by air. Thus 125 years of passenger travel by ship ended here, as it did all over the world. British passenger ships returned to a role they had played centuries earlier – the short-sea trade between the island and Europe: Calais, Boulogne, Dunkirk, Zeebrugge, the Hook, and the more distant Roscoff, Santander, Esberg, Stockholm.

For shipping lines, the end of long-distance passenger travel had not been seen until very late on. In 1960 three very large passenger ships were being built in British yards (almost the last as it turned out). These were the *Canberra* and the *Oriana* for the Australia run, and the *Windsor Castle* for the South Africa route. Like the *QEII*, built as a defiant swan-song at the other end of the '60s, they had a short life in the role for which they were principally built. Their launches, along with that of the last great *Queen*, were a lament for the old ship-building yards, too. In 1960 it was just possible to imagine a future for these, given substantial changes in work practices; by 1970, only the wildest optimist could raise much of a cheer for British ship-building. By 1970 Cunard was owned by Trafalgar House, basically a property company, and P&O had undergone a major reorganisation. But by then containerisation had made its mark on shipping and nothing was ever to be the same again.

The ordinary seaman of the merchant fleet has always had a bad image. Drinking, swearing, whoring across the world, when he returned to these shores his reputation had long preceeded him.

> I'd stayed ashore for four days. I was in the bar all day and then at night one of the women would take me back to her little flat. When I got home and told my friends what had happened they wouldn't have it, they thought I was telling a load of lies. But if you were a kid down there with blue eyes you couldn't go wrong with women ...²

Seafarers cultivate an image of derring-do, of adventure, or did until recently. It is hard to be romantic about supplying North Sea oil rigs, or criss-crossing the English Channel with a load of day-trippers. The girl to whom your remarks are being addressed has just returned from a holiday in Bali. There you have it. Until the demise of the British seafarer, faced from the late '70s with a shrinking deep-sea fleet, and an increasingly mechanised and mechanical lifestyle, 'going to sea' had a rhetoric of its own.

There were skills, too, some of which still count, others of which have died under the weight of technology. Seafaring was *not* just another job, it entailed sacrifice and considerable danger. It was, as we have noted, a young *man's* job. It involved long absences from home and hearth. Although older seafarers did – and do – exist, most have left the sea to settle down with wife and children. The romance is as much to do with a lost *youth*, those 'blue remembered hills', the 'land of lost content', as it is to do with the mystical pull of the sea.

Until very recently, as just about every one of our seafarers has constantly pointed out, it was more often than not a badly paid and filthy existence, in which the food could be inedible and the conditions harsh. The environment was relentless, sometimes close to unendurable. The surprise to anyone who has made even superficial enquiries is always that so many kept on doing it. Whilst those passengers on the great liners were enjoying a luxury hardly to be matched by anything on land, this was not matched by the over-crowded and dank cells occupied by the hundreds of stewards and stewardesses, the cooks, waiters and others. The ships' crew inhabited even darker lower deck 'cabins'.

Dick Logan was in the engine room with Cunard in the late 1940s.

> They sent me to the old *Aquitania*. When I saw the living conditions I couldn't believe it. The bunks were tied up with wire – there were ten to a cabin – and the showers weren't working.

There were some compensations remembers Jo Gallagher:

> You could have few pints and go to the cinema. We never got to have much contact with the passengers – you did cop on with women from time to time. But if you got caught you were sacked – broaching the cargo was the charge, that was always the worst crime they could charge you with, whatever it was.

The weapon which ships' masters could use was the discharge – 'very good', 'good', or 'decline to report'. If a sailor left a ship with the last he would be unable to get a job. Sometimes even getting a 'good' would be viewed with suspicion. Sometimes, masters short of crew would offer either a discharge with a 'DR' or say to the sailor, 'stay on board and I will give you a better report at the end of the next voyage.'

It is easy for the landsider to forget that seafarers came in many disguises. We tend to think of officers and ratings – deck sailors. We might, if pricked, think about the engine room crew – who with the onset of oil, then diesel, just kept on shrinking per ship. But there were so many other jobs – stewards, cooks, boys, carpenters, elec-tricians. On the passenger liners employment opportunities multiplied to the level of a small town. With the final passage of the great liners, thousands of jobs went for ever – the stewards and waiters, the cooks and their assistants being just a few. Servants of the sea-going, all, they were swept aside as if they had never been. With them went a whole way of life.

10

NEMESIS: THE SECOND SHIPPING REVOLUTION

' "They built great ships and sailed them"
sounds most brave.'

John Masefield, *Ships*

By 1992 there were just 18,000 British seafarers left (8,000 officers
and 10,000 ratings), and around 300 ships of the merchant fleet. Yet
it was only in 1975 that Britain had the greatest ever tonnage on her
register. The sudden decline of that register, in the 1980s, was sufficient to rouse parliamentary interest in a subject most MPs had long
forgotten about, if they ever knew or cared.

There were many factors which led to the destruction of the British
registered fleet – some of which can be reversed. One was containerisation, of which more below. Another, linked to the technological changes, was crew costs; European crews simply became
unaffordable. Yet another was the ending of the cross-trades through
international agreement. Finally, there was the great oil crisis of the
1970s, when the Arabs hiked the price of fuel, then hiked it again.
This led to a worldwide shipping slump in the 1980s, compounded
in Britain's case by government changes in the tax laws.

The result was that from a peak tonnage of about thirty-three
million gross registered tons in 1975, the British fleet fell away until
by 1991 it had reached 6.2 million gross registered tons, a reduction
of 92 per cent since 1989, leaving Britain with only 1.6 per cent of
world tonnage. (In 1991 it had fallen further to 4.1 million tons and
in 1991, also, few British ratings were left on the flagship of the
merchant fleet, the *QEII*.) In a hundred years, then, the British
merchant fleet had reduced from around 55 per cent of the world
total to almost nothing, the decline appearing in 1992 to be continuing. Even the cries of ship-owners that this was a strategic industry
and should not be allowed to fall below a certain level were no longer
heeded. The collapse of the Communist threat, the end of the Cold
War, the growing interest in a European fleet, all combined to make
these pleas go largely unheeded.

It was argued, as well, that British *ownership* had not declined anything as much as the register implied. British owned ships had moved out of the British register because of costs; they had gone to Hong Kong, Bermuda, the Isle of Man and even the Falkland Islands, where taxation was lower and regulations looser – especially over what nationality crews to employ. Other devices, like changing from a ship-owning company to a ship-'management' company disguised the truth about the 'real' owner and meant that there were many more 'British' ships than an examination of the register would suggest. But seafarers lost out anyway, as employment for British sailors fell away.

The loss of employment was inevitable, once the great container revolution had taken shape. This huge change in cargo handling brought to an end for ever the traditional 'break bulk' methods of loading and unloading, with their heavy dependence on manpower, either in seamen or in dockers. Logical though it may be, it has destroyed seafaring as known and understood for generations. Seafarers to a man all say it wiped out any romance that might be remaining and turned shipping, finally, into the equivalent of truck-driving – without the benefit of being home most nights.

Cargoes had always been divided into two broad classes. There were bulk cargoes, like coal, grain or oil. Then there were general cargoes which could range from machinery, through sacks of jute or cocoa, to barrels of beer, crates of whisky and on to individual parcels and trunks of books. The immense range of general cargoes, to be transported all over the world, led to a huge industry within an industry of freight agents and shippers, specialist companies who would ensure that a particular consignment would get to its destination, along with insurers and consignment agents, middle men and distributors.

On board cargo ships, loading these myriad quantities of goods and chattels was a specialist art, involving the mate in particular knowing his ship and her holds and 'tween' decks intimately. Loading was an art, in which every last space aboard a ship had to be stuffed tight. It did not stop there. At the other end of the voyage a cargo ship might be unloading in a dozen or more ports along a coast – and loading. A mate of a ship like this had to be able to work out how to load new cargo whilst still being able to get at the as yet unloaded freights. It took skill – and time. But the life it implied was to many on board the epitome of seafaring: time was not a problem and those exotic coasts could be enjoyed to the full. In far-off places like New Zealand seafarers knew they would be welcomed on their perhaps twice-yearly arrivals, like lost relatives. Families on shore would adopt a ship and invite the sailors into their homes; parties would be thrown and dances given.

Among the most evocative of accounts of these latter days of the old order, Richard Woodman's fictional 'documentary' tale of an old Blue Funnel cargo liner's trip to the Far East stands out. Woodman, who until recently commanded one of Trinity House's buoy and light-ship tenders, and who writes his own version of derring-do novels about Nelsonian sailor, Nathanial Drinkwater, tasted those final days in the 1960s. *Voyage East* is the chronicle.

He, like many of his fellow sailors, might not have guessed at the time how soon it was all to end. The Blue Funnel ship they voyaged in was a general cargo ship of some 8,000 tons and, like all Blue Funnel 'liners', she was named for a Greek hero – in this case, *Antigone*.

Woodman's description of her is worth repeating because what he writes about is to be found, if at all today, at the furthest margins of the shipping world, now long dominated by container ships. *Antigone*'s purpose was general cargo, all of which had to be stowed by hand – hundreds of dockers might be involved in the Liverpool docks whence hailed. Her officers, like Woodman, had to ensure that as she discharged her cargo in dozens of ports across the Far East, each item would come out at the right time, and that every lessening of cargo weight would not upset her balance in the water.

> She had been built, like so many of her sisters, at the Caledon Yard in Dundee in 1949, the year the Communists took over China and Holt's lost their great wharf at Pootung on the Whang-Pu River below Shanghai. She was 487 feet long with a beam of sixty-four feet. Her long black hull with its pink boot-topping had a distinctive curve to the line of its sheer and was topped by three white painted 'islands'. Amidships, the longest was known as the centre-castle and bore the main accommodation and the huge blue funnel with its black top.
>
> The scantlings of her hull were massive, row upon row of rivets strapping her plating and frames, her stringers and her beams to a specification far above the most stringent requirements of Lloyds. Holt's ships were built for anything, typhoon-proof and uninsured, the Company's confidence resting with their ships and men, rather than underwriters.[1]

Les Walker served on cargo ships trading to West Africa, and up the rivers. Like Woodman, he remembers it well:

There were lots of things hanging over from the old days. But things had improved during the war; on one ship I found myself sleeping on a Dunlopillo mattress as opposed to the old 'donkey's breakfast' which used to be lice-ridden. The food was far far better. I mean, once I sailed on a ship where we had a twelve lb tin of jam to last twelve men for a fortnight. Then conditions got to be like home.

I was mostly on tramps – average trip was about nine months. You knew your first three ports, that was all. You could never tell where you would be after that, or when you'd get home. I was with the Silver Line going for palm oil and palm kernels along the Gold Coast (Ghana). What happened there was that you took supplies in for the English up the rivers. You'd come to swamps where the workers had built their houses along the banks and when you were going through you'd sound the ship's whistle and that was a signal to them to evacuate all the furniture out of their houses for a spring clean. As we went in the wash would go through the houses: with the temperature it would soon all dry out.

Three hundred was a big village – some were about twenty people. Some of those inlets you got to the surface was like green moss. In other places the trees would overhang the ship – you know like when you are driving along in the car through a country lane. You'd sound the whistle and all kinds of life would start moving overhead. We'd pick up from these creeks.

Ships like these general cargo vessels moved at around 16 knots, lifted about 9,000 tons of cargo. They were the end of a line, though. The key to their demise lay in the loading and unloading; it was messy, prone to pilferers, of which dockers were legendary masters, prone to strikes, to damage in transit and discharge. Most of all, it was horribly slow. The travel to a number of small ports, or laying off harbours too small to take her whilst lighters came alongside was becoming uneconomic, taking too many men, too long. The replacement was soon in coming in the 1960s but it was not to be a ship but a system.

Changes in both the operation of ships and their shape and size had been continuing since the war. As costs rose so efforts had been made to find quicker ways of building ships, and of making their cargo space more accessible – and larger. Welded ships had arrived in the war; they were far quicker to build than riveted ships and whole sections could be prefabricated. In the 1950s ways were found to make much larger welded ships and the super-tanker would soon be no longer a fiction, but a fact.

The growth in size of oil-tankers, to the giant 500,000 tonners of the 1970s, was matched by a change in tramping of this kind from the old dry-hold system to 'bulkers' and 'OBO's. These ships were designed with engines and accommodation aft in such a way that cargo carrying was maximised. OBO stood for oil, bulk and ore cargoes. These ships might carry oil or oil products on one voyage and grain or sugar on another. Even though they had to operate at times 'in ballast' – that is, empty – they became cheaper than the older tramps.

With the going of the old-style cargo liners, and her tramp-ship sisters, the latter squeezed to death from the development of the bulkers, the scene was set for the greatest set of changes in shipping since the coming of the steamship – some would say since the replacement of oar-power by sail. With container ships, seafaring can be said to have died, to be replaced by what has become just another job.

Stowing cargo was not just about how much you could squeeze in: different kinds of cargo had to be stowed in different ways (some could be packed tight, other articles could not. Some cargoes would spoil others – tea was notorious for taking up the odours of other goods. Other cargoes might be full of insects, which would then infest the holds; some would sweat, some might explode if the conditions were wrong. On deck these cargo ships would have a complex pattern of derricks for loading and unloading. Through this system the container cut a swathe. The cost to the shipping world was huge. Containerisation meant a world standard 'box' had to be agreed. New ships had to be built, new ports, with new kinds of crane. Lorry trailers had to be built to take the containers, and railway trucks. A complex worldwide system of tracking containers had to be installed, so that a port might not get overloaded with empty boxes, another short. The container brought a complete change of view. Today, people may move house by stuffing their own container, conveniently left outside. As we have come to accept the skip, so too the container. People have used them to live in; they have been mobile workshops and laboratories, emergency shelter and animal pens. They have become the world's first fully integrated transport system. And they killed general cargo handling, outside remote Third World ports.

The container ships, as they developed, were larger and they could handle far more cargo, more quickly. They could be loaded round the clock. It has been estimated that, with faster turn-round, larger vessels and higher overall voyage speeds, each ocean-going container ship replaced up to twelve break bulk general cargo vessels. The British shipping industry pioneered these ships, not least because they offered a way out of the old-style docks and their endless problems of demarkation – and pilfering. But the cost of changing meant that it was not only shipping practices which came under scrutiny. From the 1970s on, shipping companies were more and more aggressively looking at ways of cutting fixed costs. With fuel prices rising, with port handling charges largely beyond their control, as with insurance, it was crew costs which could be reduced most readily.

By the 1970s the world market was getting leaner, too. From 1974, the year after the great oil crisis, an UNCTAD conference agreed that henceforth cross-trades should be restricted. Developing countries, to which cross-traders increasingly went, would now get up to 40 per cent of their own shipping trade, and a further 40 per cent was reserved to the shipping lines of the country from which, or to which, the cargoes came or went; only 20 per cent was to be left to the cross-traders. Britain, by this time, was suffering from a long-term decline in her export trade and hence gained little from the 40:40 rule. But her cross-trading shipping lines had been a crucial element of the industry and they were to suffer.

The shock of the decline was made worse because these events were taking place whilst British tonnage was still increasing. In the early 1970s, too, there had been an unprecedented demand for British sailors, ratings and officers. Shipping companies had to resort to sending unsolicited letters to retired or semi-retired seafarers in an attempt to get them back. World merchant tonnage had doubled between 1945 and 1965; between 1965 and 1975 it doubled again. Just before the 1973 oil crisis seventy million tons of new shipping had been ordered. Ships take time to build and the world tonnage continued to grow – until 1982 – when it reached a peak of 425 million gross registered tons. By this time, world trade was shrinking and there was a huge over-tonnage.

Ten years on and all this looks academic. The argument now is whether Britain will have any deep-sea fleet by the end of this decade. For seafarers the answer is plain: no. They point to the continued flagging out of the old stalwarts of the British register. More than that, they pointed to the demise of training for merchant officers. Despite a belated attempt to get more youngsters interested in a career at sea, it looked as if in the future any deep-sea fleet would be entirely manned by sailors from outside the UK.

Ronald Hope, in his monumental *New History of British Shipping*, concluded in 1990: '... History will not repeat itself ... British oceanic shipping will not rise again.'² With the final connection of the Channel Tunnel, late in 1991, another symbol of our past – the concept of an island nation, dependant on the sea, had gone. Yet shipping still provided a third of the invisible earnings, after tourism and the City.

On the other hand, these earnings had slipped by one billion pounds since 1980. Equally significant, whilst in the Falklands War the British government had been able to charter and requisition an entirely British fleet to support the Royal Navy (fifty-six ships in all), in the Gulf War they could only muster six British ships. The remaining 127 ships used to supply British forces had to be chartered from abroad.

The Gulf War had demonstrated, a hundred years on, Alfred Mahan's central thesis on the projection of power by naval forces. Sea-power was demonstrated in awesome effect with cruise-missile launches from the deck of the US battleships, and in the aircraft carriers and the strikes flown from them. Control of the Persian Gulf for the Allies was, of course, absolutely critical in getting heavy equipment into Saudi Arabia and in continuing to re-supply the troops. The Royal Navy, with around a dozen ships deployed, sank a number of Iraqi missile craft and kept a watch on the coast for any surprise moves by the Iraqis. The number of Allied warships in and around the Gulf showed clearly how important navies remained in any kind of conflict.

Twice in the past ten years the Royal Navy had been involved in a war and both times it had been outside the Nato area. Few planners would have predicted these scenarios in the 1960s or 1970s. The evidence from the world stage today is that it is in these kind of regional conflicts, probably brought about by maverick states or rulers, that the world community will have to involve itself. If Britain is to play a role, then its forces, including the RN, will have to adjust. The 1991 government White Paper, *Options for Change* envisaged more cuts in the fleet – yet failed to cancel the immensely expensive Trident submarines.

For both the Royal Navy and the merchant fleet (and one could as easily add the remnants of the British fishing fleet into this argument) the 1980s have been desperate times. It is, in the end, about whether 'progress' beyond a certain rate is what we can cope with, or need. For Britain's seafarers, then, of all kinds, what they have had to endure is an inexorable working out of a drama in which they have been pawns, never remotely the major pieces. What they have all lost is a complete and to nearly all a very satisfactory way of life. In many ways this way of life, towards the end at least, represented on sea what colonial civil servants enjoyed on land: exotic locations and a reasonable living in often very good conditions. Travel, in the best sense.

Seafaring became more and more acceptable, more civilised at the moment of passing. The last of the big-gun cruisers of the Royal Navy came home as they shut down the Empire in hand-over ceremonies across the globe. The Royal Navy became a cold-water Navy, dedicated to patrolling the North Atlantic, scene of its greatest-ever victory, above and below the seas. It became what it had always prided itself on being, the silent service, as well as the senior service.

The merchant fleet merely industrialised itself and in so doing all the old ways ebbed. For the rest, Britain began to turn itself into a maritime theme park, from the Albert Docks in Liverpool, to Chatham Historic Naval Dockyard, from Greenock to Plymouth, from Exeter to the Tyne.

VOICES FROM THE NIGHT WATCH

'And all I ask is quiet sleep,
When the long trick's over.'
John Masefield, *Sea farer*

Today there is much anger among British sailors: it applies to merchant seafarers, to servicemen in the Royal Navy, and to fishermen; bitterness can be tasted on the air everywhere. Many are confused, too, at the changes they have witnessed, happening so fast after decades – even centuries – of the old ways. There were so many uncertainties in seafaring that it may appear odd that those who chose it should baulk when change comes. But seafaring has long been a highly traditional area, trammelled by rules, beset by legal requirements. Sailors, despite themselves, crave routines, enjoy the little rituals of daily life at sea.

The crucial alteration, as far as the British merchant seafarer is concerned, has been the erosion of a life-style, first through the lack of opportunity to go deep-sea; also by the Industrial Revolution caused by containerisation. The new ships are fewer and they operate with much smaller crews. They rely on technology – something old-style seafaring has always mistrusted – to make up for manpower. As a result, one of the key elements – comradeship – has been stripped out. Crew might hardly see each other on a long voyage, then only to swap notes between watches. In ports turn-around is so fast there will be little chance to go ashore. Container ports, often purpose built and very new, are set miles away from the towns and cities they serve in green-field sites, so trips away from the ship are not what they once were – even if the turn-around timetable allows it.

The reduction of the British fleet has meant a retrenchment. Most merchant sailors now live and work around these coasts on the short-sea trades – or on the supply and service ships of the North Sea oil industry. This account is typical, not least because it ends in the North Sea:

I went to sea in 1973, as a catering boy and I left the merchant navy in

1987 to come ashore on the express instructions of a new wife who viewed my way of life a bit too nomadic for her liking.

I served on general cargo ships, on one coastal tanker – sacked after twenty days – but I eventually found 'heaven' aboard an anchor-handling tug and supply ship working one on, one off, on a six week duty rosta. I specialised on smallish ships all round: deep sea salvage, anchor-handling, dive ships, supply boats and general harbour tugs.

I came ashore in '87, as I said, and I have been working as a guard (yuk!) for BR but I have been trying to get back on the ro-ros as an AB. My chances are slim, though.

If you ask me about decline, there are many reasons, in my view, but here is one case, that I handled as an NUS rep. I don't see the unions as being 'knight crusaders' fighting a caricature of a tight-fisted British ship-owner but, at times, it felt a lot like that. This case – which led to a fall in company conditions and put a lot out of work – was partly why I left the sea.

The company began trading in the North Sea in a new line of business. It had previously worked chemical tankers. They became ship managers for TNT though it became obvious that TNT would buy in to ensure a foothold in the very lucrative offshore trades – as they were in '85-'86.

I joined a brand new ship, crewed by competent seamen (on deck) and new officers to a demanding trade and with an attitude that everything should be kept nice and peaceful to preserve the status quo.

We three ABs had between us nearly 25 years offshore experience at everything from anchor handling to supply runs, bulk sea transfers, rig ties, buoy chasing, dive support work and so on. We were all 'ticketed' ABs, all solid seamen. Leading us was a master who had had command of a chemical tanker before coming into the North Sea, a mate who hadn't even seen a supply boat before, an ex-tanker second mate with a view that all ABs were worthless. There were two engineers – good guys.

So you have the ship, no larger than a decent sized tugboat, crewed by five officers and five seamen; then the bullshit began. For instance, officers wearing woolly pullover rig with epaulettes for meals. Officers not coming on the deck at the rigs, and not chipping in. These sort of things had long gone on other North Sea ships because it was a one for all and all for one kind of job.

It riled us, as experienced hands, to be serving with namby pamby officers who refused to get their hands dirty at any time – but who were adept at handing out orders. You can't have a class structure on a 700-ton ship; it's impossible.

The attitude that they were officers and we were crew didn't work. For instance, company agent's being fêted at ship's parties but us being told we could not have drink in the duty mess. Or, us having to struggle on an icy fo'c'sle entering a windswept Aberdeen while the duty OOD passed orders from a centrally heated bridge via the intercom.

Maybe on an RFA or a passenger liner but on a supply boat? No way!

I've never agreed with the class system of officers remaining aloof from their men, something British officers did after being used to Third World crews and men 'who knew their place'; men who were not unionised and who worked all day on a cupful of rice and a thump on the jaw.

If the class system had been negated, as it has been on Norwegian and Danish ships, if companies had respected men and had not treated them like schoolboys, maybe the merchant navy would have survived. If the companies had worked with their men instead of against them, if they had worked with the unions maybe they'd be better established than they are. Then again, if the government had put money into the industry, if they dropped down on cross-trading, if they halted the free-floating of Norwegian tonnage into the UK market . . . if, if, if! I think the demise of the fleet can be firmly laid at the feet of the officer echelon – those who considered themselves an elite rather than what they were – employees.

I am not saying crews could not be inflexible, either, or the NUS. We have all contributed to the decline: we should have learned lessons from the past but we did not. We still brook no interference, reject change even when it is for the better. We cling to our conditions rather than swim with the tide.

Greed played a part, it still does. You tell a man that a six per cent loss in his wages means that, in a year, he'll be ten per cent better off and he won't say, 'sure, I'll go along with that'. What he will say is 'no way, you're not cutting my wages, they've been too low for too long'. You tell an ex-ferry boat chief officer that he'll have to muck in with the crowd on deck instead of standing with his radio and shouting orders and he'll say, 'not me. I am the mate, not an AB'.

We need a dissolution of established archaic practices. We need communal mess-rooms and the scrapping of barriers, an end to the God-given demarcation lines. We need ship-owners who want to do well instead of trying to make a fast buck and then flagging out when the profits get bad for a year or two. We need a sea-change – and we have not yet got it.

We need lots more – much of which I don't fully understand – like a ratified building system where new tonnage can be 45 per cent subsidised by a scrap grant to the owner or when dual usage – like a military facility in a ro-ro – is inbuilt and paid for by an auxiliary warship cost fee or the like.

We need flag protectionism, so that UK cargoes are carried in UK hulls, or agreement reached on cross-trades so we can still benefit. We need help: we get zero.

That's my view, a bit lower deck, but it's mine.

The great lament among seafarers is not often that the old class system should be broken up; many liked things the way they were – the lower deck here, the upper there. There was comfort in it, as well as anguish, or dislike. Of course, officers liked it best – and still do, where it applies. In many ways that old class structure has gone; rigid hierarchies are rare. If anything – and again not surprisingly – it has been among the *petty officers* where most resentment at that change has come. In P&O containers, for instance, petty officers, like the chief steward, have to share a mess with ratings. As it happens, chief steward is about to be a non-post; more 1991 cuts.

There is a good deal of thoughtfulness among many officers as to what used to be a clear-cut set of rules and how they apply – if at all – today. Ships have to have officers to make the rules stick, everyone agrees about that. You cannot run a ship, in the constant hazard she faces, by committee; democracy and sailing do not work. The old system went much further than that. Officers on the great passenger liners were living the life of Riley, waited on hand and foot, dining with the rich and famous and lauded in their own right. To some extent, cruise liners' officers enjoy exactly the same conditions today.

Merchant ships could be divided: the liner trades, and some companies, worked an officer to crew hierarchy as rigid – possibly even more so – than passenger ships. Tramp ships varied, tugboats and harbour craft, such as fishing boats, generally had a more relaxed atmosphere.

This was the situation in a cargo liner running between home and South America in the 1960s:

> We had to dress for dinner. That was particularly true of the passenger liners [cargo ships frequently carried up to twelve passengers]. We had 'Number Ones' and long white trousers, a tunic and a collar buttoned up high. It was very uncomfortable in hot weather. The company would lay down regulations – no smoking on the bridge – but it all depended on the old man. Uniform regulations were laid down, too. Sometimes the master would say 'Well, I don't care what you wear as long as you

wear your epaulettes so that everyone knows who you are'. Others were very, very keen. I remember having an argument once with a mate who expected us all to wear starched collars. A lot of people would no longer know what one of those was today.

I had just bought three drip dry Bri-nylon shirts and I spent my time roasting in them but he thought this was absolutely disgusting and I really ought to set an example.

The RFA (Royal Fleet Auxiliary), as the supply arm of the Royal Navy, was most rigid about dress. In the end, it was always down to the master on any ship, some being much more pernickety than others.

This is one experience – very recent – of a cadet officer in the RFA:

It all depends on the senior officers. You can get some who have done a lot of their time with commercial companies and who came into the RFA later and who, as a result, are quite relaxed, quite laid back. And then you'd get what we called the 'plastic' Navy – maybe it's a bit unfair but that's how it seemed. They were people who want to be in the Navy but the Navy won't have them. All the officers would call the captain 'sir' and that would be rigidly enforced. But none of the crew would. They would call him captain, or just nothing at all. Very occasionally I would get called 'sir' – say by a young rating – just out of the Navy proper and it didn't fit. I didn't like it but if someone called me 'third' or 'third mate' I'd take it as a compliment, a mark of respect.

Dress – and address – was one thing. Ships officers and crew are covered by dozens of Acts of Parliament, largely to ensure safety at sea. The need to have men instantly obey an order is as much to do with that as anything. But the old days, when sailors were often illiterate, have gone. Today's AB is as likely to have an Open University coursebook in his cabin as his chief officer. Until fairly recently crew could be quite severely punished for various misdemeanours, pay frequently would be docked. On the old Union Castle passenger liners operating between Southampton and South Africa, crew could be given the equivalent of a court martial, brought in before all the officers in full uniform, for what were petty offences.

On the officer side, life could be often equally difficult, not least because they had a 'position' to keep up; in port that meant staying firmly out of trouble. Ordinary seamen could have a high old time whilst their often younger 'masters' had to be much more circumspect.

For most seafarers, though, the adventure of going to sea – certainly before the age of mass tourism to far-off places – over-rode any concern about conditions of service. Many went because they relished not having to 'push paper around'.

Others – and they still exist – talk about that indefinable 'lure' the sea's own motion seems to bring forth; the restlessness of youth personified. The romantic nature of all seafarers, once the surface is lightly scratched, applies today as much as it did a hundred or three hundred years ago. Once again, the onset of the modern ship has torn a good deal of that out of the job. 'Boxboats' is the dismissive term for containerships. A century ago engines in sailing ships were dismissed as 'iron topsails'.

> I went first in 1959, with Royal Mail Lines. I think I always had the feeling that I wasn't going to be happy pushing paper around a desk. The usual thing at the school I went to was university entrance and I don't think I would have made that because I am not that academic.
>
> I always had an interest in ships which I got from my father. By fourteen or fifteen it was fixed in my mind that I would go to sea. I went to the old training ship – *Worcester.* I think in those days ships were far more in the national consciousness. And it wasn't difficult getting a job – eighteen out of twenty of us were taken by our first choice company. They were chasing you, then.

'Sandy' Kinghorn, now retired, remembers

> ... the three ways to sea as an apprentice or cadet had remained unchanged for generations [this in the 1950s]. You could simply leave school – with or without a school certificate – and join a shipping company. Some companies had cadets, some apprentices. Blue Funnel had midshipmen. Parents or guardians paid a £50 premium for tra- ditionally worded indentures: the apprentice 'must not enter ale houses or taverns or play at unlawful games'. A cadetship was less categorical although the basis was the same, but usually without premium or indentures.
>
> The second (sic) method of becoming an embryo deck officer was through a sea school. Various courses were offered, some residential, varying from a few weeks to a several years ...[1]

The difference between officer entry and rating entry could hardly have been more complete. Ratings either just went to a ship or to a shipping company to get in; training was on the job. Some of the large passenger companies ran training schools of a sort, though largely for catering and steward crew. Kenneth Long went via a training school, the *Indefatigable* on Anglesea. Like all seafarers, he remembers in crystal detail his first voyage:

It was out of the Victoria Wharf in Birkenhead. When we got out into the Irish Sea the vessel began to move. I had been given very few instructions as to what my duties were so I was on the bridge, she was rolling badly and I was sick on deck. I was terribly embarrassed about this so I went out on the bridge wing. Unfortunately the master – Captain Mason – followed me out and slipped on my vomit and was quite badly hurt.

He started shouting at the Chief Officer. I couldn't ever understand this, that these two seemed always to be shouting at each other. Anyway I went off to my bunk and I woke up in Milford Haven. There we loaded explosives. Thousands of tons of them. They built special compartments for them. In Number One hatch, forward, we put all the detonators but all separated in their own spaces. In Number Two there was general cargo, in Number Three, Four and Five, we put the explosives. The most volatile we put in Number Five – which happened to be adjacent to the Indian crew accommodation.

Some of what we loaded was rocket fuel because we took it out to Australia where it went to the Woomera Rocket Range. We sailed out of Milford Haven after a couple of days. Crossing the Bay of Biscay I was ill again. All through my seagoing I was always ill for a couple of days, if I had been ashore for any period of time. I found ways of coping – like laying a particular way in my bunk.

For the first few trips I simply watched what other people did. You were given no real responsibility. You turned up in the saloon and a liveried steward asked you what you wanted; you had a menu to choose from. You minded your Ps and Qs – from the other cadets – there were four of us.

We got through the Bay of Biscay and I was beginning to take much more notice of the world. I could see these snow covered peaks to the north. I went into the Chart Room and measured where they were and I found they were 120 miles to the south. This to me was part of the magic of being at sea – seeing things like that. I had been to sea for two weeks – I was sixteen – and suddenly I was seeing these things, images I had read about. It was all going to happen – to me.

We got through Suez and now we were in the Orient. I had by then figured out what I had to do. We went to Aden, then Ceylon, Columbo, then Hong Kong. I was sixteen, remember, and an officer in the making, on this great ship, doing something worthwhile. In the Bay of Bengal, on the way to the Hoogly, we picked up a pilot. I was ready for this. There was this senior man – Dutch – with a junior pilot and a bearer.

He had these big gold buttons. He had a long chat with the Captain, me standing there, while I listened. They, of course, totally ignored me. It is 125 miles up that river from the entrance. You can't go that fast because of the bow wave effect on the bank. I got up the next morning and I stood on the bridge while the captain and the master had a few Chota Pegs. Dawn rose and you are in a narrow river and I could see the people in the villages getting up and going along the bank. Making fires with cow dung – that smell – and I knew I had really arrived, I was here in the Far East. It was great.

Being at sea, as anyone who has made a long voyage will tell you, can be remarkably uninteresting. Long days and nights of nothing, punctuated by what can seem equally endless hours and days of appalling weather, when decks are permanently awash and the ship creaks and groans in every joint.

Watch-keeping – being on the bridge – either steering or checking a course, endless rounds of maintenance (a quite small ship has a huge quantity of parts all exposed to salt water) are routine but critical. Painting and scraping is what many old seamen remember best (or worst); checking hatch covers, maybe having to shovel bulk cargo to correct a list, endless greasing and, in some ships, varnishing.

I joined Palm Line in 1961 on a ship called the *Niger Palm*. She had been built in 1946 and she was actually the last of her class, designed in the 1930s, big 'Woodbine' funnel with stays and she had a triple expansion reciprocating steam engine.

In fact, I remember we were in Genoa and there were six cadets and five of us had gone across to see this super duper American ship. The chief engineer was chatting to us and he said 'which ship are you from?' We told him and he asked what kind of engine we had. When I told him he said, 'God damn, that's a floating museum', and he went and got his cadets and chased them across to have a look.

The same seafarer recalls, however, that despite their ancient power-plant

We were victims of our own success. Skippers would tell me that in the late 40s they could wander into a shed on the African coast and say 'where's that for?' and then say 'I'm going there, load it on my ship'. It was the Empire, you see, it really over-protected us. When it got cut-throat we were not used to it.

I mean, in the seven years I was in Palm Line, there was a big difference between the number of Russians I used to see in West Africa; of course, the developing countries started their own fleets – Nigeria, Ghana. We helped provide the personnel and now Palm Line has gone altogether.

We had all five-hatch ships: it was a long laborious process, general cargo went in, so you would be carrying stuff like stock fish – which is dried in the Arctic. You would be going up the rivers and unloading into lighters – or alongside. We used to go right up the creeks, carrying palm kernels, pulp, logs. When I think back to the number of logs we used to carry it's a wonder there is any forest left.

British liner trades were still everywhere, not just down the coast of West Africa. Another story:

I went to sea in 1958 when I was sixteen with Bristol City Lines. They had five ships then – at one stage they had had ten. They ran from Avonmouth to the eastern seaboard and up to the Lakes, and as far south as Charleston; otherwise the main ports were Montreal, Halifax, New York, Baltimore and Norfolk.

We used to take quite a bit of steel from South Wales a   ᴅ lot of cars – shoes, sherry, manufactured goods; then, coming back, grain and tobacco.

In those days you still mostly had wheels [instead of modern ships with 'iron mikes' and automatic steering]. I had the first wheel watch, two hours on, then an hour's stand-by and an hour as look-out. You worked the deck during the day. It was old-fashioned, in that you worked with the sailors [whilst an apprentice]. Number Three hatch was my hatch and we always opened it up and did all the rigging for the derricks, painted them – and the whole area.

We had an all-British crew, mainly off the Pool [i.e., casuals], but coming from Avonmouth. We used to get a few from the local Borstal, I think they got some kind of remission if they came with us.

He now works in the North Sea, like so many. Although the deep-sea fleet has contracted, one incentive for sailors in the North Sea supply industry is the regularity of the work. This applies as well to the short-sea trades – particularly the ro-ro (roll on, roll off) ferries. Regular hours and knowing when you will be at home has always had its attractions.

Sailoring has been largely a young man's world; as seafarers grow older, find a wife and settle down, domestic pressures reach a point where a stark choice usually has to be made: the sea or me. Wives have always been suspicious of sailing; either the all-male world from which they have traditionally been excluded, or simply the inability to find out what the old man is up to. Sailors have always dined out on their reputations as womanisers, which hardly helps.

But things have been changing at sea, beyond the size and shape of ships. Partly as an incentive to recruit – and then keep – men otherwise away from their loved ones for months at a time, some companies began, in the 1960s, to allow wives on board. More recently, there has been a serious attempt to get women interested in a sea-career.

> Just before I left [the sea] I did an eleven month trip. My daughter was three weeks old when I left and nearly a year old when I came back. I went ashore, then.

It was hard enough for married men and their wives; young sailors are often entirely cut off from life ashore. They may go to sea fairly young, at a time when their peers are out enjoying themselves, out having fun night after night. They endure a life-style few can understand when they come home on leave. Girlfriends have to be exceptionally loyal.

> In some ways, looking back on it now, I realise how much I missed through not being with my friends in my late teens and early twenties. I had friends at school whom I never really saw again, apart from the odd drink on leave.
>
> My last trip was a very long one – fourteen months. It was then that I started to think that I didn't really want to do this for the rest of my life. I tried to find a company where the trips would be more regular. I did three trips with Ben Line out to the Far East – it took about fifteen months, towards the late 60s. Ben Line were very old-fashioned, almost Dickensian. I think it was because a lot were family owned. Then I got married; I was then looking for a company where you could take your wife to sea – that was just beginning to happen. In fact, just as I left Ben they brought it in but it was only for senior officers.

This seafarer went to work for Shell so his wife could come, too. Sue remembers: 'I first met Bob on a ship and I knew he would be away a lot but you have to weigh that against wanting to have him.'

In the flush of excitement, Bob's first effort to get her along failed:

> I asked for a ship with Shell that was coastal thinking myself of our coast.
>
> What I got was a trip out of Curacao [in the Caribbean]; coastal all right but the wrong coast! It was a fabulous trip actually because we transited the Panama Canal about four or five times, went to Vancouver, to Bermuda, the five ports in Brazil and to the Virgin Islands. In the first thirteen months of being married we were apart for 11.

Sue simply could not get out to his ship. Later, she joined him.

It is a very strange life. I always signed on as a supernumerary and you used to find you were treated as one.

You do find a lot of tensions build up. I had to take a lot of things with me to do – sewing, knitting. It wasn't so bad on the coast because if you did get ashore you could go to the shops. I used to draw a lot – you need things which do not take a lot of outlay. Over two years I got a year's seatime in.

You would not be very welcome on deck when they were discharging the oil. But at sea you were free to wander around. You wouldn't go up on the bridge uninvited; you soon got to know where you could or could not go.

Being with her husband, though, was better than being stuck at home for months at a time.

Contrast this tale with another – Helga's. She has been married to a P&O captain, just retired. For years, on every trip he made to the Far East she accompanied him, loving the life of nine weeks at sea and in port, then nine weeks back home. As master he could take her every time but there were five other berths aboard this modern container ship for crew wives. The single cabins are like hotel suites, all kitted with double beds.

Life at sea separates less today than it ever has. Ships on short-sea trading are in and out of port so often that staying in touch is easy; attitudes today make that not a problem, either. Sailors want to talk to wives and girlfriends as much as the troops in the Gulf did. Like them, being 'manly' and toughing it out no longer has to falsely include a denial of the need for love.

Deep-sea sailors can talk to home too via long-distance radios. Marine VHF traffic suggests they do, just as they are now more likely to phone from foreign ports. The emphasis has shifted in part because their life is so at variance with the land-based worker. Going to sea no longer implies that cut-off isolation that until quite recently it did.

So much, though, *has* changed. Ships have become huge warehouses, loaded semi-automatically, steering themselves, checking their own engines for wear and tear. Crews have become fewer – and more foreign, because they are cheaper. The job is now much like any other, a change which technology reinforces. British sailors have become too expensive, bluntly; sailors were always cheap labour for the shipping company. Now they are not, every effort is made to reduce their number, or buy in Filipinos.

As we have seen, British seafarers have always sailed with foreign ship-mates, in part as a result of Empire. Chinese, Goanese, Maltese,

Sri Lankans, Somalis, West Indians, Malayans, among dozens of tribes and nations, all have played their part in the story of British shipping. Some made parts of the deck their own.

All the evidence is that the British seafarer was never a racist when it came to working, living and sleeping alongside men of other races. Some racial groups, such as the Chinese, kept themselves to themselves; others, like some Arabs, segregated themselves for religious reasons. Many companies employed particular racial groups in specialist roles – the traditional jobs they had always done, a kind of tribal right. This could apply to Liverpool firemen as much as Somali ones. Most British seafarers never had a bad attitude to other members of their crew, wherever they hailed from. The bonds of the ocean are strong and the number of sailors who married a girl from 'over there' is testament to a powerful integration of race and culture. Tales are still told with awe of Somalis, able to work in engine temperatures which would lay out a white. Except one breed – the Liverpool firemen who, like John Cooper, used to stoke the fires of the ships from the great transatlantic liners to the most humble tramps. They were the toughest of a very tough breed, one master told me, a law unto themselves. They, like the rest, have passed into history and into legend.

Shipping companies, those bastions of old-style certainties and old-fashioned gentility, have become businesses like any other. Many now pass on crewing problems to an agency, just like the Job Centre you find in the High Street. That has reinforced the feeling among sailors that their job – their vocation – is no longer any different to driving a bus or working as a BR guard.

The world has shrunk, making it easier and much more comfortable to see its exotic corners via a jumbo jet, or even in a cruising yacht. Seamen are corralled in far-off noisy port 'facilities' on stand-by for the next port, like land-based jobs. They find it hateful. 'What man would go to sea, nowadays?' they ask. 'What is there for a youngster looking for adventure?' Despair, anger, bitterness, much of it falling, like rain on water, into a void. Many sailors blame government – any government. They blame our failure to hang on to the Empire, if they are old enough to remember. They blame the Russians, the Americans (for the war), the Norwegians or the Greeks. Others blame the unions – notably the National Union of Seamen – either because it has fought too well for better pay and conditions, or because it has not fought enough.

Some blame themselves for having ever got into this mess, as they see it. In truth, as we have seen, what they rail against is change itself. The timelessness of the world's great oceans, its rhythms and moods, the endlessly changing sunsets and sunrises, the beauty of a new coastline, the excitement of marine life, the exoticism of discovery in ports and harbours, all have drawn men down the ages to voyage on the sea. They could come home and yarn, tell of places and people the rest of us would never see.

Once, that was true of travellers through remote towns and villages; the city and its life was as strange to men and women as the planet Mars. And once it was true of Curacao, of Rio and Buenos Aires, of Shanghai and, that most evocative of names, Surabaya. The world has shrunk beyond reason; our next-door neighbour is as likely to have been to Java as to Jersey; my children have already been to Bangkok, Singapore and Australia. Seafaring can no longer be what it once was and its loss, to those who remember, is incalculable. They mourn for more than a way of life, they grieve for life itself. Too romantic a view? Maybe, but then seafarers constantly return to this theme in their own memories. They have created this mythic quality which overcame even the worst of conditions. In wartime or in peace, seafarers have always been easy prey to hope triumphing over experience. The next ship will be better, the last – 'now I am out of that bitch' – was not *so* bad.

But there was always the bad side. Recently, seafarers have been more willing to discuss it. Captain 'Sandy' Kinghorn should be allowed the valedictory of that other way of life. He is talking about the *Dominion Monarch*, a Shaw Saville liner launched in 1938, broken up in Osaka in 1962. She ran between Britain, South Africa and Australia, carrying 525 first-class passengers with 385 crew. Kinghorn comments on those crew.

> Certainly, her crew were accommodated in 'far from luxurious conditions'. As indeed were the crew of most ships, not only large liners, until near the end of Britain's supremacy as a maritime mercantile power. The very awfulness of shipboard accommodation drove seafarers to seek delights ashore at every possible opportunity. Thus they came to meet the people, share their lives – really to see the world in a way that has never been possible since ships came to dash around, into and out of port in the unsociable way they do today.
>
> Sure, life at sea without air-conditioning, video entertainment, shipboard bars etc., was tough – but what you've never had you don't miss. Sadly, the coming of the vastly improved conditions at sea coinciding with the 'boxboat revolution', seemed to herald our decline as a

maritime power. Certainly sailors are chained to their ships in port in a way unthinkable in the past.[2]

All these comments – and they could be matched by thousands more, written, spoken, all heartfelt – imply where they do not say that Britain has suffered a catastrophe because of these changes. They add together the loss of ships with the loss of a way of life. For they all perceive that the sea gave something beyond the surface highway to adventure, that it was, unquestionably, life itself.

The craft of seamanship – being able to splice a rope is almost a lost art now – has gone with the changes. Shipping has been industrialised, as weaving once was, or making furniture. But the anguish goes further for in moving from one system to another we have thrown away our inherent lead: the decline is *not* just about standards or the old ways, but about ships. Finally, it is about us, the people who live on the land and our inability to appreciate seafaring for what it was, and what is left of it. We have grown away from the myths, from the sea chanties, the literature, the art, and the popular imagination that once brought 'going to sea' alive in mens' hearts, and chilled that of their womenfolk. Today women go to sea on British ships, as officers if not yet as ratings; they can also go as the companions of their menfolk. For the rest of us, though, seafaring has become more of a mystery than ever before.

The closest we come to experiencing it is in ferry crossings and in cruise holidays; neither give any sense of what being at sea is really like. Even the mundane opportunity of looking at ships in port has been taken away, shifted to distant and security-conscious container berths, or oil refineries well clear of the curious. Britain has prided herself, at least in theory, on having been a maritime nation. Yet we have always been ambiguous about the cost of that. On the one hand our Victorian ancestors relished the naval power it brought. On the other, as we have seen, seafarers have been treated like pariahs should they intrude too far upon landside life. In wartime merchant seafarers have had plenty to complain about. John Masefield, among others, compared seafaring to the gypsy life and that seems, at heart, to be what this ambiguity is all about. Gypsies represent an exciting world, a world of danger only a wall apart from everyday life. In some of our dreams we want to go with them, to experience those freedoms, real or imagined, which they appear to have. On the other, we are afraid of their intrusion into our settled lives, the anarchy they bring, their freedom turned into something else, something dark and untamed.

Seafarers down the centuries have been careful to cultivate this image. And for the average Briton, a meeting on the streets with a black, brown or yellow sailor, off a ship from God only knew where, must have been a considerable shock.

Today, we have grown world-weary with our own travels. The gripes of seafarers sounds like a badly played chord. *Our* experiences of the exotic are not like that, we cannot see what kind of life they describe. In any case, their experiences of far-away places is likely to be much more restricted than ours for they are more than likely to have been confined to a quick turn-around in a port 'facility' miles from the beaches, the nightspots, even the people of the land to which they have come.

Seafarers are back among us, now, more than they have been for centuries. And they are shadows, unnoticed. The British have come home at last, from the sea. Today, British shipping is much like it was in the days of Henry VIII, before Elizabeth and her bold buccaneers set out to create the beginning of the greatest deep-sea fleet the world has ever seen. Now, we are more and more coastal sailors – commercially and in leisure. Even the deep-sea fishing fleet has come home.

Does it matter? This is no place to make that judgement. The transformation of Britain from what she once was, to what she may become, is still in the balance. Seafaring is swept along by that, no more, no less, than other trades.

12

HULL DOWN:
THE FINAL RETREAT
OF THE ROYAL NAVY

'Far off they served, but now
Their deed is done.'

Henry Newbolt, *Farewell*

What of the Royal Navy while all these changes had been taking place in the British merchant fleet? For nigh on 400 years the Royal Navy had been the nation's bulwark, its shield against all comers. By contrast only a small standing Army ever stood between an invader and success. The Empire – especially the Indian Army – were where British troops were concentrated. Immediately after the Second World War in 1945 all that changed irrevocably. The Navy, at the moment of its greatest-ever expansion in ships and numbers, was about to concede to both Air Force and Army the role of the prime defender.

The ironies of history were everywhere in 1945. Bismarck's comment that were the Victorian British Army to invade Germany he would send the police to arrest it was to be thrust back at the defeated Germans as the British committed themselves to a permanent occupation on the Rhine, first as conquering police force, then as defenders of the West.

The Royal Air Force, too, would take up permanent residence in Europe and for a long time the ultimate defence of Britain would lie with them. The Navy, meanwhile, was within a few years going to have to get used to being on long, cold patrol in the North Atlantic and round the North Cape. The tropical delights of the past were all too soon to go.

But that lay a little over the horizon at the end of the Second World War. As we have seen, the Navy had a patchy war: some great successes, some firsts, many near defeats, some very bloody encounters. The best remembered, perhaps because they cast up folk memories, were those odd incidents of derring-do. Vian's attack on the *Altmark* to liberate British merchant seaman, in the dark days of 1940; earlier the Navy's successful encounter with the *Graf Spee* – even the make-shift evacuation and near disaster of Dunkirk.

Those dashing triumphs, fitted with the myths of 'Jack Tar'. The frightful attrition in the Atlantic did not; neither did the unnecessary loss of the *Repulse* and the *Prince of Wales* in the Far East; nor, earlier, the punishment from the air British warships had taken off Crete.

To return to the summer of 1945: the Royal Navy's ships straddled the world. Altogether there were nigh on 800,000 men and 75,000 women in the service. Between them they operated fifteen battleships, fifty-two aircraft carriers, sixty-three cruisers, 257 destroyers, 542 escorts – frigates, sloops, corvettes – over 1,000 minesweepers, 137 submarines, 1,400 MTBs, inshore patrol boats and other small craft. There were 5,000 landing craft, backed with 430 supply, depot and repair ships. The Fleet Air Arm consisted of 1,300 aircraft in seventy squadrons.

Against the US Navy, though, this looked less than formidable. In the Pacific alone, the US Navy had twenty-three battleships, eighty-nine aircraft carriers and over 750 destroyers and escorts. It also operated 238 submarines. Whilst the Germans had come close to beating the Allies in the Atlantic, the Americans *had* beaten the Japanese at sea in the Pacific using submarines. By 1945 most Japanese shipping was being sunk in this way and the only vessels escaping were coastal junks.

Air power, too, had worn down the Japanese, pounding their defences; then final defeat with the dropping of the Atomic Bomb. In Europe, it had been manpower – not least the huge Red Army efforts in the east – which had forced the German Army back into its citadels, and thence to surrender.

The run-down of the mighty RN fleet of 1945 began almost as soon as the war ended. A Labour government had been elected, committed to the early return of British forces from across the world. Their equally early discovery that Britain was basically bankrupt, and that the Americans were asking for their money back, ensured a violent contraction of the forces. Hundreds of vessels were scrapped, hundreds more put into 'reserve'. Hundreds were sold or given to foreign navies all over the world. India, for example, benefited upon independence from a gift of RN ships. Closer to home the Dutch, the French and the Danes all were handed warships to help them start their navies anew.

Within a year 700 planned new vessels had also been cancelled. In fact, apart from the decision to complete the *Vanguard*, only two escorts, one submarine, two survey vessels and a few smaller ships were being built in 1946. Even at that stage concern was being expressed that Britain could not put up a credible naval force against anyone. There was an acute shortage of manpower. By 1948 the home fleet could muster one cruiser and four destroyers (these were to active service standard); in the rest of the world, it was said only seventy-four vessels were operational. The public were regaled with horror stories – especially over the lack of battleships. More serious, only four aircraft carriers, two of them used for training, were in commission.

Apart from cash, the Navy was in ferment over the role they might be expected to play. The loss of India in 1947 had thrown the whole basic strategy into doubt, for it had always been the defence of the sea-lanes between Britain and India which had been a primary role. All else followed: the bases of Gibraltar, Malta, Cyprus, Alexandria, Suez, Aden were now in jeopardy. The recognition that the Pacific Ocean had been lost to the USA was no longer in doubt. But elsewhere, too, there were threats. The Argentines – along with the Chileans – had begun to get very aggressive in the South Atlantic, landing on parts of the South Shetlands in 1949. The Navy was reduced to not much more than showing the flag.

Apart from incidents in the south, warships had been employed to stop Jews reaching Palestine, a task few relished. There were training exercises, there was a voyage into the Arctic Ocean by the carrier *Vengeance* to test clothing and equipment (a rare example of Admiralty prescience). There was, too, an immense clearing of mines and wrecks from the coasts and channels around Europe, although the mine-sweeping squadrons were drastically cut by 1949.

Innovations did occur. The first landing by a jet aircraft on an aircraft carrier was made by the Fleet Air Arm – a Vampire landed three consecutive times on the deck of the light carrier, *Ocean*. Soon, the British were to invent the angled deck, now standard on all but the smallest carriers, the steam catapult, and the mirror-landing system. More important, they were to pioneer the use of gas turbines in warships, although it was to be the 1970s before they were installed in all British warships of any size. There is no doubt that the Navy still felt itself to be the senior service in the post-war period. Although it might have contracted it was still the world's second largest navy, patrolling as of right, across the oceans. All that was to change in the next decade.

The three forms of naval warfare which now had principally to be addressed anew by the Royal Navy after 1945 were the aircraft carrier, the submarine and the mine. The latter was to be a popular weapon for the weaker, poorer powers – witness both Argentina and Iraq. Then, there was the Bomb – by 1950 still an atomic bomb, but shortly to become the thermo-nuclear (H-) bomb. Borne on its back, so to speak, would come ballistic and guided missiles.

Finally, there were geo-political realities. Mostly this came down to the retreat from the Empire and the economic costs of keeping warships on station all over the world, often in hugely costly bases (like Singapore). Of all this hodge-podge of change, the onset of nuclear weapons created the greatest crisis. As it became clear in the early 1950s that nuclear weapons were growing in power and numbers, so it seemed that navies might have no strategic future. One nuclear weapon dropped on or near the fleet would simple annihilate it.

The Americans had tested the effect of atomic weapons on ships at Bikini Atoll in the late 1940s. The British followed suit in the Montebello Island tests off the north-west coast of Australia. Their first A-bomb test actually placed the weapon inside HMS *Plym*, a *River*-class escort. The ship was vapourised. Other tests had ships bombarded by radiation to see how much penetrated armour. As a result ships were fitted with 'citadel' sealed superstructures and high-power wash-down sprinklers, once the sealing had been applied. None of this really helped, in so far as the basic premise remained true: an atomic weapon exploding within a few miles of any ship would overwhelm it with blast or the subsequent tidal wave, even if the radiation could be washed off. As a result, the Royal Navy went through a phase, in its core planning, of theorising over 'broken-backed' warfare. Put bluntly, this meant warships would be scattered well away from the land if a major conflict broke out. In the aftermath of a nuclear exchange, they would return to deal with enemy ships which tried to land invasion forces, or to escort friendly convoys.

Few dared ask what these ships would be defending on land; or how the convoys would unload radioactive cargoes onto radioactive docksides – were any of the latter still to exist. All in all, it was a depressing scenario and the Navy hated it. Outside of strategic considerations the Navy had to come to terms with the tactical realities. Many were not to become 'real' until the Empire, and its requirements, faded. The mine-countermeasure ships were a decade away in the early 1950s, as were modern anti-submarine specialist frigates. Anti-submarine warfare was one of the central concerns, though. There were many conversions of wartime destroyers to the new role; new weapons – Hedgehog, Squid, Limbo – and newer asdic systems (renamed sonar) for detection, all came into play. The helicopter, as an anti-submarine detection and weapons platform, was mooted.

Right up until the 1970s the Royal Navy had never been happy with submarines, other than as a necessary addition to a balanced fleet. Like the mine, their use had been considered un-British and unfair. Although there were highly successful British submarine sorties in the Second World War, perhaps the only ones which gained public acceptance were the X-craft and one-man human torpedoes; guts against guns.

Post-war development of British submarines was hampered, too, by some dreadful accidents: the *Truculent*, and the worst, the *Affray*. The *Truculent* was rammed at night in the Thames estuary by a Swedish ship; she sank in minutes and those who managed to get away died of exposure in the strong tides. The *Affray* simply disappeared in the Channel, whilst on a routine exercise. Only with the onset of the nuclear-powered submarine did Britain's Navy take, still reluctantly, to the deep.

It was with the aircraft carrier that the Navy experimented most at that time. Aircraft carriers had become the single most powerful projectors of naval power. In 1950, just before the Korean War broke out in June, Britain still had nine, with three in reserve. The fleet then still consisted of twenty-six cruisers, those archetypal warships of Empire. Although India had gone, the bases remained and the Navy expected to take part in action in any theatre. The Korean War was no exception. The War led to a Labour goverment decision to re-arm, continued by the Conservatives when they came to power. It was a turning point because it committed Britain to maintain a worldwide stance, not ended until the 1970s.

The Navy played a large role in the war. Its ships used to bombard the coast, its aircraft to bomb the Communists. Navy ships supplied troops on shore, landed them, evacuated them, entertained them, treated them on hospital ships. Aircraft carriers proved their worth once more. Casualties – for the Navy – were few. The War demonstrated a pattern to be repeated: the use of naval forces in an off-shore role, either in a large-scale conflict, or in what came to be known as 'brush-fire' wars. Outside of the Armageddon of nuclear war, post-war navies had found one of their purposes.

The two other major tests of the Royal Navy – before 1991 – were both to be amphibious task-force-led invasions. Meanwhile, it carried on as it had for centuries, in a global posture, expecting and intending to be wherever it might be needed. Because the roles of the Navy have contracted so much, it is worth taking a snap-shot portrait of just what it was doing. If I pick 1949, rather than 1950, it is not just because of the Korean War messing up the picture. There was, in 1949, one of those quintessentially Royal Naval moments, the dash down the Yangtsze by the *Amethyst*. The year is significant for other reasons: the Western European Union – in which Britain took part – was to lead directly to Nato and the acceptance that the Navy would play a part in a multi-national force defending European shores. It saw, too, the first explosion by the Soviet Union of an atomic weapon; and the loss of China to the Communists.

In February 1949, the cruiser *Sheffield* took a party of British troops to land in Belize following a threat by Guatemala to seize the territory (the British still defend Belize from the same threat). In Malaya a growing emergency – caused by Communist guerrillas – meant warships bombarding the coast. In Antarctica, following trouble with Argentina and Chile, a British warship – the frigate *Sparrow* – on general duty got temporarily trapped in ice in the South Shetlands. At home the Soviet Union returned, belatedly, the battleship *Royal Sovereign*, lent to them in the War. It was by all accounts in a terrible state; rusting live shells had been abandoned in the breeches of some of the guns.

The Navy were now experimenting with replenishment at sea, as they were with gas turbines in small, fast patrol ships. New methods of escape from sunk submarines were being tested. Three MTBs made a 3,000-mile voyage around ports in north Norway. The Navy tried out its first jet aircraft, the *Attacker*. Meanwhile four piston-engined Sea Furies flew 1,300 miles non stop from Britain to Malta in three hours.

Flogging was still a possible punishment in 1949, but Prize Money for ships seized had been ended four years earlier. Conscription had been extended to eighteen months; sailors going ashore were forced to wear uniforms at all times. At sea they still slept in hammocks in often poorly ventilated spaces.

But *the* naval event of 1949 in popular imagination was the escape of the *Amethyst* down the Yangtsze. The situation in China had been deteriorating; the Communists were on the verge of winning. For months a guardship had been on station in Nanking, protecting the British embassy and the local British business community; this, even though the city was 200 miles from the sea up the immense Yangtsze river.

In April the *Amethyst*, a *Black Swan*-class sloop, was ordered up the river to relieve the destroyer *Consort*. When still sixty miles from Nanking the ship was fired upon and severely damaged, running aground in the process. In all, seventeen officers and ratings were killed, another ten injured, two of whom, including her captain, died. The *Consort* came down river to try to help and suffered damage with nine killed and three wounded. The day after that the cruiser *London* and the *Black Swan*, *Amethyst*'s sister ship, tried to get up river; they too were forced back with a further fifteen killed and twenty-two injured.

After a pause, sixty-three of *Amethyst*'s crew were evacuated by flying boat; the ship, meanwhile, had been re-floated. Shortly after, the Assistant British Naval Attaché, Lt Cmdr Kerans, arrived from Nanking to take charge. He began a lengthy but futile attempt to negotiate the ship's passage with the Communists. Food and fuel was running out.

On 7 July Kerans signalled in clear (all the code books had been destroyed) to his Commander-in-Chief asking what to do 'if there was a typhoon'. Suspecting his intentions, Admiral Sir Patrick Brind replied 'make an offing and get sea-room'. On 30 July the *Amethyst* slipped her cable and followed behind a local steamer in the dark, when the river was running high. A gunboat fired on her and was sunk; she remained under attack for three hours from shore batteries; she also had to run through a boom across the river.

Five hours after leaving she signalled she was a hundred miles down-river; two and a half hours after that and she signalled: 'Have rejoined the fleet. No damage or casualties. God save the King.' Kerans received an immediate DSO and the ship and crew were given a huge public reception on their return to Britain. The general public loved it; Nelson lived, the Navy had put some polish on a tarnished and fading image. The real message was missed in all the excitement: the Navy had run away from China, no further gunboats were sent to deal with the Communists. The truth was we had celebrated another retreat, a defeat. This time, there would be no triumphant return.

The Korean War ended in an uneasy truce in 1952. The Navy continued to do its jobs around the world. Increasingly, these were supporting the troops dealing with the local emergency, wherever it might be, clashes between the servants of Empire and the apostles of Communism or, as it frequently turned out, the more lasting and penetrating passion of nationalism. There was to be much bloodshed and many clashes as the British painfully held on to, then detached themselves from, their old colonies.

Egypt was a special case; the Suez Canal had a value in British eyes that transcended anything physical, anything directly related to economics, or even politics. The Canal was the artery to and from the heart of the old Britain, the old ways. The fear of its sclerosis under Arab rule sent a coronary shock through the nation.

The Egyptian government had abrogated a Treaty they had made with Britain in 1951, following British rejection of the demands that British troops should leave the Canal Zone. As a result the Mediterranean fleet sailed. Warships arrived at Port Said to take over from striking local workers. The Navy took over the running of the Canal. To begin with, the cruiser *Gambia* acted as the guardship and 'office'; later she was relieved by the cruiser *Liverpool*. By the end of 1951 the Navy had overseen 2,600 merchant ships passing through the Canal. The Navy stayed on until the last British troops were withdrawn from the Canal Zone, in 1956.

Shortly after that withdrawal, on 26 July, Nasser nationalised it. Much muddy water, which might have come from the Canal itself, then obscured events. France and Britain signed a secret pact with Israel, sabres were much rattled in public about freedom of navigation. Thereafter events moved, much as in the Gulf crisis of 1990, with a sedate but deadly pace. Ships were requisitioned, warships were brought out of reserve, the task force – a joint Anglo–French one – was assembled. By the last week in August the twenty-three ships of the British Mediterranean fleet had been reinforced by the carrier *Bulwark* (joining the *Eagle*), landing and depot ships. Further carriers (*Theseus*, and *Ocean*) had brought troops from home to Cyprus; in September, the *Albion*, another carrier, left home waters for the Mediterranean.

The Israelis attacked – as the task force knew they would – at the end of October. The British and the French governments then called for the two parties to separate and, using this excuse, invaded Egypt and the Canal Zone. Losses, considering the size of the operation, were slight. It was to no avail. The Americans threatened to pull the plug in the international markets on their support for sterling. Britain, the old lion, was tamed. It was a brave last imperial cast; the dice were loaded, however.

In all, 105 warships and auxiliaries (bigger than the entire 1990

RN ocean-going fleet, incidentally), 20,500 officers and men and fourteen squadrons of the Fleet Air Arm, along with fifty merchant ships, took part. After the cease fire the Navy was involved in clearing away the wreckage from the Canal; the Egyptians had sunk numerous ships in the Canal itself, and at the entrances – twenty-one in Port Said alone. Flotsam and jetsam from the Suez Operation were to dog the British for decades. For many at home the result was a humiliation; finally, the Americans had shown who really was in charge. Some saw the American attitude as part of that same desire to see the British Empire destroyed, part and parcel with the ending of Lease-Lend, the Washington Naval Treaty, and beyond, back maybe to American resentment over the war of 1812, even some atavistic recall of 1776.

The British were becoming paranoid, now, seeing plots in every turn of the screw against them. The world, long our oyster, was giving the body politic food poisoning. The repercussions were felt at home in other ways, too. Never again could Britain plan for such a large-scale amphibious operation; for the most part, in the future, any major military moves were likely to be made with allies in Europe or Nato. There was another price to pay for Suez. The Soviet Union used it as an excuse to invade Hungary, then struggling to find its own freedom. In the early days of 1957 the British achieved another first: more self-deception, one might say. We exploded our first hydrogen bomb, off Christmas Island in the Pacific. It was to be followed by a White Paper which spelled out the theory of broken-backed warfare for the first time. But the real sting was that, for the first time, too, the Royal Navy was to have no part in the delivery of the exciting new weapon. Coming in the aftermath of Suez, many saw this as the end.

That view was reinforced when it was announced in the same year that the reserve fleet of 550 ships would largely be scrapped or sold; that the Navy was to be reduced to 75,000 officers and men. All the cruisers then in commission were to go (the end of Empire, truly), and all the battleships in reserve. The three *Tiger*-class cruisers would be replaced by heavy destroyers of the *Daring* class. Costs had been soaring; ships were very expensive to build; even more expensive to maintain. They needed frequent re-fits; that natural requirement was made worse by the rapidly changing technology which could mean a ship being out of date before it entered the water.

Decision-taking in the armed services at planning level has never been that good; some would argue it has been continuously bad. Ship planners in the late '50s, though, were hampered by a failure in government to give a clear lead, along with an increasing desire to hold down costs. As we have seen, the concept of a post-holocaust Navy was not a very positive one. The truth was that the weasel of all-out thermo-nuclear war was hynotising the rabbits of government and those who advised it. For the first time in history one reason for having a government – to defend the people – was gone. Governments could only offer a hope that nuclear weapons would *deter* aggressors. If that failed, all failed.

British defence planners were in a dilemma here. Constantly exhorted to cut costs, it seemed that through nuclear weapons we could have a cheap alternative to the expensive and overmanned conventional forces. Lots of nuclear weapons could be made and stored all over Europe; thus they would deter, and very cheaply, too. The delivery of these weapons, other than the increasing number of short-range tactical weapons, would be by air, using the new guided missile technologies coming forward. Once Britain had decided not to go ahead with her own missile, the Blue Streak, only the USA could act as a source.

We opted for a stand-off weapon, Skybolt, to replace our aging V-bomber force, of Victors, Valiants and Vulcans. Skybolt was a crude early variant of what we now know as cruise missiles, except it was launched high in the stratosphere. Having once decided to buy it, the British government found to its horror that the Americans had decided to cancel its development in favour of the new submarine launchable ballistic missile, Polaris. At the threshold of the '60s, Britain found herself faced with the huge cost of developing her own credible delivery system for her nuclear bombs. What happened, of course, was that the Royal Navy found, at the moment of its potential demise, a new strengthened and permanent role, as the carrier of the British deterrent. We, too, were to have Polaris.

The Royal Navy's first nuclear-powered submarine, though, was not the carrier of ICBMs (intercontinental ballistic missiles). *Dreadnought* was launched (with an American reactor) on Trafalgar Day (21 October 1960 and her arrival signalled acceptance by the Admiralty that, henceforth, the real capital ship of the late twentieth century was to be the hunter-killer nuclear submarine, the SSN. These sinister black hulls, with no pennant number (so one can never know, just by casual observation, which is which), can stay at sea for months, submerged all the time. Their role is to sink other ships, more than probably enemy nuclear submarines carrying nuclear missiles. Their flexibility as a weapon system has developed over the past thirty years so that now they may be equipped with all manner of guided missile, not just torpedoes. The latest British SSNs have sub-Harpoon an anti-ship missile installed, for instance.

The sophistication of submarine warfare has increased beyond the point where most laymen or women can follow the debate. The key to it was the development of nuclear reactors small enough to fit into a submarine. The parallel development was of the submerged launch of missiles – starting with Polaris. A future naval battle could easily be fought entirely underwater. The nuclear submarines which followed *Dreadnought* became even faster underwater, and much more silent in running. The seabeds across the ocean gaps between Greenland and Iceland, and Iceland and Norway were laid with a highly secret – and probably nuclear-powered – system of electronic alarms, each of which gave Nato information about the passage, in and out, of Soviet submarines on their way to the Atlantic.

Those who have seen the recent film *The Hunt for Red October* will recall an American sailor listening to a sonar set and saying he thought he could detect a Soviet *Typhoon*-class SSBN (a ballistic missile submarine). That was no exaggeration; in fact, sonar systems can analyse individual submarine noises. Whales, shoals of fish, surface ships, almost anything can be picked up as sound, fed into computers and analysed.

Underwater navigation, using SINS (submarine inertial navigation systems), has become a science. Submarines carry sophisticated charts of the ocean bottom, its ridges and valleys and they use them as a Tornado fighter will use the terrain, hugging it, staying out of sight except when ready to attack. This hidden war game has been played across the North Atlantic and into the shoaling waters off the Kola Peninula, whence Soviet submarines once emerged. Passive arrays, that is sonar which emits no signal to betray its source, are towed by both surface and sub-surface ships, huge networks of sensors, miles long, towed behind the ship. Immense effort has gone into ensuring silent running so a submarine can track another without giving itself away.

Dreadnought, for the Royal Navy, was the beginning of this secret war. Sadly, for all of us, it has meant the complete disappearence of the real heart of naval power. The odd glimpse from the shore, perhaps, of one our submarines, the occasional sequence of shots on television; that is all.

When the *Conqueror* came home from the South Atlantic, having sunk the *General Belgrano*, it was a rare sighting, as she steamed to her Scottish base at Faslane. Equally, old controversy was stirred when she flew the 'Jolly Roger' from her 'sail', an old British submariner tradition but one which provoked distaste. We still cannot really accept these new and deadly battleships and their work, it seems.

Alongside the new SSNs of the 1960s, Britain invested in SSBNs (the ballistic missile submarines) and Polaris. This American weapon had been hastily substituted for the aborted Skybolt missile. Unlike Skybolt, Polaris had been successfully tested. It was a highly innovative weapon and increased its possessor's power for a second strike immeasurably. It was, in that sense, a 'war-winning' weapon. Britain argued strongly with the Americans for having these weapons. Prime Minister Harold Macmillan finally persuaded a reluctant John Kennedy. We got Polaris. At a stroke the Royal Navy moved back into the forefront of defence. At the same time, as became apparent only much later, having responsibility for running this country's only credible nuclear deterrent could also be a burden.

The débâcle of Suez, political more than military, forced a debate about the future role and structure of Britain's 'mobile' forces. The commitment to Nato meant much of the core of the armed forces was already spoken for; the remaining question was over our responsibilities for any possible operations 'out of area'. The decline of the Empire had, by 1960, become a rapid and often disorganised retreat, nearly a rout in places. Macmillan's 'wind of change' speech in Africa had merely flagged the inevitable in that unhappy continent; whatever the cost, the British were going to leave the natives to battle for their own patch.

In the Far East, after India, there was a growing realisation that we would sooner or later be leaving Malaya and Singapore. Hong Kong, of course, was under a lease and its future could be safely left for the time being. All this was leading to a conclusion about out-of-area military force: the fixed bases of the past, Cyprus, Aden, Singapore – even Malta – could not be relied upon. From now on, local politics would dictate whether we stayed or went.

The Navy's response was first of all to develop aircraft carriers for a mobile lift role, carrying troops and helicopters and all their equipment; next specialist ships, with command and control built in, for the same purpose. Thus it was that the carriers *Bulwark* and *Albion* converted to the commando-carrier role; then, that the assault ships *Intrepid* and *Fearless* were laid down. The role of the fixed-wing aircraft carrier was also in doubt. Largely from a cost and manpower point of view, these giants, like *Eagle* and *Victorious*, did provide that huge projection of power that had been classic naval theory. Plans were made to build a new carrier (coded AVA01), the first that would be laid down since before the end of the war.

In 1964, however, a Labour government was elected. Many of its senior cabinet members had served in the Labour governments of 1945–51, albeit as junior ministers. They were afflicted with visions of finally putting an end to 'colonialism'. It was the economy, though, that remained their central worry; its decline had now become steep. The public began to hear more and more about the export 'gap'. By 1967, when this Labour government had been re-elected, Britains' economy was in a dire condition. Cuts, in all government departments, were the order of the day. Defence was an obvious choice. The recent Malaysian 'confrontation' with Indonesia, in which naval forces had played an important supporting role, had died down. Plans were advanced for us finally to leave Aden.

Then the government announced, early in 1968, that after 1971 there would be complete withdrawal 'east of Suez'. Only in Hong Kong would our Far East military presence be felt. Almost as an afterthought they announced there would be no new carrier. The end of fixed-wing naval aviation was now in sight. The Singapore Prime Minister, Lee Kuan Yew, managed to get the east of Suez withdrawal postponed until after the last possible date for a British general election; dismay at the decision, in both Singapore and Malaysia, was considerable. This was the time when a Communist threat, through Vietnam, Laos and Cambodia, was perceived by many of the smaller countries in the region as their biggest headache. And by the late 1960s the more perceptive analysts could already see that the battle for Vietnam was being slowly lost.

As part of the re-alignment a final retreat back from the Far East entailed, the Royal Navy now found itself having to concentrate far more on its role within Nato. This created enormous headaches – and much heart-searching. The Navy had been told, in effect, that its global role was at an end and that, henceforth, it was to act as a glorified coastal force with concentration on anti-submarine and anti-mine warfare.

Even the possession of the nuclear deterrent did not help as it was clear that this specialist task was very separate from 'normal' naval duties. Worst of all, the cost of Polaris was still borne on the Navy Estimates; the RN was having to pay for the nation's last-ditch defence and, although, as Defence Ministers have never tired of stressing, the deterrent is relatively 'cheap', it built in a distortion to all the figures – and all the planning.

In the gloomiest picture, it became obvious that the Navy might in the not too distant future end up with a small number of corvettes and mine-hunters, the four Polaris SSBNs constituting a parallel but distinct force. There came, then, by the late 1960s, a period in which the Navy was being wrenched from its traditional goals and purposes and forced to think in an entirely different way. The glories of the Grand Fleet were far away; as was the long and valiant history of keeping the sea-lanes free for British and other merchant ships. No longer was there any purpose in having cruisers, those archetypal protectors of colonies abroad; the frigate, as a long-range outlier, checking for hostile action, was now to hunt for submarines in the cold waters off Iceland and Greenland.

The carriers had no place, neither did their protective screen of destroyer-escorts. Horizons had shrunk: recruitment would change as potential matelots could not be tempted with 'join the Navy and see the world'. Now, only the grey waters of the North Atlantic, the freezing ice-laden seas around North Cape were on offer. Trips to the exotic Far East and the Caribbean were to be replaced with sojourns in Hamburg or Narvik. Harsher realities than even these emerged. The 'new' Royal Navy, minus its carriers, would be smaller than the French whose fleet was still developing new weapons. The RN, by contrast, had just cancelled a tactical anti-ship missile programme. Once the aircraft had gone, no medium-or long-range anti-ship capability was available.

The reduction in fleet size meant that ships would have to be longer at sea; crudely, they would wear out more quickly and maintenance time would increase, another burden on over-stretched crews. Then came news that even the nuclear SSN fleet was being scrutinised for possible cuts. All of this meant redundancies ashore, especially in ship-building, but also in the Navy yards and shore bases. It was a gloomy prospect.

Times have changed so drastically it is worth recalling that the decline of the Royal Navy in absolute numbers, in the late 1960s and 1970s, had to set against the rise and rise of the Soviet Navy, in the 1960s seeking out a global role – much of it based on a Soviet version of Mahan. The Royal Navy had to watch this massive increase in surface ships, as well as the submarine fleet, and to contemplate what it would be like trying to assist convoys across the Atlantic in the event of a European war, with very few escorts indeed. No amount of theorising about efficiency of weapons systems could disguise the fundamental fact that the Soviet submarine fleet alone had vastly more vessels than the Germans had calculated they needed in order to destroy the British economy.

The fall of the RN as a world fleet 1951–1981.

	1951:	1961:	1971:	1981:
Battleships:	5	–	–	–
Carriers:	12	9	5	2
Cruisers:	26	10	3	–
Destroyers:	111	52	12	14
Frigates:	162	98	65	37
Submarines:	56	53	36	22
Minesweepers:	63	203	58	34
Minelayers:	3	3	–	–

Some numbers are approximate.

The end of 1970 saw a Conservative government in power in Britain, led by Ted Heath. It was determined to get us into the EEC; determined to get British industry fighting fit, at whatever cost. In naval defence it reversed the Labour government plan to withdraw from east of Suez. And it reversed the decision to end fixed-wing naval flying, although, in the event, only the carrier *Ark Royal* was kept on. The last of the Polaris submarines, *Revenge*, was launched in 1970; plans were well under way to build a new kind of warship. These had been dubbed 'through-deck cruisers' when first mooted so as to fool Labour politicians into not realising they were light-aircraft carriers, capable of flying vertical take-off Harriers. In the event another invention, eventually accepted by a very reluctant Admiralty, the ski-jump, meant Sea Harriers would be able to operate more easily from these ships, principally designed to operate helicopters. In the short-term it ensured continuity of purpose, although the primary role of the *Invincible* class was anti-submarine warfare. Once again, though, these plans were thrown in jeopardy by the incoming Labour government of 1974. Withdrawal from Singapore was then taking place, as it was from Simonstown, the old naval base in South Africa.

Simonstown 'covered' the South Atlantic – and Antarctica. It also covered the Falkland Islands, all then perceived with indifference from London. Events were to change that – not least the realisation that in a world running out of oil, minerals and fish this vast area was almost entirely unexploited, and available. Both Argentina and Chile had already seen the potential. The miners' strike and the three-day week of 1973–4 came – and the Conservative government of Mr Heath went. The Labour governments which followed only wished to cut defence as far as possible to aid the ailing economy. This gloomy record, stuck in a seemingly endless groove of decline had by the mid-70s reached its nadir. Britain, just inside the protection of the EEC, was in a mess.

The Labour Defence Review of 1976 planned for no warships to remain in the Mediterranean, for a cut of one seventh in destroyers, frigates and mine counter-measure vessels. There were going to be no replacement for the commando carriers, or the two assault ships. Once again, the credibility of the Royal Navy as other than a glorified coastal force was being challenged. When the Conservatives were re-elected, in 1979, navalists might have sighed with relief. The Conservative Party, while not totally consistent, has tended to back a bigger, rather than smaller, Navy. If that were true of the past it was not going to be true any more.

In 1981 John Nott, a name as vilified as any in the Navy's own lexicon of hate figures, announced in his Defence Review that he was planning to cut the Navy again. Both the assault ships would go, as would one of the *Invincible* carriers. *Hermes*, last of the commando carriers, was to be sold (to India). Chatham Dockyard was to close, Portsmouth run down. The number of destroyers and escorts was to be levelled off at 'around fifty'. The cost of the new Trident missile submarines (the replacements for Polaris) meant a new class of diesel patrol submarines, the first planned for decades, would be scrapped. Almost as a footnote, the Review noted that the ice-patrol ship *Endurance* would also not be replaced when she came to end of her life in a few years. Far away, in Buenos Aires, heads came up, dark thoughts began to be spoken aloud.

Analysts in Britain looked at the proposals less emotionally than Keith Speed, the Navy Minister, who resigned over the matter. The plans outlined the future for the Royal Navy, as an anti-submarine force inside Nato. One major group, ASW2, consisting of one carrier and fourteen escorts, would deploy to the north, in a war with the Soviets, to protect the planned landing on the Kola Peninsula (to prevent a Soviet thrust through Norway). This was part of a new concept of forward defence, aimed at de-stabilising Soviet intentions by taking part of the war close to their submarine bases around Murmansk.

Because Nott intended to scrap the assault ships, the Royal Marines and others, to be sent north, would have to travel in requisitioned North-Sea ferries. This caused much derision. Other ships of the Royal Navy were to protect the North Atlantic convoys; one group, of a carrier and four escorts, would seek out Soviet submarines; the other, of four to six escorts, would be the convoy supports. There would be elements of the Dutch, German, Belgium and French navies but their combined strength, even if all could be used, would hardly match the opposition. It all looked horribly bleak. Once again the carrier force, such as would be left after 1986, was to be primarily an anti-submarine force. Even this was problematic for other, largely technical, reasons.

As we have all seen in the movies, the early form of anti-submarine warfare was conducted by asdic 'pinging'. A sound was bounced off a submarine, its return recorded. A convoy escort would home in, drop depth charges and wait. But when aircraft joined the hunt, everything was transformed. Submarines had to surface; when they did they could be easily located and sunk from the air. Underwater technology went on getting better. Helicopters could, by the 1980s, 'dunk' sonar in the water, pick up a submarine and then drop homing torpedoes. The command and control systems available to the humble escort, now designated ASW frigate, were highly sophisticated – and increasingly heavy.

The 'top hamper' of modern warships is the characteristic most recognisable. Instead of sleek low-slung grey shapes, today's warships have become ugly boxes sticking high above the water, festooned with huge radars and oddly shaped domes. All of this has meant an enormous weight penalty and, far worse, the lifting of a ships' centre of gravity high in the hull. At the same time, the introduction of gas turbines has reduced the weight of engines, and their associated fuel-oil (kept in the bottom of the hull). The loss of armour, the removal of heavy guns and their ammunition has all forced the centre of gravity higher and higher. Big warship radar antenna can weigh forty tons; positioned fifty feet up, when a big sea is running (as in the North Atlantic in winter) and serious stability problems arise.

The weight of modern equipment alone could do damage. The old Second World War cruiser, *Swiftsure*, was three and a half million pounds and several years into a re-fit when it was found her frames were buckling under the weight of the new structures and equipment.

She was scrapped as a result, in 1960. There have been persistent reports that Type 21 frigates have suffered from buckling problems in the hull at high speed in heavy seas.

To traditionalists something else was wrong, too. These modern ships lacked fire-power, much of it sacrificed in the search for a balance between tracking an enemy and shooting at him. They looked at Soviet ships, armed to the gunwales and then compared them with British ships. It did not add up. An argument developed that if shorter, fatter ships were built, their stability would be assured and their ability to carry more arms guaranteed. This argument was countered by the hydrodynamic fact that length gives speed through the water. To make a ship go faster, apart from giving her bigger engines, you have to lengthen that part of the hull in the water.

Two opposing camps of navalists and strategists, quite a few of them armchair based, grew out of these arguments. There arose what came to be known as the short-fat lobby. They made the fairly devastating point that RN frigates and destroyers in the 1980s were the same length as they had been in the First World War; they travelled no faster, despite their hugely enhanced engine power, but they lacked good old-fashioned guns. The argument also raged over numbers. Short-fat lobbyists believed the British should build dozens of their design, to act as the Nato equivalent of the old Second World War corvettes; their sole purpose to kill submarines. The frigates being built by the Navy, they argued, were hugely costly, and served little purpose if they were opposing an enemy relying on numbers.

Eventually, the Admiralty caved in, commissioning a report on the merits of their designs versus the short-fat designs. It concluded long and thin was best. This did not quell the short-fat lobby who argued that the questions asked by the panel had been the wrong ones. The Navy went on designing – and building – long ships. All was to be put in abeyance, though, by the Falklands War.

If one of the triggers that set General Galtieri off on his quest to liberate the Malvinas was the knowledge that the British were scrapping the *Endurance* one of the others was the 'invasion' of South Georgia by the scrap metal merchants in the early part of 1982. That this party had been landed from Argentine warships, that it had all happened before (just after the Second World War, as we have seen); that, indeed, the Argentine press were portraying it all as the beginning of the campaign for the Falklands, was missed. This is not a book about the Falklands War; the details leading up to it, and the overall military campaign have been well documented elsewhere. The part played by the Navy in all the weeks of preparation and fighting is what we have to examine.

It was, from the start, a naval 'show'; only the Navy could get the troops to the South Atlantic; only they could provide the cover for an invasion. Their aircraft would clear the skies of Argentines; their ships would maintain the supply link. To begin with, all went well – better even than many expected. The Navy was stretched but not desperately so. The Task Force had two carriers, a fair number of escorts, a huge fleet train. There were at least two nuclear hunter-killer submarines on station; the Argentines were led to believe there were more. The Navy they faced was ill-equipped, largely a coastal force. There was the ex-British *Colossus* carrier, *Veinticinco de Mayo*, an ex-US heavy cruiser, the *General Belgrano*, a few modern destroyers and escorts, a few conventional submarines. It was the Air Force, equipped with the sea-skimming French anti-ship missile, Exocet, that posed the real threat.

First blood fell to the Royal Navy – or rather the Royal Marines – on South Georgia. The submarine *Santa Fe* was effectively sunk. Soon would come a much more controversial sinking, this time by a submarine: HMS *Conqueror* sank the *General Belgrano*. This caused great anguish in Britain: the 'fairness' issue. The *Belgrano*'s captain ought to have the final word, though:

> By no means do I have any feelings of anger ... I realised from the outset that the 200-mile limit [the Total Exclusion Zone] had nothing to do with the mission I had to accomplish ... it was all the same, in or out.[1]

The sinking started the naval war of attrition. The next day Argentine aircraft attacked the *Sheffield* with an Exocet; it later sank but not before demonstrating a number of faults in design. Aluminium, extensively used in modern warships, burned more quickly; bedding gave off toxic fumes (this had been known about years before and nothing had been done). Smoke, of which there was plenty from all kinds of sources, killed a lot of sailors. As the war continued other ships fell – all to aircraft bombs and missiles: *Coventry, Ardent, Antelope*, the container ship *Atlantic Conveyor*. Worse in a way were the near misses and damaged ships: *Antrim, Argonaut, Brilliant, Glamorgan, Glasgow, Plymouth, Sir Galahad* among the immediate naval forces, and the tanker *British Wye*. Other ships had close calls, some from Argentine submarine operations.

The Admiralty had planned its campaign to allow for the loss of at least one carrier and had negotiated an immediate replacement via the Americans, should that have happened. *Atlantic Conveyor* turned out to be the 'carrier': the pilot believed, as do many Argentines to this day, that it was *Invincible* that was sunk in that attack. The most worrying outcome for naval planners was the degree to which conventionally dropped 1,000-pound bombs could make their mark on the lightly armoured decks of modern warships. If the Argentines had corrected the fuses on these bombs most of the damaged ships would have moved to the sunk list. It might, just might, have encouraged the Argentine Air Force to keep going.

The lessons learned were applied: frigates and other ships got a close-in weapon system, like Phalanx, designed to shoot down incoming sea-skimming missiles. Lack of weapons, especially close-support, was now glaringly obvious: some seamen had taken to trying to shoot down incoming jets with machine-guns, mounted Heath Robinson style along the ships' rails. Re-design of interiors – replacement of cable sheaths so they would not give off fumes, the mass provisioning of smoke hoods, the removal of formica table tops, which could let fly lethal splinters – went ahead because of what happened 8,000 miles away. Far more important in the long run, the Navy had to re-assess its future out-of-area requirements, as did the government. Although some frigate and destroyer cuts were continued, the third aircraft carrier – *Illustrious* – was saved. The assault ships were, too, and now new plans are being drawn up for their replacement. It all proved necessary, eight years later as, once again, an out-of-area conflict flared in the Gulf. By then the Cold War had been declared officially dead, the Americans and the Soviets were in general agreement over the Gulf crisis, the Warsaw Pact had collapsed, Germany re-united. The world was seeking a new order for the new century. What was still clear was that navies would be playing a critical part in policing that order. Their futures had never been so certainly assured.

For Britain's Royal Navy, these global re-positionings cannot remove the doubt about its own long-term future. The Cold War was the principal justification for a long-range and relatively large deep-water fleet. Now all that has to be in doubt. The coming together of Europe and Britain's place within the growing federalism of the twelve lends weight to a view that the Navy is likely, by the year 2000, to be a largely coastal force, more gunboats than aircraft carriers or frigates.

In 1992 public arguments – over whether forty escort ships were in truth available at any one time – had died down a little but the central question – what are these for – had not yet been fully addressed. Meanwhile, there were innovations, one in the unlikely shape of the Wrens. The decision to allow women a role at sea from 1990 gave back the RN a little of that rakish air it had so often forgotten since the War. It was an historic moment, too. The reason was a manpower shortage of a chronic kind. The Navy, that most traditional of the armed services, had joined the trend. What effect it would have, in the long run, was hard to predict. One event, however, demonstrates in good measure what a mixed crew are like in action. No one could have realised, when the decision was made, that within a few months of the first women starting service on a commissioned British warship, they would be off to war for real, in HMS *Brilliant*. That grey winter's day, 14 January 1991, as *Brilliant* left Plymouth Sound, marks a moment of great significance for the Royal Navy.

In the forty-five years since the end of the Second World War it had suffered a lot, changed a lot. Weapons were different, ships were altered beyond dreams, the nature of war had changed. And yet it was still the same war, for the sea does not change. Now women were to join that ancient battle. The Royal Navy, though, was a victim not of its failures – or even in some cases successes – but of the huge changes that had been taking place in British economic and political life. The Navy followed trade – as it had in the beginning. The two world wars had destroyed the old British economy, at home and abroad. Like the merchant ships, the 'Grey Funnel Line' had to grow smaller. But compared with the merchant fleet, the Navy had managed to hang onto a remarkably large tonnage, still a world Navy, still among the biggest.

13

VOYAGES

'O farther, farther, farther sail ...'
Walt Whitman, *A Passage to India*

This story of Britain and the sea could not be complete without experiencing something of today's ships and the men who work them. What follow are three sketches of the merchant navy. There are great contrasts in these tales but they demonstrate something of what has been left.

The last is a lament of a kind – for a way of life that will not come again – but I hope the overall tenor is upbeat. Seafarers always make the best of their lot; and we should give thanks that they do for otherwise little of the goods and services we take for granted would have come to us.

The container revolution: *Peninsula Bay*

Alongside berth 205 in Southampton's container port sits a ship of a size similar to the *Queen Mary*: she is 900 feet long, 100 feet wide and when fully loaded she draws forty feet. She is not, however, a particularly pretty sight, with a huge elongated bulb where the bow enters the water, ugly squared-off flaring above and then hundreds of feet of flat plating. Her stern is huge but also squared off. The superstructure is near the stern, rising steeply to a functional single funnel.

None of this is what catches the eye first of all. Most of her lines – including her superstructure – are dwarfed by what she carries, loaded up to five high on deck, before and aft of that funnel: 'boxes', up to 3,800 of them. *Peninsula Bay* is a 'boxboat' – one of the very newest, third-generation, container ships. A P&O liner, she carries an all-British crew; nonetheless, she is registered in the Bahamas, another victim of the cost of British registration. This, it might be added, in

spite the desire of P&O's chairman to get the British shipping register
in better shape.

Peninsula Bay is in Southampton to unload and load, more or less
at the same time. The container revolution is never more apparent
than in this extraordinary sequence of events. First, one is struck by
how few people are involved. The ship is unloaded and loaded in an
eerie silence hardly punctuated by human voice. Huge container
cranes loom over her decks and deck cargo. Boxes suddenly appear
out of the hold, swing high, then back, and drop onto the quay. A
straddle carrier (made in Finland) appears from the acres of desolate
storage, plops over the container, lifts it and is gone.

A sudden squeal, somewhere in the vast deck spaces; another box
is proving a little harder to lift but it hardly stops the rhythm of crane
and container. It goes on all the time, day and night, until the ship is
ready to leave. She came in at 18.00 hrs the night before; she will
leave at 05.00 hrs tomorrow – for Le Havre. Thereafter, in a rapid
sequence, she will go on to Rotterdam, then Hamburg. After that,
having discharged her cargo from the Far East and reloaded with a
new set of containers, she sails for Suez, thence Jeddah, Singapore
and Japan. Nine weeks from Southampton to Southampton.

To do this she will maintain a steady speed of around 19 knots
(she can go at 23 knots, flat out). Hidden inside that superstructure
is a single huge marine diesel engine of nine cylinders. It turns a single
huge propellor at eighty-nine revolutions per minute (flat out). On
the shaft is a generator: it can develop two million watts of electricity
for the ship. Otherwise auxiliary generators do the work. Ships of
this size make enough power to light a small town. Some is needed
to help the ship steer herself, some for lights and heat. Some is needed
for the immensely complex communications equipment which keeps
her in touch with ports all over the world, should her officers desire.
More can be used to keep the refrigerated boxes cool. *Peninsula Bay*
has no dedicated refrigerated holds; individual containers now have
their own built-in compressors; once loaded, they are simply plugged
into the ship's power supply.

Boxes have to be loaded according to a plan which takes account
of stability – which means every box has to be weighed and then
placed accordingly. In the ship's office a computer screen tells the
mate exactly where each box is, what it weighs and where it is going.
This is necessary for loading and unloading, to prevent, if possible,
restowage. But, today, he is checking the ship's stability using a
programme out of the same computer. He devises the almost

inconceivable situation of a thirty degree roll in a period of sixteen seconds. The programme winks back: the ship would recover. The same system also tells the mate how much extra lashing he needs for each deck-stowed box, to ensure that in storm conditions no container would be torn free. In all the years they have operated container ships, P&O have lost almost no containers.

The ship's office is opposite the engine control room; both are on the main deck. The engine runs itself; there is no need to have a control room deep in the ship. Here, the room is accessible to the whole ship. It needs to be because the most startling thing about the *Peninsula Bay* is her crewing: just twenty. The latest cut – of the catering officer – has reduced her complement by one more. He is retiring, after forty-two years at sea. 'On my first ship,' he notes, 'we had sixty-five Chinese stokers; now look at what there is. We even had five Chinese running the laundry.'

But he adds that delivering food to the engine room mess meant that everything was covered with a fine layer of coal dust. Stokers have gone, so have specialised 'greasers'; the ratings on this ship are general purpose, expected to work on deck or in the engine room. But then there are only five seamen for the whole ship. On the bridge there are four officers, including the master, one radio operator. Four engineering officers run the power systems; an electrical officer assists. There are now just two stewards, one cook. Next year the radio operator will no longer be a legal requirement when the new world-wide GPS satellite emergency service comes into force. It will identify any ship in the system, worldwide, much as aircraft are identified now, by an electronically transmitted code.

A group of officers – with the ship in Southampton it is crew change-over day – discuss these changes. One wonders whether there will be a job for a navigating officer soon (second mate). Electronic systems are constantly improving – as a glance around the bridge will testify. But the main concern is over uniforms. That age-old status issue still manages to employ much of the discussion time, even as the ship discharges and loads around them. If anything illustrated the traditionalism – the concern, albeit subdued now, with hierarchy – here it still was.

Boiler-suited officers (for port working) wondered whether their current master would insist on their wearing reefer jackets or whether the increasingly ubiquitous blue Navy-style pullover would be accept-able. All with the requisite epaulettes in place. This is in a ship with more officers than men (twelve to eight). It is, of course, facile to dismiss their concern. Underlying this talk was a deeper worry that with the continuing erosion of numbers, jobs, not status, were at stake. Nevertheless, the removal of the catering officer meant more paperwork for the officers – and less service.

And although the cost of one man (£20,000 a year, maybe) has to be set against the cost of each transit of the Suez Canal (costing the *Bay* a staggering $215,000 a time), men can be sacked; the Egyptian government cannot.

Peninsula Bay was built in Japan; her engine is German (Sultzer). She carries a lot of British equipment, of course, on the bridge, on deck as fire-fighting kit. She is the state of the art: huge, impressive, efficient. But she is, as I have suggested, a warehouse on the move, her design by computer programmes ennabling her to maximise her speed under minimal fuel consumption. Her crew quarters are luxurious – hotel suites for everyone, including the wives she carries each trip. There are not many berths, though.

Each time she closes a coast maintenance workers may board to begin their tasks, all aimed at preventing, for even one hour, her delay. She is a self-contained world, and because of that she is cold, inhuman even. Her lines might be appreciated by Brunel for what they have achieved; no nineteenth-century painter would wish to linger with his brush over her. Her lifting capacity is 40,000 tons, five to eight times what an old general cargo ship could manage. Her real power is in the rate of discharge and load; for a week or a fortnight, substitute thirty-six hours. Hard though it is to judge, she is probably 'worth' as many as twenty to twenty-five of those old ships. That is one reason you see so few, these days.

It had to happen; that does not make it any less sad. The container port is sterile because it is so efficient; that quality makes it lifeless, barren. Swarms of dockers may have been a nightmare of a different kind but they provided a human touch. The old cargo ships swarmed with crew, rigging derricks, checking valuable or fragile goods were safe. Now it is all hidden in those endless lines of anonymous boxes.

If one wishes to find why the heart has gone out of seafaring, this is where to look. I cannot condemn it; like the weather, like the sea, it is what it is. Shipping is the most advanced of transports: and here it has been realised. We all want exotic fruits twelve months a year, exotic meats, Japanese stereos, cars, computers. That is how it all started, sea transport, bringing the first spices, the first silk and Damasks, the first Cognac.

We all willed this. Late twentieth-century consumer society created the container ship, the huge ULCC – ultralarge crude carrier – ro-ro and bulker; because we wanted the things they bear, in greater number, with greater ease. What made the *Peninsula Bay* was the unstoppable logic of progress. But as a sage once pointed out, progress means going forward; who ever said that would necessarily lead to a better way of doing things?

Mucking out: *Consortium I*

Down in the wasted docklands that was once Liverpool's pride is a sewage works, as yet incomplete. Whilst it is still being built *Consortium I* will have a role for she takes out, day and night, the sewage sludge of Liverpool and Manchester, to dump it off the coast.

It is a 'trade' registered in the Port of Liverpool as an export: one and half million tons each year. 'Well,' says one of the *Consortium's* masters, 'you have to remember, it goes out but doesn't come back.'

North West Water used to own other ships; now they just have two, of which only *Consortium I* is in use. She was built by Ferguson Brothers in Glasgow, and left there in May 1972; her first 'cargo' was carried in July that year. Just under 300 feet long, and forty-six feet wide, she draws just under twenty feet when loaded.

Her dimensions were calculated so she could fit into the Manchester Ship Canal in which she and her crew had many adventures. Today, with six years to go before dumping becomes illegal, she works out of the Sandon Dock. To get into the River Mersey she has to pass through the old Canada Dock, past the Brocklebank, Alexander and Hornby Docks before swinging into Gladstone Dock which allows her out.

She has a complement of fourteen – a master, chief officer and first officer, chief, second and third engineer, cook, mess boy, leading hand and five seamen. They work a week on, a week off and *Consortium I* can work seven days a week depending on the demand for her services. Sludge dumping has been controversial for some time – in the Thames similar ships work up and down, dumping off Southend. The Mersey dumping ground is about fifteen miles off the coast in a tightly defined area.

Bridge monitors can determine if the ship has dumped where she should not; inspectors may come aboard at any time to check the system and the ship are being worked legally. The waste they dump is only 5 per cent solid matter but it is the quantity that bothers people: 3,000 tons a time. It takes only a short while to load and an

even shorter time to dump – around ten minutes. The tanks, of which
the ship has nine, empty by gravity. As the tanks discharge, the valves
on their tops turn in an eerie dance, squealing and squeaking. It is all
over before it has begun. Some sea-water ballast is allowed back in
to the wing tanks to ensure an even keel, the *Consortium I* swings
back on her normal east-to-west track, and we are headed toward
Liverpool again.

The crew make many jokes about their work, as you might expect.
The Port of Liverpool's motto 'Business in Great Waters' is the cause
of much merriment. 'You can't be proud when you're doing a job
like this', says one sailor. 'It's a dirty job but it has to be done,' laughs
another. Most have been deep-sea sailors at some time or another.
Like thousands of seafarers before them, they returned to the land
for a while, got bored, looked for a more regular sea-going post.
Some were attracted by the conditions of work. But all agree it is the
one week on, one week off aspect which is most attractive.

'We have been given the longest redundancy notices in history,' one
of the officers says. They have known for some years now that there
would be no work after the European convention on dumping sewage
waste was finally applied by the British government. They are unlikely
to lament it when it comes; most will be able to take early retirement.

The seamanship skills the older men learned in their youth still
apply here. Moving *Consortium I* in and out of the river is a tricky
job; fog, bad weather, strong tides and a shifting estuary mean they
must constantly be on their guard. Although the number of ships
using the approaches to the Mersey has fallen, there are enough to
make each journey out and back that bit different. A drilling rig has
arrived of late, a sign of the times. The huge Morecambe Bay gas
field will extend southwards and another part of our coast will look
like the Bay of Mexico.

The ship is fully fitted for life on board; like all working ships she
has a utilitarian air in her topsides. There are comforts but little in
the way of luxuries. She is spartan, spare, but still a beautiful artifact.
Meals are substantial, as is the way of ships: lots of mash, lots of
filling. The officers are served and eat separately from the crew. But
there is less of a hierarchy than would have been true years before.
'The best set of friends a man could hope to sail with,' says the master,
and he means it.

The ship swings into the Gladstone Dock; it is Saturday afternoon
and there will be no Sunday working this week. We have passed a
couple of fishing boats and one chemical carrier on our journey out

of what was Britain's second port for decades. A few men are fishing
off the dock; otherwise it is an empty scene we survey. Coming back
through the wasted docks to our berth, all that can be seen is twisted
metal, wrecked wharves, empty berths. Life has moved on; *Consortium* moves in a world of her own, untroubled by the mundane
work she has to do, for there are no ships here on more exotic runs.

Yet it would be a profound mistake to see this ship, her company,
in anyway a less important part of our story, doing a lesser job. Ships
will go where they must; *Consortium I* is just a small but still necessary
element in the bigger picture. She is on the British register and she
has an all-British crew. Those facts alone make her special in the
1990s.

The last lightship: *Patricia* and *No. 23*

The English Channel is never still; even when it looks calm, an
underlying swell, or the notorious short-wave chop, gives it a labile
quality that has turned many a hardened seafarer's stomach.

It is the busiest stretch of open water in the world. Hundreds of
ships use it every day and after an horrific series of collisions in the
early '70s, which showed that many ships were not keeping bridge
watches, or only minimally, separation lanes were introduced.

These are enforcable by international law and they are springing
up all over the world's seaways to try to enforce some order to what
would otherwise be dangerous chaos.

The Channel light vessel, in June 1989, was the last manned
lightship in Britain and she marked the western end of the lanes which
run up the narrowing Channel to the Dover Straits. In that month,
the last of the old lightship keepers were taken off, ending a maritime
tradition of many years.

Her vague familiarity to millions of land-lubbers stems from her
daily place in the shipping forecasts. Light vessels have numbers, not
names. *No. 23* was the vessel on station in that warm June day; *No.
19* was her automatic replacement. Like lighthouses, lightships have
increasingly been re-supplied by helicopter.

But to tow in a lightship needs another ship. Trinity House still
keeps a couple of large ships to maintain buoys and to do other
important supply and maintenance work. For the task of overseeing
the change-over, one of these, the *Patricia*, was detailed to tow in *No.
19*; *No. 23* would be towed away afterwards by a commercial tug.

The master of *Patricia* for this trip was Richard Woodman, he of the *Voyage East* I have quoted and of the Nathaniel Drinkwater novels. Like many of the Trinity House marine staff he was sadder than he let on that this trip was the last of its kind.

Trinity House's main depot in the south is located in Harwich, that rather seedy east-coast town, now faced across the river by the space-age container terminal of Felixstowe. It is a neat illustration of much of what I have discussed. Before the war, and for a long while after, Harwich, in the shape of Parkestone Quay, was the glamourous gateway to Holland and other more distant continental ports.

But the rise and rise of Felixstowe, whose explosive growth depended on being outside the old Dock Labour Scheme, has eclipsed the older town. While Parkestone Quay still hums with activity, while ferries still come and go, Felixstowe looks like the future.

The Trinity House quay is at the very end of the land. Just offshore, in neat rows, are dozens of light vessels awaiting allocation, being repaired or revised in some way. Here they look dinky, bright red paint giving them a quality of gaiety their working life denies them.

At sea, their locations, which they wear like badges on their sides, speak a rare language, delineating the British coastline by its shoals and underwater banks: Dowsing, Galloper, Inner and Outer Gabbard, the Sunk and the Goodwins and the most exposed of them all, the Seven Stones, off Land's End. One of those last light vessel crewmen, Peter Hocking, a lamp 'trimmer', remembers the Seven Stones well. As he watched *No. 19* being towed in to replace him and *No. 23*, his eyes lit up.

> I've done twenty-six years in light vessels, and twenty-one years and ten months in her, *No. 19*, when she was on the Seven Stones. I've got some fond memories and some very frightening ones. In one storm we had 275 fathoms of cable down [three-quarters of a mile] and she still dragged for a mile.
>
> We had 140 mile an hour winds that time and a wave recorder on the land went off the scale at sixty-five feet.'

No. 19, sliding sedately into place as he talked, had been thrown around like a cork attached to a piece of string.

Light vessels are especially built for the job. Automatic stations have been taking over since 1982 when the east coast Shipwash came on station. Existing light vessels were gradually converted and the crew of five replaced by a GEC radio telemetry system. Diesel generators on the vessels run continuously to provide the power; they continue to be re-fuelled by tenders like the *Patricia*. Emergency repairs to the equipment, should any fail, is provided by engineers flying in by helicopter.

At its zenith Trinity House ran fifty-four light vessels, the largest fleet in the world. But, as we have seen, this number has been reducing for years. The old lightship crews are sceptical of this, as of many things. Like *Consortium*'s crew, many are ex-deep-sea men. They have seen the world, they know about ships. In the Channel, they bemoan their removal, predicting disaster. As if to prove part of their point, as we came through the Dover Straits towing down *No. 19*, two ships passed us, in that narrowest of seas, going the wrong way in the separation lanes.

The old lightsmen are bitter because they say that despite it not being their primary job, they used to be able to spot this kind of disaster in the making and radio the ships to warn them. They claim that the old manned South Goodwins light vessel north of the Dover Strait, for example, saved many ships from running directly onto the sands.

That June day *Patricia* lined herself and her tow up, to drop *No. 19* exactly on the location marked on the charts. *No. 19* had her own anchor hanging just a few feet above the bottom. Meanwhile, I had been dropped off in the working boat to go over to *No. 23*, drifting off station with her own anchor now slowly being raised.

To come alongside one of these bluff ships, with a good deal of tumblehome, in even a slight sea, is some achievement. On board *No. 23*, there was much sorrow. The hissing, panting tones of the old engine as she strained to lift the immense cable and anchor was the only sound. The five crew stood on the deck, watching, remembering. They all loved the job. The idea of spending a month tied to a lump of metal deep in the Channel and taking what the weather threw at them was offset by the peace, and by the fishing. They knew, too, that every month they could look forward to a month off. It was a poorly paid job but it was, in a sense, only a half-time one. Living conditions were crude: the iron ships hardly had any linings to them and ancient gas stoves provided the cooking. Despite the ratio of size of ship to number of men aboard, it was all rather cramped. Charlie Woods, *No. 23*'s master, at sixty-one a wiry nut-brown testament to a life of sun, sea and salt, used to work on coastal tankers. For every weekend off he would be three months at sea. 'I got married, that was the main thing. I decided to come ashore but there were no jobs.' He started to work for Trinity House in 1954.

Perhaps the most poignant moment of that day was just after

No. 23 had been taken in tow by the tug which was to pull her back to Harwich with her crew. The Casquets lighthouse, some twenty miles to the south and herself now automated, put in a VHF call to the lightship. The lighthouse keeper talked to Peter Hocking, one of the lightship crew. Peter Hocking could be heard saying he no longer knew what the future held. But, he added, sadly, 'They call it progress, anyway ...'

His words hung in the ether, an epitaph for a race of men that have passed us by, like ships in the night.

MEMENTO MORI

*'For we are bound where mariner has not yet dared to go
And we will risk the ship, ourselves and all.'*

Walt Whitman, *A Passage to India*

Farewells are hard. Hard on those who have gone but harder on those who remain. What we have mourned in these pages is the passing of the old ways: the days of British shipping, when it was still possible to voyage out to discover New Worlds, new people, new life; when it was possible to believe in the romance of it. This does not have to be sentimental. Much of that world was harsh; men died, they plundered, killed, took what they wanted with little thought for the morrow. Being the world's greatest shipping nation was a mixed blessing.

It should not detract from the fact and the achievement which in its best moments touched life with art. Sailors carried more than a crude jingoism in their bags, returned with better than just a yarn. Their work enriched not just our material world but our culture. Some of this went unnoticed no better nor worse than any other activity; others saw in it the seeds of immortality; still others nothing more than tawdry materialism. Sailors were exploited, as they from time to time exploited others.

In today's world, where time flashes past in the jet-trails criss-crossing the skies, the luxury of the sea, its slow beat, can be missed. It is better to travel hopefully than to arrive: we simply cannot allow ourselves to believe that any more. Sailors lived that philosophy for centuries.

This book has been about saying goodbye. We have to face that, squarely, before we can face any future in which British shipping plays a serious part. The flotsam and jetsam of our maritime glory has increasingly hampered our progress. In saying goodbye – properly – we might finally recognise our progress from youth to maturity.

To return for a moment to the past – the great Battle of the Atlantic. There was little enough glory in it; it was a long, dirty, desperate fight, over many years. Men died in thousands, dreadful dark deaths in the cold seas. The ships which won this battle were small, insignificant, their officers and crew often volunteers, part-time sailors. The merchant fleet they shepherded was battered, old, carrying unglamorous war material. Yet it kept Britain alive.

Perhaps only Joseph Conrad can end a book such as this because, as so many seafarers have appreciated, he was a sailor, too.

> ... they were the everlasting children of the mysterious sea. Their successors are the grown-up children of a discontented earth. They are less naughty, but less innocent; less profane, but perhaps also less believing ... But the others were strong and mute ... They are gone now and it does not matter ... a generation of men goes ... and it does not matter!

NOTES

Place of publication London unless otherwise stated.

INTRODUCTION

1. From *The Seafarer*, an eighth-century poem.
2. *The Cruel Sea*, Nicholas Montsarrat, Knopf, 1951.
3. *Naval Tracts Concerning the Abuse of Seamen*, Monson (ed. Oppenheim), NRS, 1893.
4. Quoted by Ronald Hope in *A New History of British Shipping*, John Murray (Publishers) Ltd, 1990.
5. *Sea Fever*, John Masefield.

CHAPTER ONE

1. *The Rise and Fall of British Naval Mastery*, Paul Kennedy, Macmillan, 1976.
2. Hope, op. cit.
3. Ibid.

CHAPTER THREE

1. Quoted in Hope (op. cit.), from *Beneath the House Flag of the P&O*, R. Padfield, 1981.
2. *50 Years Too Soon*, J. Donaldson, Whitcombe and Tombs, Melbourne, 1948.
3. *Ships and Women*, Adams, Lovet Dickson, 1936.
4. Donaldson, op. cit.
5. *A Million Ocean Miles Apart*, Edgar Britten, Hutchinson, 1989.
6. *Tramps and Ladies*, James Bisset, Patrick Stephens, Yeovil, 1989.

CHAPTER FOUR

1. *Their Lawful Occasions*, Herbert Edwards, Percival Marshall, 1956.

CHAPTER FIVE

1. *Sailors at Sea*, Harold Hickling, William Kimber, 1965.
2. Edwards, op. cit.

CHAPTER SIX

1. *Committee of Inquiry into Shipping*, Rochdale, HMSO, Norwich, 1970.
2. Article in *Ship's Monthly*, James Boyce.
3. *The Last Grain Race*, Eric Newby, Martin, Secker & Warburg Ltd, 1981.
4. *Schoonerman*, Richard England, Penguin, Harmonsworth, 1983.
5. *Seafaring in the 30s*, Captain R.F. McBrearty, Book Guild, 1989.
6. McBrearty, op. cit.
7. *Captain of the Queens*, Harry Gattridge (with Richard Collier), Old-bourne Press, 1957.
8. Britten, op. cit.
9. *The Romance of a Modern Liner*, Edward Diggle, Patrick Stephen, Yeovil, 1989.
10. Quoted in *Grand Luxe, The Transatlantic Style*, John Malcolm Brinnin and Kenneth Gaulin, Henry Holt, 1988.

CHAPTER SEVEN

1. *It's Really Quite Safe*, Geoffrey Rotherham, Hangar Books, 1985.
2. Edwards, op. cit.
3. Rotherham, op. cit.
4. *The U-Boat Peril*, Bob Whinney, Blandford, 1986.
5. *Able Seaman, RNVR*, Herbert Messer, Merlin Books Ltd, 1989.
6. *In His Wake*, Molly Passmore, Merlin Books Ltd, 1948.

CHAPTER EIGHT

1. Messer, op. cit.
2. *The British Sailor*, Kenneth Poolman, Arms and Armour Press, 1989. (Quoted by permission of Watson, Little Ltd.)
3. Whinney, op. cit.

CHAPTER NINE

1. Article in *Ship's Monthly*, Trevor Verner, December 1990.
2. *Grey Dawn Breaking, British Merchant Seafarers in the Late Twentieth Century*, Tony Lane, Manchester University Press, Manchester, 1986.

CHAPTER TEN

1. *Voyage East*, Richard Woodman, John Murray (Publishers) Ltd, 1988.
2. Hope, op. cit.

CHAPTER ELEVEN

1. *Before the Box Boats*, Captain 'Sandy' Kinghorn, Kenneth Mason Publications Ltd, Emsworth, 1983.
2. Article in *Ship's Monthly*, Captain 'Sandy' Kinghorn.

CHAPTER TWELVE

1. Quoted in *The Fight for the Malvinas*, Martin Middlebrook, Penguin, Harmondsworth, 1990.

GLOSSARY

AB — able-bodied seaman

aft/after — sternwards; the rear end of the ship

asdic — anti-submarine detection investigation committee: an early form of sonar

ASW — anti-submarine warfare

barbette — an armoured cylinder below a turret on a warship that protects the revolving structure and foundation of the turret

bulker — bulk carrier: a ship that carries unpackaged cargo, usually consisting of a single dry commodity such as coal or grain

bunt — the baggy centre of a fishing net or other piece of fabric, such as a square sail

cabotage — reservation of coastal navigation to a country's own ships

citadel — a specially strengthened part of a warship

clipper — any fast sailing ship

confused sea — waves with no single direction; dangerous conditions

conning tower — 1. a superstructure of a submarine, used as the bridge when the vessel is on the surface
2. the armoured pilot house of a warship

fo'c'sle — forecastle: the part of a vessel at the bow where the crew is quartered and stores, machines etc. may be stowed

GPS — geographical position system; satellite navigation for ships

GRT — gross registered tons

ICBMs — intercontinental ballistic missiles

MTB — motor torpedo boat

MV — merchant vessel

OBOs — oil, bulk and ore cargoes

OOD — officer of the day

Q-ship — a merchant ship with concealed guns, used to decoy enemy ships into the range of its weapons

ratings — a sailor who holds neither commissioned nor warrant rank; an ordinary seaman

red duster — an informal name for the Red Ensign, the ensign of the British Merchant Navy

RFA — Royal Fleet Auxiliary, the supply arm of the Royal Navy

RNVR — Royal Navy Volunteer Reserve

ro-ros — roll on, roll off ferries

SIN — submarine inertial navigation systems

SSBN — nuclear-powered ballistic missile submarine

SSN — nuclear hunter-killer submarine

tramp ship/steamer — a merchant ship that does not run between ports on a regular schedule but carries cargo wherever the shippers desire

tumblehome — the 'bulge' in a ship's sides from waterline to deck

ULCC — ultralarge crude carrier

UNCTAD — United Nations Conference on Trade and Development

windjammer — a large merchant sailing ship

BIBLIOGRAPHY

Place of publication London unless otherwise stated.

Adams *Ships and Women*, Lovat Dickson, 1936.

E. H. H. Archibald *The Fighting Ship of the Royal Navy*, Military Press (New York), 1987.

Correlli Barnett *Engage the Enemy More Closely*, Hodder and Stoughton, 1991.

Paul Beaver *The Modern Royal Navy*, Patrick Stephens (Yeovil), 1988.

Dea Birkett *Jella, a Woman at Sea*, Gollancz, 1992.

James Bisset *Tramps and Ladies*, Patrick Stephens (Yeovil), 1988.

John Malcolm Brinnin and Kenneth Gaulin *Grand Luxe, The Transatlantic style*, Henry Holt, 1988.

British Maritime Charitable Foundation *The Merchant Fleet and Deterrence*, 1988.

Edgar Britten *A Million Ocean Miles*, Hutchinson, 1989.

James Cable *Britain's Naval Future*, Macmillan, 1983.

G. C. Connell *Jack's War*, William Kimber, 1985.

Department of Transport *Merchant Fleet Statistics*, 1990.

Defence Committee of the House of Commons Sixth Report – *The Royal Navy's Surface Fleet, Current Issues*, HMSO (Norwich), 1989.

Ernest Diggle *The Romance of the Modern Liner*, Patrick Stephens (Yeovil), 1989.

J. Donaldson *50 Years Too Soon*, Whitcombe and Tombs (Melbourne), 1948.

Bernard Edwards *The Merchant Navy Goes to War*, Robert Hale, 1989.

Herbert Edwards *Their Lawful Occasions*, Percival Marshall, 1956.

Richard England *Schoonerman*, Penguin (Harmondsworth), 1983.

Tony Gibbons *Complete Encyclopedia of Battleships*, Salamander, 1983.

Harry Grattidge (with Richard Collier) *Captain of the Queens*, Oldbourne Press, 1957.

A. Cecil Hampshire *The Royal Navy Since 1945*, William Kimber, 1975.

Harold Hickling *Sailors at Sea*, William Kimber, 1965.

Ronald Hope *The Merchant Navy*, Stanford Marine, 1980.

Ronald Hope *A New History of British Shipping*, John Murray (Publishers) Ltd, 1990.

Ronald Hope *Sea Pie*, The Marine Society, 1984.

Jane's *Fighting Ships*, 1986/87; 1989/90; 1990/92.

Joint Working Party of the Department of Transport *British Shipping, Challenges and Opportunities*, HMSO (Norwich), 1990.

John Keegan *The Price of Admiralty*, Hutchinson, 1988.

Paul Kennedy *The Rise and Fall of British Naval Mastery*, Macmillan, 1976.

Captain 'Sandy' Kinghorn *Before the Box Boats*, Kenneth Mason Publications Ltd (Emsworth), 1983.

Tony Lane *Grey Dawn Breaking, British Merchant Seafarers in the Late Twentieth Century*, Manchester University Press (Manchester), 1986.

Peter Liddle *The Sailor's War, 1914–1918*, Blandford, 1985.

Christopher Lloyd *The British Seaman*, Paladin, 1970.

Lloyd's Register *Statistical Tables, 1988, 1990*.

John Masefield *Sea Poems*, Heinemann, 1978.

John Maxtone-Graham *Cunard, 150 glorious years*, David and Charles (Newton Abbot), 1989.

Merchant Shipping Act, 1988, HMSO.

Herbert Messer *Able Seaman, RNVR*, Merlin Books Ltd, 1989.

Martin Middlebrook *The Fight for the Malvinas*, Penguin (Harmondsworth), 1990.

Martin Middlebrook *Task Force, The Falklands War, 1982*, Penguin, (Harmondsworth), 1987.

Captain R. F. McBrearty *Seafaring in the 30s*, Book Guild, 1989.

Bernard Mccall *Coasters around Britain*, Bernard Mccall, 1989.

Richard Natkiel and Anthony Preston *Atlas of Maritime History*, Gallery Books, 1987.

Molly Passmore *In His Wake*, Merlin Books Ltd, 1948.

Kenneth Poolman *The British Sailor*, Arms and Armour Press, 1989.

Gordon Prange *Miracle at Midway*, Penguin (Harmondsworth), 1984.

Philip Pugh *The Cost of Seapower*, Conway Maritime Press, 1986.

Dave Quigley *Under the Jolly Roger*, Portmouth Publishing (Portsmouth), 1988.

Geoffrey Rotherham *It's Really Quite Safe*, Hangar Books, 1985.

Royal Navy Broadsheet 88 and Broadsheet 90.

B. Smith *Merchant Ship Design Since 1945*, Ian Allan (Shepperton), 1984.

S. G. Sturmey *British Shipping and World Competition*, Athlone Press, 1962.

Geoffrey Underwood *Our Falkland's War*, Maritime Books, 1983

Derek Hamilton Warner *A Steward's Life in the RN*, Arthur Stockwell, 1990.

Desmond Wettern *The Decline of British Sea Power*, Jane's Information Group (Coulsden), 1982.

Bob Whinney *The U-Boat Peril*, Blandford, 1986.

John Winton *We Joined the Navy*, Maritime Books, 1988.

Richard Woodman *Voyage East*, John Murray (Publishers) Ltd, 1988.

INDEX